D1614952

C334258244

Understanding Sharia

Understanding Sharia
Islamic Law in a Globalised World

Raficq S. Abdulla and
Mohamed M. Keshavjee

I.B.Tauris
LONDON AND NEW YORK
in association with
The Institute of Ismaili Studies
LONDON

Published in 2018 by
I.B.Tauris & Co. Ltd
London • New York
www.ibtauris.com

in association with The Institute of Ismaili Studies
210 Euston Road, London, NW1 2DA
www.iis.ac.uk

Copyright © Islamic Publications Ltd, 2018

All rights reserved. Except for brief quotations in a review, this book,
or any part thereof, may not be reproduced, stored in or introduced
into a retrieval system, or transmitted, in any form or by any means,
electronic, mechanical, photocopying, recording or otherwise, without
the prior written permission of the publisher.

ISBN: 978 1 78831 319 3
eISBN: 978 1 78672 405 2
ePDF: 978 1 78673 405 1

A full CIP record for this book is available from the British Library
A full CIP record is available from the Library of Congress

Library of Congress Catalog Card Number: available

Printed and bound in Great Britain by
T.J. International, Padstow, Cornwall

MIX
Paper from
responsible sources
FSC
www.fsc.org   FSC® C013056

The Institute of Ismaili Studies

The Institute of Ismaili Studies was established in 1977 with the object of promoting scholarship and learning on Islam in historical as well as contemporary contexts, and a better understanding of its relationship with other societies and faiths.

The Institute's programmes encourage a perspective which is not confined to the theological and religious heritage of Islam, but seeks to explore the relationship of religious ideas to broader dimensions of society and culture. They thus encourage an interdisciplinary approach to the materials of Islamic history and thought. Particular attention is also given to issues of modernity that arise as Muslims seek to relate their heritage to the contemporary situation.

Within the Islamic tradition, the Institute's programmes promote research on those areas which have to date received relatively little attention from scholars. These include the intellectual and literary expressions of Shi'ism in general, and Ismailism in particular.

In the context of Islamic societies, the Institute's programmes are informed by the full range and diversity of cultures in which Islam is practised today, from the Middle East, South and Central Asia, and Africa to the industrialised societies of the West, thus taking into consideration the variety of contexts which shape the ideals, beliefs and practices of the faith.

The objectives of this research are realised through concrete programmes and activities organised and implemented by various departments of the Institute. The Institute also collaborates periodically, on a programme-specific basis, with other institutions of learning in the United Kingdom and abroad.

The Institute's academic publications fall into a number of interrelated categories:

1. Occasional papers or essays addressing broad themes of the relationship between religion and society, with special reference to Islam.
2. Monographs exploring specific aspects of Islamic faith and culture, or the contributions of individual Muslim thinkers or writers.
3. Editions or translations of significant primary or secondary texts.
4. Translations of poetic or literary texts which illustrate the rich heritage of spiritual, devotional and symbolic expressions in Muslim history.
5. Works on Ismaili history and thought, and the relationship of the Ismailis to other traditions, communities and schools of thought in Islam.
6. Proceedings of conferences and seminars sponsored by the Institute.
7. Bibliographical works and catalogues which document manuscripts, printed texts and other source material.

This book falls into the second category.

In facilitating these and other publications, the Institute's sole aim is to encourage original research and analysis of relevant issues. While every effort is made to ensure that the publications are of a high academic standard, there is naturally bound to be a diversity of views, ideas and interpretations. As such, the opinions expressed in these publications must be understood as belonging to their authors alone.

'A valuable work, elegantly written, raising issues which help to explain the ethical underpinnings of sharia and its workings in the modern world. It's a book that should be read and reflected upon by both Muslims and non-Muslims.'
Dr Maulana Shahid Raza Naeemi, OBE Chair of MINAB (The Mosques and Imams National Advisory Board) and Executive Secretary and Registrar of Muslim Law Shariah Council (UK)

'I loved this book. It gives the reader an introduction to the thinking behind sharia, and the evolutionary nature of its interpretation. And it makes clear how different authorities at different times in history have had wholly different approaches. The fact that the law is not a terrifying, immutable, and uncompromising whole, but has to be interpreted by human beings, is strongly emphasised, and changes in interpretation and practice are well laid out. Everyone, Muslim and non-Muslim alike, can learn from this elegantly written, well-researched volume.'
Rabbi The Rt Hon The Baroness Neuberger DBE

'*Understanding Sharia* is a thought-provoking yet accessible overview of one of the most misunderstood and contested concepts of our time. The authors raise the kinds of questions that can open a much-needed conversation and show why and how sharia is always work in progress.'
Dr Ziba Mir-Hosseini, Legal Anthropologist and Activist

'Accessible, informative and wonderfully enlightening, this book is a must-read for anyone, Muslim and non-Muslim, who wants to acquire an unprejudiced perspective on the meaning of sharia for today. The authors, refusing slavery to either lifeless literalism or unthinking relativism, introduce the reader to sharia's contested origins and multiple cultural embodiments. They also point out continuing misapplications and relevancies for committed Islamic and wider critical consciousness. The book concludes with a trenchant plea for fresh thinking which has the potential for engaging sharia more flexibly and productively in the light of the many hitherto unimagined issues that are emerging in our globalised and interdependent world.'
The Revd Canon Dr Alan Race, Theologian and Interfaith Specialist

Contents

Preface and Acknowledgements

This work has been inspired by our recognition of the need for an accessible book on a topic that today occupies the minds of so many people, both Muslims and non-Muslims. We realise that books on this subject tend to be specialist and academic and generally do not take into account the range of subjects covered by sharia. We hope our book enables its readers to obtain a broad understanding of the subject, encouraging them to look further. We feel that we shall have succeeded if we provide a platform for interested people (and we believe that sharia is a 'hot' topic today) to gain a more informed understanding of the subject, which may help to allay fears and misconceptions that abound in the media and indeed generally across the world, including the Muslim world. We wish this work to be a staging post towards a real engagement with both the topic and the world in which it is embedded.

This book is therefore not academic, nor is it a textbook of the law; but we hope that it provides a perspective for the general reader, showing how sharia has developed historically and how it responds to particular issues that emerge both as general principles and in daily life. We also provide a critique that covers the role of sharia today and its interface with modernity through various legal systems, as well as setting out our own legal position and a contextualising world view.

Sharia in its Sunni and Shi'i manifestations is covered in this work, as well as its relationship to the modern world, in a manner which is descriptive and reflective without being polemical or binary. We hope our book will help to encourage debate and discussion, and enable its readers to discover new ways of engaging with sharia.

As we intend this book to be for the general reader, it has been decided to simplify the diacritics that are usually employed to represent Arabic names and terms in the Latin alphabet. Unless within a book title or quotation, all diacritics and the use of the Arabic *ayn* (') have been avoided, except where it begins a syllable and within the terms 'Shi'a' and 'Shi'i'. All dates given are CE years. We have also chosen to refer to sharia, rather than 'the sharia' for ease of reading, and to use the term in Roman rather than italics. This applies also to our use of the term hadith. Furthermore, we have used for our Qur'anic references the interpretation of the Qur'an by Seyyed Hossein Nasr, with some slight modifications.[1]

We should like to thank Dr Ziba Mir-Hosseini for enabling us to correct some errors with regard to her work, and finally we would like to thank the Institute of Ismaili Studies and all its staff who have enabled us to work in a congenial environment. Our thanks go particularly to the Director, Dr Farhad Daftary, whose encouragement has been invaluable; to Russell Harris for his invaluable editorial expertise; and to the librarians, Khadija Lalani and Alex Leach, who were always available to provide us so efficiently with all the books we needed. Our thanks also go to our respective spouses, Marianne Rohlen and Amina Jindani, for their constant support during the writing of this work.

While we have had immense help and assistance in writing this book, we must point out that this book reflects our own viewpoints and although the book appears under the imprint of the Institute of Ismaili Studies, London, the contents reflect our own research and understanding of the issues about which we have written. Any errors and shortcomings are solely ours.

Introduction: Islamic Law in the Contemporary World

'Islam is a clear stream with well defined characteristics which are the same everywhere. But the soil over which the stream flows can be varied. Moreover, in each case, the water will take on the colour of the shores, the sand or the earth which forms its bed.'

Jacques Jomier[1]

Preamble

Sharia has been a perennial source of misunderstanding and misconception in the Muslim and the non-Muslim worlds. In the former, its literal interpretation has sometimes been an excuse for repression, and in the latter it is often an icon for vilification and a classic representation of the demonised and demonising 'other'. This book attempts to explore the reality behind these confrontational appearances. We endeavour to examine the notion of law in general and the principles and practice of sharia in particular.

By way of introduction it is necessary to provide the reader with a brief definition of sharia and a few other vital terms. According to John Esposito in his *Dictionary of Islam*, sharia is 'God's eternal and immutable will for humanity expressed in the Quran and the Sunnah; the ideal Islamic law.' It is the human effort to codify Islamic norms in practical terms and legislate for cases not specifically dealt with in the Qur'an and the Sunna (the example of the Prophet) that involves the application of *fiqh* (jurisprudence). Esposito adds, 'Although human-generated legislation is considered fallible and open to revision, the term *shariah* is sometimes applied to all Islamic legislation.' Esposito defines *fiqh* as the human attempt to understand divine law. To do this, the jurist (*faqih*) employs *usul al-fiqh*. The *usul al-fiqh* consist of the 'body of principles and investigative methodologies through which legal rules are developed from the foundational sources.' For the four main Sunni schools of law these are the Qur'an, the Sunna, the consensus (*ijma'*) of the scholars of law on a legal issue not covered in the Quran or Sunna, analogy (*qiyas*), which is used in reasoned argument to deduce legal prescriptions. The Ja'fari Shi'i school of law adds reason (*'aql*) and the sayings of the Imams as a source. There is also custom (*'urf*), which may be the custom of Medina in the time of the Prophet or local custom in a given area, although there has been debate on the acceptability of this last source.

Schools of Law in Islam (*madhahib*)

There are eight schools of law (*madhahib*) in Islam. These are the four Sunni schools, three Shi'i schools and the Ibadi school. The Sunni schools are made up of the Maliki, the Hanafi, the Shafi'i and the Hanbali. The Shi'i schools consist of the Ja'fari, the Ismaili and the Zaydi. The Ibadi stand alone, belonging neither to the Sunni or the Shi'a schools of law. All these schools are also known as *fiqh*, or jurisprudential understanding, which connotes the understanding of sharia as developed within a particular school. The Sunni schools are all known by the names of their founders.

To understand the notion of *madhab* or *fiqh* one has to know the significance of the word 'sharia', which is often translated as 'law'. The term derives from the Arabic word for path or way and encompasses the totality of obligations incumbent on a Muslim. As Islam developed and expanded, a common set of stipulations evolved to guide the believers in their lives, and this process was undertaken by Muslim thinkers who formulated their ideas largely within the framework defined by the Qur'an, hadith (reported sayings of the Prophet), the Sunna (customs of the Prophet) and rational arguments that took place among scholars and others with a view of reaching the best solutions suited to the circumstances of time and place. This resulting framework is generally known as sharia, which encompasses a number of relationships such as the individual with God, with other human beings and with the environment in general. Therefore, sharia has a wider connotation in that it regulates life for Muslims within the community and also between themselves and others.

Sharia operates at various levels. At the political level, it aims to define the nature of the Muslim state and those responsible for government including institutions which are mandated to safeguard the well being of the populace. At the social and personal levels, it provides guidelines affecting economic, social and family life. It prescribes in detail the religious obligations which all Muslims are obliged to follow. During the course of Islamic history, Muslim political authorities provided courts and judicial functionaries whose job was to mediate disputes and to oversee the workings of sharia with the result that, over time, the totality of political, moral and social order in Islam acquired a more specific definition. Sharia was not meant to be a fixed body of rules and regulations, as it always looked at the wider purpose of the public good (*maslaha*) that was determined by the demands of necessity (*darura*), which Muslim scholars identified and analysed in accordance with their understanding of sharia's higher purposes known as *maqasid* (purposes). This led to its theoretical understanding (*fiqh*), which itself was meant to be fluid and responsive to changing conditions.

The Hanafi school, founded by Abu Hanifa al-Nu'man (d. 767), is the largest Sunni school and is mainly found in central and Western Asia, and more particularly in countries such as Turkey, Bangladesh, India, Pakistan, Tajikistan and Syria.

The Maliki school, founded in Medina by Malik ibn Anas (d. ca. 796), is predominant in Upper Egypt, North and West Africa, particularly in Morocco, Tunisia, Libya, Algeria and many of the countries of sub-Saharan Africa, such as Senegal, Mali and northern Nigeria.

The Shafi'i school, founded by Muhammad ibn Idris al-Shafi'i (d. 820), is predominant in Lower Egypt, East Africa and South-East Asia, particularly in Indonesia and Malaysia.

The Hanbali school, founded by Ahmad ibn Hanbal (d. 855), is predominant in Saudi Arabia but has adherents in many countries in the Arabian Gulf, such as the UAE, Kuwait and Qatar. Oman follows the Ibadi school of law. Of the three Shi'i schools, the Ja'fari, whose founding principles were formed by Muhammad al-Baqir (d. 733) and Ja'far al-Sadiq (d. 765), is found mainly in Iran, Iraq, parts of Lebanon, as well as on the subcontinent of India and East Africa where many Ithna 'ashari Muslims live today.

The Ismaili school of law in the form of the Da'a'im al-Islam is the chief legal text for the Tayyibi Musta'lian Ismailis, including the Daudi Bohras of South Asia, while the Nizaris, known popularly as the Ismailis, have followed the guidance of their living Imams, known today as the Aga Khans, in their legal, normative and ritual practices.

The Zaydi school of law is found predominantly in Yemen and is followed by the Shi'is of that country.

However, readers should be aware that this book is not a comprehensive textbook of law focusing on individual issues from the perspectives of particular schools of Islamic law, nor is it an account of dispositive laws (laws applied to dispose of a legal matter) as practised in the courts of various countries – in short, this is not a textbook of legal practice.[2] Instead, much of what this volume is concerned with will be the explanation and expansion on the brief definitions supplied here, the history, and application of these terms and a brief outline of the people who were or are involved in the development of Islamic law. In short, this work aims to provide an overview, an exploration of sharia's role and a critique that considers the nature and practice of sharia in the contemporary world. We hope it will encourage further reflection.

While Western systems of law may have had religious origins, they are now essentially secular: the sovereign body that enacts laws is a legislative body that is recognised by citizens as having the power to enact legislation and ensure its implementation. This sovereign body includes the courts which, in Anglo-Saxon legal dispensations, interpret and create the law, through the application of precedent. Laws are found in texts,[3] and they are both created and implemented by a recognised process of interpretation. If the law is not to be mob rule or some other sketchy device for settling disputes and imposing order, it must follow an agreed and respected choreography of legal process, of court hearings, of evaluating evidence and responding to the exigencies of society. In this way, legal decisions more or less fit the legal requirements of a society. This process differs from jurisdiction to jurisdiction even as it applies a single legal system. In the case of sharia, the system is infused with variations in substance, and those countries applying sharia have been influenced or affected by Western modes of argument and process: for example, in the Moroccan and Turkish courts French legal procedures and secular laws are respectively applied. When we consider Western legal systems in the modern era, we are concerned with a secular formation of law that is now embodied in the notion of the state. However, sharia does not sit comfortably within the ambit of a modern nation state where sovereignty attaches to the state itself, whether through democratic process or more authoritarian fiat. For sharia, sovereignty lies exclusively with the divine, whose edicts are imposed from above rather than through law that emerges from human needs as developed and understood by the community. This is the theory; but in reality the situation is more complex and sharia also obtains its legitimacy from social requirements. It is often stated that Islamic law is both a divine law and a jurists' law. This, as we shall see, produces its own challenges.

Our Approach

We consider that our approach enables us and our readers to think about or rethink the nature and reality of sharia in the modern world, and especially in the Muslim world. This process entails raising issues that offer a critique but are not intended to be polemical or partisan in ways that provoke or obscure. The importance of understanding the complex nature of sharia cannot be overstated in a world of over 1.6 billion Muslims, some of whom live as minorities in non-Muslim countries, in various cultural, linguistic, economic and ethnic communities and who are struggling to reach new levels of material, intellectual and spiritual development without abandoning the values and ethics of their faith. These issues cannot be understood as an abstraction, and they should be situated in an historical framework of understanding that takes into account the origins of Islam and sharia and their development from the classical period to modernity within the context of other civilisations and other legal systems. This study aims to provide different perspectives rather than prescriptive answers to particular issues in the contemporary world, such as finance, social governance, environmental problems, criminal justice, alternative forms of dispute resolution, Human Rights biomedical ethics and the role of religious law in the establishment of modern states – all these raising important ethical questions about and practical problems around the development of sharia.

This exploratory approach will enable us to understand the dynamic processes that underlie sharia. Commonly misunderstood as being static, eternally valid and immutable, in fact sharia and *fiqh* (jurisprudential understanding) are constructs that must be adapted to new circumstances while adhering to the universal ethical principles which are their basis. This understanding is essential where religious laws are concerned, in order to avoid the tendency to regard them as a fixed corpus, as this, whether in theory or in practice, is simply not the case. Our book aims to provide a broad overview of the main schools of sharia in the Sunni and Shi'i as well as the Ibadi school of Islam.[4] It will demonstrate that there is no single or fixed body of Islamic law called the sharia, but that there exists a set of principles, some of which may be claimed to be permanent in terms of the values and ethical norms they promulgate. These principles form the basis of a variety of interpretations by human agents who are responding to the context of their time. Therefore, sharia is always a work in progress. We argue that sharia is not a symbol for regressive or repressive agendas; indeed viewing sharia symbolically in this way misconstrues and abuses its nature. As part of this analysis, this book will address certain fundamental jurisprudential questions such as what law is, what legal reasoning is, how law and society relate to each other, and what the role of politics is in shaping the law. Finally, we address the central question of what makes law Islamic, and whether the call to Islamicise laws is realistic or simply a rhetorical device for legitimising a particular ideology that politicises religion through a society's legal processes.

The notion of universal rights and universal values, while attractive and indeed necessary, is not easily identified and accepted by all. And at a certain level of abstraction, philosophical words and abstract ideas that aim to establish what is good and cure our perennial frailties may in reality mislead and confine.

The word 'sharia', depending on the context, can evoke a host of negative connotations, portraying Islam as a backward faith that espouses a system of law that is inimical to all the notions of civilised behaviour that are associated with modern, liberal and enlightened thinking. This is largely because of controversial interpretations of its sanctions, coupled with the use of images of its egregious application in the media, which today, in a digital age, has a potentially instantaneous global reach. This impression of sharia therefore infiltrates all levels of civil society, and the very mention of the word lends itself to disinformation, polemics, hysteria and controversy.[5] According to the historian of Islam Suleiman Mourad: 'much chaos in the Muslim world today is because most people don't know what Sharia is'. Each school of law creates its own understanding of sharia. Sharia touches almost every aspect of life: for example, when someone dies they have to be buried in accordance with rites propounded by 'the Sharia of the school they followed'. Mourad argues that today these distinctions are no longer clear: Muslims state they are Muslims and they follow sharia without knowing exactly what this means or how it is defined. He continues: 'The eclectic practices in the modern Islamic world are more a reflection of its chaos than actual observance or clarity about what Islam is.'[6]

Muslims themselves often conflate sharia (which they consider to be divinely ordained as inscribed in the Qur'anic text) with *fiqh*, its man-made, time-marked jurisprudential understanding, as expressed in the various schools of law that were developed more than a thousand years ago by different communities of interpretation with their own notions of legitimacy and authority. These ideas of sharia and *fiqh* are further conflated with *'urf* (customary laws), which in many cases pre-date the revelation of the Qur'an and in some cases were infused with Islamic norms. In many

Muslim countries these customs continued, and still continue, as a separate but parallel system of law that at times contradicts sharia and its *fiqh*. From Indonesia in South-East Asia to Morocco on the shores of the Atlantic Ocean, Muslim countries today apply a panoply of laws, including sharia, in pluralistic societies that espouse their own form of legal pluralism. Thus, in most countries we find the application not only of sharia, but also of *'urf*, colonial laws and laws enacted by the governments of newly independent states as part of the need to create legal and administrative structures that enable modern social governance.[7]

Viewing the concept of sharia ahistorically and acontextually, as an exclusively God-given command not requiring any form of human interpretation according to the exigencies of time and place, prevents it from co-existing harmoniously with other systems of law or with contemporary needs. In these cases, sharia as a symbol of permanent divine dispensation fails to adapt to the modern demands, needs and stresses that assail all societies.[8]

Why has this Situation of Apparent Stasis Arisen?

The development of sharia has been hindered by a number of factors, not least of which is that the classical doctrine, according to professor of Islamic law Noel Coulson, posits that 'Law is the revealed will of God, a divinely ordained system *preceding* and not *preceded* by the Muslim state [and] *controlling* and not *controlled* by Muslim society.' Hence, in Islamic discourse there is an insufficient notion of law itself evolving as a historical phenomenon that is closely tied to the historical changes in society.[9]

According to Muslim legal philosophy, such as it is today, law is imposed by God and postulates the eternally valid standards to which the structure of state and society must conform. This contrasts with the Western modernist approach that posits law is constantly shaped by the needs of society and that its function is to address social problems appropriately. We argue that this more flexible notion of law did indeed exist in classical times of Islam, especially when one considers concepts such as *darura* (necessity), *maslaha* (public interest) and *maqasid* (purpose of the law) which shaped Muslim thinking at various times, and indeed are beginning to shape new thought today. The issue of the nature of law has also preoccupied Western jurisprudence, perhaps more intensely than Islamic legal theory has done.

For the most part, early Islamic law developed largely in isolation from legal practice, and legal history does not feature in its study.[10] The notion of historical process was alien to classical Islamic jurisprudence. However, research in the early 20th century by scholars such as Ignaz Goldziher and others, coupled with statutory and judicial developments in the Muslim world over the last hundred years, has thrown new light on this historical approach to the study of Islamic law.

Need for a Clear and Easy-to-Read Book

There is thus a need for an accessible book on Islamic law that will help readers to understand that there is no single, monolithic understanding of sharia that is followed by all Muslims. We aim to show here how jurisprudential understanding developed over a period of three centuries following the Revelation of Islam in the 7th century, both within the Sunni and the Shi'i interpretations of the Qur'an. We shall see how deeply involved and influenced Islamic law was in its formative stages with a number of different laws and legal systems that pre-dated it and with which it co-existed, and continues to co-exist, more or less harmoniously. It will become clear that there is no such thing as a pristine corpus known as 'Islamic law'. In most areas of the world where Muslims are settled, different colonial laws were introduced over time and gave rise in many countries to a form of legal pluralism. This, in turn, has been subject to continuous change and reappraisal. In the 19th century, for example, the Ottomans realised that classical sharia was becoming inadequate to meet the needs of Muslim societies that were interacting with an increasingly dominant Western world; therefore they introduced the *Tanzimat* reforms.

In turn, these reforms became the precursor to important changes in the law that were brought about in the 20th century largely in the Muslim Middle East but also elsewhere in the Islamic world. Calls for greater Islamisation of laws in the last quarter of the 20th century must be seen in the context of these earlier changes. Coupled with this phenomenon, there have been new developments in various fields of law in the Western world, such as the International Protection of Human Rights, laws dealing with biomedical and information ethics and Alternative Dispute Resolution (ADR), which have had an impact on Islamic law and its application both in Muslim-majority countries as well as other areas of the world where Muslims live as minorities. This book aims to cover some of these issues to enable the reader to better understand Islamic law as a system that has developed in the context of history and, like all other legal systems, has had to accommodate the forces of time and place. In this way, we hope to open doors of perception, interpretation, understanding, reflection and exploration that go beyond the tired polemic that surrounds most of the discussion about sharia today, and in doing so we hope to indicate new, more constructive, collaborative and complex ways of regarding this important body of law that prevails in many parts of the world.

What this Book Aims to Do

The book aims to provide the reader with a sound background to Islamic law, highlighting its origins, evolution and the issues that have affected its growth and nature. It covers sharia's long and sometimes complicated history, starting in the 7th century at the time of the revelation of the Qur'an, when it came into existence in the context of existing laws in Arabia and those of its nearby imperial neighbours, taking into account the changes that Islam made to the customs and practices of this area. We shall see how in the early Qur'anic period the Prophet Muhammad and his immediate successors, the Rightly-Guided Caliphs, played a decisive role in interpreting the law for a nascent Muslim community or *umma*. The early legal practice will be discussed, showing how the Umayyad Caliphs (r. 661–750), as practical administrators, dealt with the need to govern a cosmopolitan polity and, consequently, to rule through the imposition of law. The development of the early court system will be discussed, revealing that sharia was not the only dispositive law of the

Muslim polity but that *siyasat al-sharia*, or as Coulson puts it 'government in accordance with the revealed law',[11] constituted a parallel system for social governance, and that this dimension of public law was governed by the political authority in charge rather than by the religious scholars or jurists known collectively as the *'ulama*. The work of Muhammad ibn Idris al-Shafi'i (born 767), the eponymous founder of one of the four major Sunni schools of law, the Shafi'i school, and generally thought of as the 'Master Architect of Islamic Jurisprudence', will be discussed in the context of its impact on consolidating the practice of law as well as the long-term consequences for its development, which is termed 'closure of the gate of *ijtihad*' or legal interpretation.[12] This remains a contested notion.[13]

The historical development of sharia covered by this book also highlights the major reforms of the 19th century and how they presaged the 20th-century developments that were brought about by the influences of thinkers such as the Egyptian jurist and reformer Muhammad Abduh (1849–1905) and the Egyptian legal scholar Abd al-Razzaq al-Sanhuri (1895–1971). This is followed by a discussion of the major developments in the latter part of the 20th century, raising some important questions for reflection and further research. While, as mentioned earlier, we do not comment on the positive laws of various countries,[14] we aim to cover some of the more controversial expressions of sharia, and to analyse some of the cases that have risen in the context of the difficulties that emerge when Muslim countries proclaim in their constitutions that sharia is *the* source of law as opposed to *a* source of law, claiming an exclusivity that often tends to deny the legitimacy of existing laws. We also provide some basic observations regarding constitutional development, in the context of discussing the main issues that some high-profile cases have engendered.

This book therefore endeavours to give the reader a basic background to sharia but, more importantly, helps to situate this background within the context of Islamic history as well as within the interface between Muslim, Western and other countries – and the effect this has had on the development of Islamic law as we understand it today.

The Structure of the Book

Chapter 1: Sharia – Origin through Revelation, Historical Development and Change focuses on pre-Islamic Arabia, the advent of Islam and its impact on society, the inception of Qur'anic legislation and the role of the early authoritative figures such as the Prophet, the Rightly-Guided Caliphs and the Companions of the Prophet, including the Shi'i Imams. It aims, inter alia, to answer these questions: What did Islam do? Did it make major changes? Is the Qur'an a comprehensive code of law or is it a preamble to a moral universe for which successive Muslim generations had to provide the operative parts? This first chapter covers such issues as *mahr* and women's rights, *tha'r* and disproportionate retaliation, testamentary principles and the effect the Qur'an has had on women's right to own property.

Chapter 2: Legal Practice under the Ummayads (661–750) explains briefly who the Umayyads were, the nature of the expansion that took place during their rule and the inception of the *qadi* system coupled with the *siyasat al-sharia* and social governance. The chapter highlights the early difficulties faced by the *qadis*, proto-judges subordinate to the Umayyad rulers who considered themselves as masters rather than servants of the law. It shows how the *qadis* evolved from lowly administrative functionaries, dealing with a multiplicity of administrative tasks, to judicial officers with greater authority, despite the Umayyad Caliphs' attempts to relegate them to a subordinate status. The chapter will argue that religious law and courts dealing with sharia at this time were not supreme or exclusive. This hybrid status of sharia remains in place to this day.

Chapter 3: Consolidation of the Schools of Law under the Abbasids (750–1258) explains briefly who the Abbasids were and how they came to power. The chapter concentrates on notions of authority and legitimacy. It further discusses the role of *usul al-fiqh* (legal theory and legal methodology) and shows how legal diversity developed. The seminal contribution of Muhammad ibn Idris al-Shafi'i is discussed against the backdrop of the *mihna* or inquisition initiated by the Abbasids who took power in the 8th century. During this time, there was an impassioned debate about the relative merits of reason and revelation, which ended in favour of the traditionalists who supported the latter. This led to the so-called closure of the gate of *ijtihad* (a phenomenon by which interpretation was set aside in favour of imitation, or *taqlid*, which is perceived as one of the causes for the failure of sharia to adapt to contemporary issues and demands). The hegemony of the classical notions of the law, which created a static and reified legal system in the Islamic world, is further discussed here.

Chapter 4: Developments after Shafiʻi – touches on the notions of *taqlid* (imitation) and *ijtihad* (new interpretations of legal texts), and the difficulties that Islamic societies faced as they began to encounter the West where new philosophical and material developments were taking place, challenging old notions. The chapter also discusses those encounters between the West and the Islamic world that led to new developments. It highlights the need for reform and the developments that took place in the 20th century with reference to various legal scholars. By showing these developments as part of an historical process, we aim to demonstrate that the classical notion was an outcome of complex historical developments that took place over centuries. The chapter will also show that the notion of an immutable and rigid law became progressively unsustainable in the light of new pressures on Muslim societies. This led in the 20th century to the development of ideas by Muslim legal modernists that contrasted with those held by the traditionalists, whom it is easy to dismiss as being out of touch. However, we aim to take into account their concerns because they go to the heart of the notion of Islamic identity as they see it, and explain their fears over the introduction of new ideas that they feel run against the traditional notions referred to by Muslims as innovation, or *bidʻa*, in a world already beset with instability. It would be wrong to disregard the traditionalists, who continue to represent large and vociferous sections of the Islamic world. While we believe that change is needed, real change can only be achieved by the creation of honest exchange and courageous self-examination by all parties, including the non-Muslim world, whereby a new consensus, or *ijma'*, can be created through a constant dialectical and dialogical process.

Chapter 5: Further Geographical Expansion and Cultural Accommodation discusses the developments that took place in various regions and how sharia adapted to these changes. As Islam expanded into new areas, newly converted peoples were expected to adhere to sharia both in terms of *'ibadat* (worship) and *mu'amalat* (transactions between people). The classical formulation of sharia as it took place in a very circumscribed geographical and cultural context did not always find favour with societies which, though they adopted Islam as a faith, continued to hold on to cultural practices that predominated over classical formulations of the law. This chapter explores how *siyasat al-sharia* and sharia operated in tandem and how customary law (*'urf*) and sharia developed a modus vivendi whereby they accommodated each other and, through this process of accommodation, were able to bridge legal practice and legal theory – something that occurred in the Maliki courts of north-west Africa through the *qadi*s, who contributed towards the development of a lived sharia, and through the *mufti*s, by way of their legal opinions or fatwas.

Chapter 6: Call for Reform – from the *Tanzimat* to the Arab Spring is concerned with the various reform movements dealing with sharia from the *Tanzimat* reforms in the Ottoman Empire in the 19th century to the present-day Middle East, highlighting the reasons for the call for the reintroduction of sharia in various Muslim countries as part of their search for a more credible social governance system.[15] This chapter shows how Western laws were used mainly to reform the Islamic legal system emerging from sharia, and how important accommodations were formulated to placate non-Muslim minorities who held entrenched positions in the Ottoman Empire. These reforms were a precursor to many changes that took place later in the 20th century. They are the reasons, in part, for the backlash of revivalist Islamist responses we witness today. This theme also permeates other chapters.

Chapter 7: Shi'i Legal Understanding and Theory of Law is concerned with the way sharia is dealt with by the Shi'i branch of Islam using its own legal theory and methodology and its understanding of the notion of authority. It also explores the role the Qur'an played in introducing a new legal dispensation. The position of the Shi'i Imams as interpreters of the law and their role in the transmission of Prophetic hadith (sayings and traditions of the Prophet), coupled with their own teachings, are covered here. The chapter elaborates on the doctrine of Imamat and provides a broad overview of 11th-century Fatimid jurisprudence which was the first endeavour to codify Shi'i Ismaili law within the context of a political state.

Chapter 8: The Multiple Manifestations of Sharia highlights some of the more controversial cases which have occurred in recent times and analyses the major issues raised in the context of Human Rights and international law as well as exploring the impact of various international treaties on Muslim countries. Analysis is carried out to explore the tensions inherent between the constitution of a modern Muslim state and its commitment to the principle of Universal Human Rights, this latter existing in a tense relationship with the rigours of classical Islamic law which a Muslim state may choose to follow, as a result of its constitutional commitment to Islam and the particular school of law obtaining in that country. This chapter also covers the role of female Muslim social activists in the field of social justice.

Chapter 9: Neo-*Ijtihad* focuses on Islamic finance, explaining how it works and its role within the context of the international financial system, including its growth potential and the regulatory, interpretive and definitional problems related to it. This chapter also covers Alternative Dispute Resolution (ADR) and some challenges faced by the civil justice system globally. It also discusses the 1980 Hague Convention on International Cross Border Child Abduction and how the various protocols related to this are given effect through mediation and judicial collaboration in situations where one of the disputants is from a Muslim country that is not party to the Convention. It shows that with international collaboration and the use of mediation as a dispute resolution mechanism we are beginning to see an expansion of the notion of *maqasid al-sharia* – the wider purpose of the law – and that recent Muslim scholarship in places as diverse as Indonesia, Malaysia, Qatar and the United States is focusing on a new approach to the understanding of sharia based on the principles enunciated by Muslim jurists of earlier centuries, culminating in the work of al-Shatibi, a 14th-century Andalusian Maliki legal scholar.

Chapter 10: Sharia and Human Rights provides a broad background to the evolution of Human Rights in Western juris-prudential culture and the Islamic critique of this notion, with references to writers such as Mawlana Abul Aʻla Maududi and Sayyid Qutb and the Universal Islamic Declaration of Human Rights (UIDHR) on the one hand, and modernist Muslim writers such as Abdullahi an-Naʻim and Bassam Tibi on the other. After commenting on the various viewpoints, the chapter concludes that the terms 'human rights' and 'Islam' are locked in a binary discourse,[16] and the ability to cut through major issues aiming to capture the original principles will help this discourse assume a more principled position in its approach towards Human Rights. Modern scholarship by Muslims in the diaspora, coupled with ongoing discussions in social media, is beginning to show that mutual demonisation often takes place between antagonists who wish to indulge in arguments that aim to denigrate the opposition rather than come to grips with the real issues through a process of dialectical and dialogical exchange. Here again, the work of female Muslim scholars is highlighted.

Chapter 11: Criminal Justice in Islam provides a background to the so-called *hadd*, or capital offences. It highlights how criminal law developed in the classical period and explores its interface with the political authority through the practice of *siyasa*. It also covers changes that took place largely in the Ottoman Empire, which produced its own *siyasa* in the form of *qanun-nama*s, a body of legal rules and state-enacted laws. The chapter describes the various penal laws promulgated in colonial times and their abolition in some Muslim countries with the reintroduction of

Islamic criminal law, and the impact on Human Rights in various Muslim countries today.

Chapter 12: Islam and Ethics examines the role of ethics in sharia, describing how ethical values inform sharia both in theory and in practice. Ethics is distinguished from morality which, we argue, is a set of rules and obligations established by an accepted sovereign authority, while ethics is a form of moral reasoning. We show how ethics plays out in some practical issues, such as biomedical concerns, in conjunction with sharia using the notions of *adab* and *akhlaq*. The chapter also highlights how major breakthroughs, resulting from a knowledge society and driven by today's digital revolution, present new ethical problems for Muslim communities both in Islamic countries and the diaspora. These revolutionary changes that are taking hold today cannot be adequately addressed by a rigid interpretation of sharia, just as they are not able to be addressed by modern secular laws.

Chapter 13: Critique raises issues that Muslims will have to address in the 21st century, emphasising the need for a new epistemology that moves from the onerous literalism that affects many aspects of the Abrahamic community of faiths, to a broader consideration of the constant dialectical processes that are bound to the notion of ethics. It also discusses why this approach is imperative in the new knowledge society that is developing today and how such an approach can be nurtured. The chapter contends that interpretation is an essential part of reading texts, and that this is in itself a complex practice. We discuss some of the inherent problems that arise when a religious law that was originally meant for a frontierless society of believers is applied to the cosmopolitan demographies of modern nation states, and how this may be resolved. The work of female Muslim scholars, coupled with their social activism in various fields, is presented with reference to its impact on some governments. The chapter calls for reflection on the viability of religious law today when it is based on epistemological principles that may be at odds with a prevailing culture shaped by a new digital reality. The problems that affect all societies, including Muslim societies, require new thinking and new ways of approaching global dangers. Modernity, as understood in the West, is therefore itself open to critique. We should be aware of this critique of the West and its values by Islamic thinkers in order to gain a balanced view of the issues involved. The nature of sharia and its role in modern-day legal systems require rethinking, which will affect the Islamic world view. We argue that sharia needs, and is able, to adapt to the contemporary world if it connects meaningfully with the values that underpin it.

Questions Raised by the Book

Our book does not raise new issues, but we hope that the questions we ask will help the reader to gain a degree of clarity on the subject. We aim to contribute to the discourse on the role of religious law in the contemporary world, more particularly showing how sharia, which is essentially a path to a better life, can inform Muslims in the quest for a more credible identity in the 21st century.

Sharia – Origin through Revelation, Historical Development and Change

The Advent of Islam

The 7th century in Arabia was a watershed – the Roman Empire
had declined, the Sasanian and Byzantine empires were in decay
for reasons that are beyond the scope of this study, and a new
civilisation was coming into being thanks to the mysterious and
dynamic revelations received by an Arab from the Quraysh tribe
of Mecca, who claimed an inherited connection with Abrahamic
predecessors who had been prophets in the previous millennium
and were part of the narrative of the Bible. This man, who was a
trader employed by his wife Khadija, was Muhammad ibn 'Abd
Allah. In the course of his life he developed the practice of meditation, for which he would retreat to a cave in the hills surrounding
his city of Mecca. It was on one of these retreats that he was
assailed by the appearance of the Angel Gabriel, who ordered him
to read – *iqra!* – although he was said to be illiterate. Thus began
the revelations that became the core of the Qur'an, the holy book
of Islam.

At first, these revelations were ignored by the people of Mecca.
Only Muhammad's first wife, Khadija, recognised them as the
words of the divine, a mystery that had the potential to change the
world. As time passed, Muhammad's revelations were accepted by
a few of his close companions, even though the notions therein
were revolutionary and challenged the traditional tribal ways
of his people. In due course, Muhammad and his followers had

to escape from his enemies in Mecca, and some took refuge in
Christian Abyssinia and then later he and a few of his very close
companions were received in the oasis town of Medina. What
began as an exhortation to people to believe in the One God and
to follow a path of righteous faith and action became the basis of
a grand religious discourse which continues to profoundly influence hundreds of millions of people today. The Revelation opened
a powerhouse of spiritual and practical energy that swept across
the world, spreading from Mecca and Medina into the Sasanian
and Byzantine empires, and reaching as far as Spain and India
within a hundred years.[1]

The new religion challenged everyone. First, it affected the
local Arab population in the peninsula who were forced to
change their mode of behaviour, to adapt to, and adopt, the
more universal ethical and practical demands of the faith. Later,
it affected wider populations across the world, in Byzantium
and in Persian lands including Central Asia, with whose populations the newly energised Arabs had to find a modus vivendi
as conquerors and occupiers. This mélange of values, demands
and expectations revolutionised societies and brought great
changes in attitudes amongst many people who were now faced
with new norms that both challenged and integrated old values,
enriching both them and itself. Thus were born the foundations
of sharia, which at first was regarded as an ethical path but,
over the course of three centuries, developed into a system of
legal practice and conventions that has moulded the identity
of Muslims.

Sharia

Sharia signifies a path to a watering hole, a point of departure,
a journey – a straight and bounded path that leads to a desired
and desirable destination – which demands from the faithful
proper action and right belief according to the precepts sent
down in the Revelation. It also entails a duty to submit to the
will of the Almighty, but the term sharia is mentioned only twice
(as *sharī'a* and a synonym *shir'a*) in the Qur'an,[2] the supreme
holy text for Muslims, or the *umma*, which consists today of a

vast, diverse and multifaceted community of believers living in some 58 countries across the globe as well as in non-Muslim nation states. Sharia is, in a sense, law – but not law as we understand the term in modern secular societies. According to the American scholar of Islamic law Bernard Weiss, the scholars of Islam, independent of the caliphate,[3] aimed to control the development of a grass-roots spiritual leadership. In this sense, they were more than jurists in the usual sense of the term, for they attended to much more than the law. Their horizon encompassed an entire way of life and of day-to-day living that went beyond what usually counts for law in the modern world. This included a set of norms, legal, moral and ritual, which over time came to be known as sharia. For this reason, Weiss feels it would be 'incorrect to equate Sharia and law *simpliciter* as is often done'. He concedes, however, that law is clearly part of sharia in Muslim thinking and therefore must always be understood as such.[4]

Legal Content of the Qur'an

While the Qur'an was, and continues to be, the moral compass for Muslims, strictly speaking it does not provide a code of law. The legal content of the Qur'an amounts to about 10 per cent of its text.

The Qur'an, a book of dynamic tension, of great beauty and practical wisdom and advice, mentions sharia, as we have said, only twice. It should be noted that it does not dwell comprehensively on this aspect of the Islamic faith, as Noel Coulson points out: 'No more than approximately eighty verses deal with legal topics in the strict sense of the term.'[5] Sharia thus evolved and developed over the early centuries of the faith from a nascent, flexible process at the origins of Islam into an apparently hard-and-fast body of sacred law (to which are attached its various modes of implementation into positive law, known as *fiqh*) which informs the identity of Muslims today. This process did not take place immediately but evolved over three centuries. It should be reiterated that the word sharia does not have the same connotation as law as understood in the secular Western sense. The following diagram gives an idea of what we understand the term to encompass.

Sharia – An Interconnected System
RELATIONSHIPS

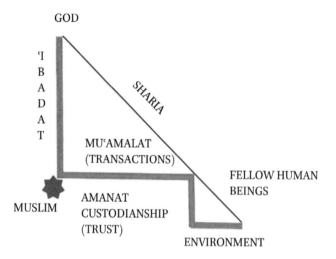

In this diagram, the vertical co-ordinate represents the individual's relationship with his or her creator, which is exemplified by worship and other acts of personal and communal piety, known as *'ibadat*. This includes praying, almsgiving, fasting, pilgrimage to Mecca and the affirmation of faith – the *shahada*: 'there is no god but Allah and Muhammad is His Messenger'.

Muslims also have a transactional relationship with their fellow beings, known in sharia as *mu'amalat* and covering commercial transactions such as contracts, civil actions including torts, domestic issues that affect inheritance and marriage, and other issues of a civil nature. In this part of sharia, of course, we should include criminal offences, which today in some cases have become problematic. This issue will be dealt with in Chapter 5.

The third relationship is based on Muslims' duty of responsibility to God's creation, to the planet, to all living creatures and to the environment. This dimension of the faith is called *amanat*, which means trust or acting as a trustee responsible for the upkeep of the environment to enable future generations to enjoy a healthy inheritance.

Sharia encompasses all these relationships, and the line in the diagram above that links all these points is the straight path labelled sharia. Muslims are obliged to adhere to this path, which has to be continuously assessed and interpreted according to the circumstances of the time.

Interpretation

Interpretation, which is a disciplined, dynamic and dialectical process, is essential to understanding the nature of sharia and, indeed, the faith of Islam as a whole. For observant Muslims, that is to say most Muslims, sharia arises from the parts of God's speech inscribed in the Qur'an, containing His voice in Arabic and collated a few decades after the death of the Prophet into a single volume (*mushaf*). The law, therefore, is distilled from God's speech into a text and has been later interpreted and expanded by certain legitimate and communally accepted processes which contain and affirm its pre-eminent standing. Clearly, sharia is distinct from law as understood in modern secular societies where its nature is subject to continuous examination and is a matter of philosophical and practical speculation and debate without a final answer.

From the earliest days of Islam the need for clarification and interpretation arose, and in keeping with the Quranic injunction, 'obey God, obey the Prophet and obey those who hold authority from amongst you',[6] the early community of believers (the *umma*) turned to the Prophet through whom the Qur'an was revealed, as he was closest to it in terms of time and reception. Thus the Prophet Muhammad became the medium of the Revelation and, in fact, its original interpreter.

Metonymic discourse (in which a concept or object is referred to by one of its attributes) was common in Arab societies of the time, as it is today, and so the reference to the watering hole of sharia alludes – as one would expect in the mainly arid environment of the Arabian Peninsula – to a place of succour, water being a precious element that sustains and enables an individual to survive; the water itself is limpid and clean since living creatures drink from it. This is a striking metaphor. However, to get to that place of serenity and redemption one has to follow the straight path that leads towards it.[7] This consists of practice and understanding, which is reached by interpretation. It is arrived at by personal effort and realisation guided by communal knowledge and the precepts of the law derived from the ordained readings of sacred pre-modern texts. We should note that interpretation is not an entirely subjective process but is legitimated and regulated by legal scholars – a process that is partly mediated through necessity and public interest. In theory, sharia is something given by God and its *fiqh* (jurisprudential understanding) is something made, a communally agreed construction of meaning and purpose in society and an ethical endeavour.

This process of evolution took place over many years, but immediately after the Revelation practical issues and problems arose that required ongoing clarification and resolution. To understand this state of affairs and acquire an insight into the early evolution of Islamic law, some background about the complex nature of Arabian society at this time is essential.

Arabia at the Beginning of Islam

Islam did not have an easy birth. Battles were fought, treaties were made and broken, and clans clashed with each other. Soon after the death of the Prophet in 632, war broke out. The so-called *fitna*, or period of internecine wars of early Islam, was largely concerned with issues of succession, legitimacy and power.[8] The extraordinary irruption of a new faith, which aimed to upset the world view of the mainly pagan Arabs, continued to hold its place and began to expand by way of conquest into new and contiguous territories within a few years. The old Sasanian and Byzantine empires, and political entities further afield, were overrun by a vibrant new society of Arabs who showed valour, martial skill, energy and political acumen of a high order. Soon an organised system of laws and rules was needed to define rights and obligations under a new socio-political order that was inspired by the new faith. With this expansion of territories and the growing number of new Muslims, new issues arose: new property was acquired, new family relationships came into being, new claimants for inheritance emerged and new principles of governance were required. The conquests, which brought with them social revolutions, set in motion major demographic shifts that created nominally Muslim societies which contained a great number of conquered peoples who were allowed to retain their own religious faith and traditions.

As already said, less than 10 per cent of the Qur'an is made up of verses of a strictly legal nature and yet a polity had to be formed that was inspired by the newly received Revelation in whose name the society would be shaped. Since the source of law was seen to be embodied in the original holy text, interpretations of the text, initially the Qur'an and later the life and sayings of the Prophet, became essential. After the Qur'an, the second most important source of law is the example of the Prophet, or Sunna. This was derived from the accounts of events in his life, his actions and his pronouncements which were initially handed down in the Muslim community by word of mouth. These are called *hadith* (a term used both singly and collectively in English), and a complex field of learning evolved around this subject, which included the means of judging the reliability of any particular *hadith* based on its 'chain of authority' (*isnad*) of oral or written transmitters and how trustworthy or otherwise they were adjudged to be. A number of these Traditions were invested a few centuries later with canonical status and further implemented into jurisprudence, called *fiqh* in Arabic, through the process of *usul al-fiqh*. This was a legal theory through which Muslim exegetes and jurists 'discovered' God's law through a process of reading the Qur'an and examining other texts which set out the sayings and deeds of the Prophet, collectively known as the Sunna and embodied in hadith. This was carried out by resorting to a notionally agreed community-generated consensus that was gained by discussions and practice amongst the legal scholars known as *ijma'* and, by way of *qiyas*, the process of analogical and deductive reasoning which has similarities with English Common Law. Therefore, the 'discovering' of the law through this process gave rise to jurisprudential understanding in the form of the positive law called *fiqh*, which was at the time a dynamic and fluid process for establishing the law.[9]

Initial Period 610–661

However, in the first 50 years after the Revelation, this process of 'discovering' the law was fluid and took place largely by way of informal consultations. These led mainly to extemporary solutions based on the Qur'anic injunction to 'obey God, obey the Prophet and obey those who hold authority from amongst you'.[10]

Muslims turned primarily to the Prophet, as divine ordinance required constant assessment from the beginning and the necessity for legal interpretation arose at an early stage after the Revelation – and continues to do so. The need to translate God's command into actuality became more acute with time and, more particularly, when the Prophet moved from Mecca to Medina in 622 where the first compact, known as the Constitution of Medina, was drafted.

Since the principles of the faith are set out in certain essential sacred texts, interpretation is a necessity, and interpretation was pursued actively from the early years of Islam. But interpretation gradually settled into an orderly and circumscribed practice over time, so that the key element of reading and understanding the Qur'anic stipulations and wisdom was conducted through the lens of the Prophet Muhammad's life in the Sunna as understood from the deeds and sayings ascribed to him. However, with the unequivocal endorsement of the Qur'anic Revelation, the importance of the Prophet's voice was established early in the development of the faith.

While pre-existing laws based on systems developed in the ancient empires continued to exist, some of these laws came into conflict with the specific rules that were coming into existence as the result of the Revelation. This was most apparent in family relations, where a new set of claimants arose who had not hitherto been granted any personhood under the tribal rules to which most Arabs of the Arabian peninsula were subject. The nature of pre-Islamic Arab society provides an essential backdrop to the challenges that Muslim administrators of the time faced. It also gives us an insight into the nature of the social reforms that took place on account of the new dispensations created by the Revelation, and which led to the call for the transformation of a society that had hitherto been bound together solely by kinship and tribal loyalties. Islam aimed to displace this old order with newly defined relationships based upon membership of a common faith, creating the notion of individual loyalty to one God over and above loyalty to a tribe. The individual's responsibility was based purely on doing good and avoiding bad.[11] A dynamic faith had come into being; the Islamic Revelation was swathed in new ideals, which included an overarching notion of justice and equality under the umbrella of a new understanding of monotheism.

Pre-Islamic Arab Society

Pre-Islamic Arab society is often described by Muslims as a period of *jahiliyya*, literally ignorance, and a benighted time before the Qur'anic Revelation, which claimed to return pagans, aberrant Christians and Jews back to the true faith of the first monotheist Ibrahim (Abraham). However, the notion of *jahiliyya* is misleading and simplistic; it reduces the stupendous changes brought about by the appearance of Islam to a sort of schematic step change. It imposes an imagined dichotomy between a time of impurity and a new era of purity and light discovered by the new Muslims, whereby darkness and oppressive paganism, replete with egregious decadence, are wiped away by the new faith. The truth is more complex, more contradictory and more interesting.

According to Wael Hallaq, a leading contemporary legal historian of Islam, the Muslims of the Arabian Peninsula who conquered the populations of the Byzantine and Sasanian empires were familiar with the cultures that had permeated their own, more austere, societies. Islam was the new revelation, but it was not something that arose *ex nihilo* to capture a totally alien world. Hallaq argues in his 2005 work *The Origins and Evolution of Islamic Law* that the new Islamic dispensation came about with Revelation, but it was in the context of an existing world formed by great civilisations. He writes: 'Prior to the Arab expansion in the name of Islam, Arabian society had developed the same types of institutions and forms of culture that were established in the imperial societies to the south and north, a development that would later facilitate the Arab conquest of this region.'[12]

Hallaq further makes the point that 'the Peninsular Arabs were not mere nomads subsisting on a primitive desert economy. While there were tribes ... who did lead a nomadic lifestyle, the majority of the Bedouins ... engaged in pastoral, agricultural and trading activities.'[13] Indeed, most of the Arab social groups at the time (and it could be argued that this condition exists even today in some areas) were tribal and sedentary, living in towns and at major oases, of which Mecca and Medina were important examples that lay on essential trade routes. This fact endowed these cities with a degree of cosmopolitan dynamism and culture. Complex groups or societies necessitated appropriate laws to ensure their orderly functioning.

Hallaq informs us that there were two types of law, one serving sedentary societies and another more Spartan system serving nomadic groups who looked essentially to customary laws. However, these laws and the prevailing culture were infused with what he calls 'the general legal culture of the Near East',[14] a culture that was already well established. Arab society of the time there-fore had a degree of social order supported by systems of laws both customary and derived from surrounding civilisations, and by a strong sense of identity that had been formed and delineated by the ancient practice of story-telling, which gave a framework or sense of a special world view and reinforced moral virtues suited to the time. This practice of narration, which formed a communal identity, helped to create the kinship and tribal loyalties which cemented the various groups within themselves and between themselves.

These ancient oral traditions, setting out heroic stories, memo-rialising noble tribal lineages and suggesting pagan values, built layers of meaning for the tribal communities and created precious self-understanding and self-presentation.

Pre-Islamic Practices

During the early years of Islam the relationships in the majority of Arab society by and large continued to be based on tribal lines.

The Qur'an itself refers to certain practices extant in pre-Islamic culture and extols the faithful to set them aside, an example being the brutal practice of female infanticide. The Qur'an states:

> When the female (infant) buried alive is questioned
> For what crime she was killed;
> When the Scrolls are laid open;
> When the World on High is unveiled;
> When the blazing Fire is kindled to fierce heat;
> And when the Garden is brought near
> (Then) shall each soul know what it has put forward.[15]

Prior to the advent of Islam, the tribe was the main pivot around which society revolved and individuals owed their allegiance to the tribe, which in turn protected them. In fact, a person's very identity and sense of selfhood were tribal, and so existing outside a kinship group was almost inconceivable – such a situation meant that one was an outlaw without status or recognition, less than a slave. The tribe provided norms which in effect controlled the behaviour of individuals without recourse to any legal sanctions. There was no real legislative authority and the enforcement of the law, as far as it existed, was the responsibility of the private individual who had suffered injury. Disputes were settled by force of arms in the case of intertribal antagonism and by the appointment of a suitable ad hoc arbitrator in the case of intra-tribal problems. Mecca and Medina, as important commercial centres, possessed a system of commercial law of sorts, but the sole basis of law lay largely in the tribal recognition of customary practice known as *'urf*. This source of legal application remained in force for centuries after the Revelation of Islam. Indeed, it played an important role in the development of the early stages of sharia and continues to be of importance in the shaping of the law even today.

Sharia as an Identity Marker

Sharia is therefore seen by many Muslims as a cornerstone of their identity. This continues to have force today and drives most Islamist discourse. According to Hallaq, writing in 2005:

One of the fundamental features of the so-called modern Islamic resurgence is the call to restore the Shari'a, the religious law of Islam. During the past two and a half decades, this call has grown ever more forceful, generating religious movements, a vast amount of literature, and affecting world politics. There is no doubt that Islamic law is today a significant cornerstone in the reaffirmation of Islamic identity, not only as a matter of positive law but also, and more importantly, as the foundation of a cultural uniqueness. Indeed, for many of today's Muslims, to live by Islamic law is not merely a legal issue, but one that is distinctly psychological.[16]

Writing almost 50 years earlier, Joseph Schacht states:

Islamic law is the epitome of Islamic thought, the most typical manifestation of the Islamic way of life, the core and kernel of Islam itself. The very term *fiḳh* [*fiqh*], knowledge, shows that early Islam regarded knowledge of the sacred Law as the knowledge *par excellence*. Theology has never been able to achieve a comparable importance in Islam; only mysticism was strong enough to challenge the ascendancy of the Law over the minds of the Muslims, and often proved victorious. But even at the present time the Law, including its (in the narrow sense) legal subject-matter, remains an important, if not the most important, element in the struggle which is being fought in Islam between traditionalism and modernism under the impact of Western ideas. Apart from this, the whole life of the Muslims, Arabic literature, and the Arabic and Islamic disciplines of learning are deeply imbued with the ideas of Islamic law; it is impossible to understand Islam without understanding Islamic law.[17]

This particular search for identity, which is fixated on a system of law, is problematic not only because it over-simplifies the notion of self-understanding or recovery, but also because sharia is itself a complex entity made up different schools of law, different modes of interpretation, and competing and sometimes conflicting modes of implementation. None of this can be glossed over by rhetorical calls to an imagined unity without creating a disjunction at the heart of what it means to be a person. Moreover, sharia does not cover, and has never covered, all aspects of a Muslim's or a Muslim society's experience and needs, and this is certainly even more the case in the modern world. Sharia has never been the sole legal system in Islamic societies, and in today's world there is no state where sharia is the exclusive legal system or legal order, not even in such countries as Saudi Arabia or Iran.[18] The central thrust of Islamic law which has evolved into fundamental elements of the faith is accounted for by the various schools of Islamic law, which we shall discuss in Chapter 2.

If sharia, as mentioned by Hallaq and by the earlier scholar of Islamic Law Joseph Schacht, is so critical to Muslim identity, we need to understand the basis of this notion and its origins, and to know more about Muhammad as prophet and ruler.

The Advent of Muhammad as Prophet and Ruler

In 622 Muhammad fled from Mecca to Medina, where he and his followers were welcomed by the Medinan Arabs and where his new role as prophet, leader and lawgiver started in earnest. A new society was in the making, and the newly formed Muslim state, which transcended kinship and tribal loyalties for a bond of a common faith, was born. The Prophet was thus able to establish a basic, mainly ethical, standard of behaviour as set out in the precepts of the Qur'an which, as Coulson points out, modified and creatively combined pre-Islamic customary laws for the new Muslims. In Coulson's words, the so-called legal matter of the Qur'an is not extensive, but 'consists mainly of broad and general propositions as to what the aims and aspirations of Muslim society should be'. Essentially, it is 'the bare formulation of the Islamic religious ethic'.[19]

These propositions included right conduct, compassion for the weak and needy, fairness, good faith in commercial dealings and incorruptibility in the administration of justice. But these ethical principles were not translated into a legal structure with corresponding rights and responsibilities. Violations, such as consuming alcohol and indulging in usury, are declared as forbidden (*haram*) in the Qur'an. However, no punishment is ascribed in this life for them. This is also true of the verses in the Qur'an that deal with polygamy and interest (*riba*). 'The primary purpose of the Qur'an', according to Coulson, 'was to regulate not the relationship of man with his fellows, but his relationship with his creator'.[20] Where the Qur'an deals with a number of subjects with legal undertones, they are in the nature of extemporary solutions rather than attempts to deal with specific topics in a comprehensive or legalistic way. A large part of the piecemeal nature of the legislation follows from the circumstances of the Revelation and the official compilation of the Qur'an, which took place some years after the death of the Prophet, whereby the longer *suras*, or chapters, were ordered from short to long, regardless of the time when they were revealed.[21]

The Early Period and the Need for Interpretation

By 628, having gained in political strength, Muhammad decided to make the pilgrimage from Medina to Mecca, which at the time was a centre of pagan pilgrimage.[22] The Meccans did not accept this state of affairs readily. The Prophet had to enter into a pact with them based on compromise and negotiated settlement. Therefore he now enjoyed the new status of being a recognised prophet by many of the Peninsular Arabs and of being regarded as the head of state of the first Muslim polity in Medina. The new political arrangement, reinforced by the Revelation granted to Muhammad, gave rise to a multitude of issues which required legal clarification.

Some Early Examples of Legal Interpretation

In the early days of Islam a number of legal systems co-existed, including Sasanian, Byzantine and Roman laws and customary practices. However, the Qur'an established a new set of norms by which the actions of the new Muslims could be assessed. An important part of these new legal arrangements dealt with inheritance, whereby a new set of claimants who formerly had no rights to inherit were now empowered by divine decree. These new rules inevitably conflicted with some of the tribal customs by which the Peninsular Arabs lived. Thus, whenever a conflict arose, Muslim administrators and dispute resolvers looked to the Prophet for clarification, based on the injunction embodied in the Qur'an.[23] Most of the legal issues during this period of Revelation concerned issues of inheritance in the family (including granting women specific rights for the first time) or matters to do with booty, as conquering Muslim armies returned from conquests with spoils that needed to be allocated. A second important innovation brought about by the Revelation in the Qur'an concerned divorce, which was permitted for the first time amongst Arabs, and it recognised new family relationships and rights based on who one's mother was and affinities of blood, which took precedence over traditional tribal norms.

The Prophet's decisions were derived from the Revelation he received, but these decisions also required thought and reason, especially when dealing with situations that were not explicitly dealt with in the Qur'an. This hermeneutic practice, which took hold with jurists in the early years of Islam amongst those in authority who had adequate religious knowledge, was called *ijtihad*, meaning to exert oneself in understanding the signs of God. This principle is reinforced by a verse of the Qur'an that supports this process of elucidation and interpretation, which is the basis of Qur'anic exegesis. The verse states:

> Behold! In the creation of the heavens and the earth; in the alternation of the night and the day; in the sailing of the ships through the oceans for the profit of mankind; in the rain which Allah sends down from the skies, and the life which He gives therewith to an earth that is dead; in the beasts of all kinds that He scatters through the earth; in the change of the winds, and the clouds which they trail like their slaves between the sky and the earth; (here) indeed are signs for a people that are wise.[24]

The practice of *ijtihad* is reinforced by a hadith of the Prophet. It concerns Mu'adh b. Jabal who was sent to Yemen as the designated head of a group of missionaries at the request of the king of Yemen. Mu'adh was reputed to have responded to the Prophet about the hierarchy of authority that he would follow during his mission. The hadith reports the Prophet questioning Mu'adh:

> 'According to what will you judge?'
> 'According to the Book of God,' he replied.
> 'And if you find nothing therein?'

'According to the Sunna of the Prophet of God.'
'And if you find nothing therein?'
'Then I will exert myself to form my own judgement.'

The Prophet was pleased with this reply and is reported to have said:

'Praise be to God who has guided the messenger of the Prophet to that which pleases the Prophet.'[25]

Some Specific Cases

The faithful approached the Prophet for certain practical decisions, such as inheritance issues, which were bound to arise given the transitional nature of tribal society. For instance, one Sa'd b. Abi-Waqqas is said to have sought the advice of the Prophet as to how much of his property he should bequeath to charity when his only relative was a daughter. The Prophet set the limit at one-third. There is another matter on inheritance, which is referred to as Sa'd's case. A widow of a soldier, Sa'd Rabi', who had died in the cause of Islam, found herself in dispute with her husband's brother, who was trying to deny a share of her husband's estate to two of their daughters.[26] On hearing this case, the Prophet decided that, according to a Qur'anic revelation, two-thirds should be allocated to the daughters, one-eighth to the wife and the rest to the brother. The process was largely informal at this time and the decisions were generally ad hoc; yet such decisions, being accepted as ordained, formed the foundations of the Islamic law of inheritance.

Matters were also referred for resolution to the Caliphs who succeeded the Prophet as the titular heads of the Muslim polity. From the nature of the cases and the names ascribed to them, one can observe the extemporary characteristics of such cases and the context of the interaction. For example, in the *Minbariyya* (pulpit) case – so-named because the case arose when the fourth Caliph, Ali, was interrupted as he was giving a sermon from the pulpit (*minbar*) – an elaborate device was proposed to reduce proportionately the fractional shares in inheritance as set out in the Qur'an when they totalled more than the whole. Abu Bakr, the first Caliph, allocated a whole estate in the first instance through a maternal grandmother, thus completely excluding a paternal grandmother, only to revise his decision later when one of the members of the family raised the issue that the Qur'anic disposition would unwittingly deal unfairly with the paternal grandmother. Another matter concerning inheritance affected a family where the new Qur'anic rules, such as they were, appeared to exclude the full brothers from inheritance. The case, known as the *Himariyya* (the Donkey), took its name from the way in which the full brothers explained that they wished to claim in their capacity as uterines (having the same mother) and waive their position as agnates (being descended from the same male ancestor). They asked Umar, the second Caliph, to assume that their father did not count. 'Consider him a donkey', they are reported to have said.

From these cases and others, it is evident that there was a growing tension between ancient customary rules and the new Qur'anic rules which had to be dealt with by those who had been in close proximity to the Prophet and by the Caliphs who succeeded the Prophet.[27] This was not dealt with in absolute terms, but the Caliphs were prepared to be flexible when they deemed it necessary. It should be noted that the power of positive legislation lay with the Caliphs only on the strength of the Qur'anic verse that states: 'obey God, obey the Prophet and obey those who hold authority from among you.'[28] Consequently, during the Medinan period (622–661), by way of a supplement to the Qur'an, the successive Caliphs Abu Bakr, Umar and Ali fixed penalties for the consumption of wine which Umar and Ali compared with the offence of the false accusation of unchastity (*qadhf*). All this was done in the interest of public order (*maslaha*). To the Caliph Umar is also ascribed the foundation of a fiscal regime, with the institution of the *diwan* or payroll register for dealing with the distribution of stipends. Umar also decided not to divide conquered territory and the booty arising from it. This constituted the foundation of the concept of land tenure in which the government was the fundamental holder, as is deemed in English law.

We do not want to give the impression that all these Caliphs only dealt with issues of inheritance and *hadd*-related (or, capital) offences.[29] Abu Bakr, the first Caliph, was in conflict with a group of followers who did not wish to pay taxes. Unfortunately, this dispute led to the Ridda Wars (632–633).[30] His advice to the military leader Khalid ibn al-Walid (585–642) after a campaign was to protect the women, children, elderly and worshippers of the conquered territories, a precursor of some of the principles of the Geneva Conventions which we respect today. The compact of Umar, the second Caliph, with the orthodox Patriarch Sophronius, when he entered Jerusalem and prayed outside the Church of the Holy Sepulchre, contained the principles of what today we regard as a pluralistic ethos, in that he did not wish to deprive the Christians (in this case) of their places of worship. The Arbitration of Siffin (ca. 657), in which the fourth Caliph, Ali, took part, was based upon principles which are used today in arbitration agreements. The arbitrators are required to be independent, the process must be approved by all parties to the arbitration, and arbitration takes place with reference to a specific legal system.

Since the new religion changed the affiliation of Muslims from that of exclusive tribal groups to the ties of family and a common bond of faith, the longstanding customary law arrangements of inheritance were disrupted for the new laws (Qur'anic rules) which gave rights to family members (Qur'anic heirs) who previously did not enjoy such rights. Umar, the second Caliph, also dealt with the issue of booty, which was becoming increasingly problematic due to the military successes of the Muslim armies. Furthermore, both Caliphs Umar and Ali played an important role in other legal rulings of a civil and criminal nature.[31] It should be reiterated that the Qur'an's legal content was minimal, and therefore at the end of the Revelation there was no fully formed Islamic law: this only developed subsequently, over the centuries. In the early years, much of the law was made in a piecemeal manner, when opinions were given to particular problems and those in authority used their personal insight and reason to create the law, in a process called *ra'y*.

During this initial period, customary law, the pre-Islamic legal system, continued to play an important and often decisive role in judgements. It was only with the onset of what is regarded as the classical period in the 10th century, when Islamic law and process took a definitive shape, that the preponderant influence of Arab customary law declined. This was only in certain contexts, however, because even in Arabia, notably Yemen, principles of customary law remained in use and continue to be applied today. It should be emphasised that there was no sudden change with the arrival of Islam, but there was a long period of evolution and a complex relationship of inclusion and containment between the growing formulation of Islamic law and the ancient practices of customary law.

Therefore, we see pre-Islamic customary law, administrative rulings, Sasanian and Byzantine laws and laws derived from the Qur'an all existing together in uneasy juxtaposition. While Malik ibn Anas, the eponymous founder of the Maliki school of law, respected and encouraged diversity in legal opinions as a legitimate phenomenon, there were others who felt this would lead to a dilution of law as a coherent force in society and thus deprive it of its necessary predictability. This sense of discomfort later opened the door for a more doctrinaire formulation of the *usul al-fiqh* in the time of Shafi'i, which is said to have led to the closure of the gate of *ijtihad*.

Important Characteristics of this Initial Period

This initial period of development of the law (622–661) coincided with a great deal of internal political strife concerning the relationship between the Rightly-Guided Caliphs, as they came to be known, and other members of the Prophet's family, who jockeyed for power following his death (632) when the issue of succession became important.[32] This period of about 39 years was less a Golden Age than a power struggle characterised by family rivalry, jealousy, intrigue, manipulation and political assassination.[33] However, despite these initial difficulties, the Caliphs were able to provide legal guidance and comparative stability, through a process of interpretation of the Qur'an and accommodation with customary law, to the nascent Muslim community. This took place in collaboration with the Companions of the Prophet (known as *sahaba*), and laid the basic foundations that helped the next stage of evolution of Islamic law under the Umayyad dynasty.[34]

Changes Islam Made to Customary Practices of the Peninsular Arabs

Pre-Islamic Arabia was a time of pagan practices, including female infanticide, disproportionate retaliation, polygamous marriages and the denial of inheritance rights to women. The Revelation brought certain changes, but their true effect has to be assessed in the context of what the Prophet was able to achieve in the short period of his life when he was receiving the Revelation. As we have stated, it should also be noted that the period immediately after his death was one of strife and uncertainty.

Apologists for Islam often claim that Islam brought about considerable changes in people's lives and their rights, particularly women's rights; but legal practices in Islamic history do not attest to such major changes. As mentioned above, the idealisation of a Golden Age created by the advent of Islam, according to which the ignoble values and practices of the old were swept away by the new faith, continues to capture the minds and hearts of many millions of Muslims today, creating a degree of cognitive dissonance that distorts the reality of history and, indeed, of political and cultural practice in the contemporary Islamic world. Self-justifying dreams are taken for ideals and ideals are taken for reality, and these have created, and are still helping to create, a vortex of misunderstanding and mayhem in the Muslim world.

To obtain a real appreciation of the revolutionary contribution made as a result of the Revelation, one has to understand the rooted nature of tribal society and the short lifespan of the Prophet after he assumed the stewardship of the Medinan state. This was just ten years, but during this time Islam brought fundamental changes to the lives of the Arabs of the Arabian Peninsula. For example, Islam accorded women a new status: as opposed to being objects of exchange and exploitation, they now became 'subjects' capable of contracting in their own right. They now had property rights, achieved mainly through the creation of a dower right which was revealed in Qur'an 4:4: 'Give women their dower'.[35]

The obvious intention of the Qur'anic rules, according to Coulson, was not to abolish the agnatic system (i.e. heirs in the male line) but merely to modify it, with the particular objective of improving the status of female relatives by imposing upon the male agnates an additional class of new heirs. The legislation, then, is by way of a supplement to, and not a substitution for, the existing customary law, which remained part of the culture and continues to do so.

This modification to customary practices is also apparent in the way Qur'anic rules significantly changed the whole notion of divorce by introducing the waiting period (*'idda*), whereby a husband could no longer discard his wife on a whim but had to wait until the expiry of the waiting period – three menstrual cycles if the wife was not pregnant, and the delivery of the child if she was. Apart from the equity of this, a practical effect of such a principle was that it provided for a period of reconciliation if the marriage could be salvaged, and enabled paternity to be established if she was pregnant. In the field of compensation for homicide, the Qur'an lays down the standard for just retribution in an echo of the maxim from Deuteronomy 19:21, which states 'life for life, eye for eye, tooth for tooth, hand for hand, foot for foot'. The Qur'anic version states in Q 2:178: 'O you who have believed, prescribed for you is legal retribution for those murdered – the free for the free, the slave for the slave, and the female for the female.' The verse also warns against disproportionate retaliation, which is regarded as a transgression. But here, while the Qur'an accepts *lex talionis*, or retributive justice, in its seemingly Deuteronomic form, it goes further in that it changes the pre-Islamic practice of rough justice by providing for proportionality through exacting a life for a life. Furthermore, the Qur'an states that it is more meritorious for the individual who has been harmed to forgive than to exact his rights under the *lex talionis* stated above. The terminology was also changed: the customary term *tha'r* (blood revenge) was replaced with *qisas* (just retaliation).

This principle of *qisas*, however, is open to abuse, all the more so since homicide in Islamic law is primarily a civil law offence rather than a crime, and the penalty may be commuted into a monetary payment. This entire process raises the issue of justice and fair punishment. The principle of compensation also contains a positive element of distributive justice, whereby the offended party is involved in any negotiated settlement. In terms of the negative aspect, a problem can arise when a Muslim commits a murder in a non-Muslim country and returns to his country of origin. Should a person be extradited for murder, for example in the United Kingdom, if he raises the defence that homicide under Islamic law is a delict (violation) and not a crime, and that he is ready and available to seek pardon from the victim's family? Difficulties can also arise in the case of crimes of honour committed in countries where homicide is a crime and extradition is called for from the country to which the perpetrator has moved and where murder may be considered to be a tort.

The changes brought about by Islam took centuries to establish, and arguably have still not been fully achieved. Some changes, such as those regarding women's property rights, occurred at the outset, while others took longer. It is important to emphasise that much of the tribal social fabric continued to exist and function, and that transformation took place gradually over centuries – although many of the practices and procedures of pre-Islamic Arabia were profoundly influenced by Qur'anic norms of fairness, justice and equity. This evolutionary process is known as change in a steady state. However, whereas the Sunni interpretation posits that customary laws should remain in place unless the Qur'an explicitly stipulates change, the Shi'i interpretation posits that the Qur'an changed the entire tribal legal culture and brought in a new dispensation, and therefore only when the Qur'an specifically endorses a traditional cultural practice should it continue. This differing attitude to the Revelation and its impact on pre-Islamic legal culture has important legal ramifications today in various areas of the law, and particularly with regard to inheritance and divorce. To a large extent, this influences the level to which pre-Islamic cultural practices today can vitiate the influence of the principles of sharia and, more particularly, *fiqh*. Developments in Islamic jurisprudential history show that the Qur'anic precepts 'form little more than the preamble to an Islamic code of behaviour for which succeeding generations supplied the operative parts'.[36]

What we see then in this initial period is that there was no specific corpus of law known as sharia or Islamic law as such, but we witness the origins of an Islamic legal ethic which begins to infuse society and the interrelationships between people, entailing general ethical principles such as fairness, compassion for the poor and social justice. While these principles were not law per se, the Prophet and the early Caliphs took political and pragmatic decisions based on the authority of the Qur'an, which enjoined the faithful to obey the Prophet and later the Caliphs by virtue of their close association with him. The Qur'an's revelations remain at this stage direct and monumental, without being mediated through later exegeses. The early Caliphs combined pragmatic decisions of statecraft with practical guidance on relationships between individuals and groups. The entire notion of the theory of law (*usul al-fiqh*) was yet to be formulated and articulated over the following centuries. The nascent Muslim polity resorted to the Rightly-Guided Caliphs for directions. Their practical decisions embedded in the ethics of the faith, coupled with their own exemplary behaviour, provided the necessary moral compass for the new Muslim world that was coming into existence. Islamic legal practice as such had yet to evolve, though direction in the form of guidance to administrative commanders was given by the Caliphs Umar and Ali respectively to the Companions Abu Musa al-Ash'ari and Malik al-Ashtar, who became governor of Egypt.[37] In these directions one can discern the rudiments of a legal/ethical culture of justice. The requirement for those who judge to be fair and beyond criticism was to follow these instructions.

Questions that Arise about Law and Legal Development Under the First Four Caliphs

One of the important questions arising from this formative period concerns the nature of legal practice during these early days of Islam. Were there any formal courts of law or were disputes resolved through informal methods of dispute resolution? In brief, were there formal structures existing side by side with informal ones? What was the nature and effect of the legal advice given by the early Caliphs to their administrators and legal functionaries? Was it binding or was it like a fatwa, simply a judicial opinion that was open to debate? Were the parties free to accept or ignore these legal utterances and what were the sanctions if they were not adhered to? The evidence is difficult to extract from a past that does not contain a plethora of writing or other physical imprints. While existing research suggests that there were no Islamic courts as such, forms of advice were given to governors by the Caliphs Umar and Ali on how to adjudicate on issues concerning the people governed by them. The advice did not take the form of technical or detailed legal opinions but exhortations to high moral virtue; these early Caliphs were intent on ensuring that governors acted with honesty, integrity and fairness.[38]

Evidence from this period also suggests that the Caliphs themselves submitted to forms of adjudication on certain matters – as for example when Umar dismissed a judge who had favoured him by offering him a cushion to sit on while the deliberations were taking place, and when Uthman lost a case that he could not prove, which also suggests that a process of providing evidence in a case was already formed. These particular instances demonstrate that even the Caliphs, who were held in great esteem by the Muslim population, were not above the law even at this early stage of its development. There are various examples of how the Caliphs in this period avoided any conflict of interest, either real or perceived. Ali's letter to Malik even today is viewed by many as a major cornerstone of social governance within the notions of Islamic principles.[39]

However, much of what we know about the beginnings of Islamic law is conjecture and hopeful discourse. There is a certain amount of information, more myth-making and hopeful construals, but a dearth of evidence. Writing of the early years of Islam, Wael B. Hallaq tells us:

we possess no court records or any other source that can inform us of how the judiciary operated during the formative period, or what went on in courts of law. We have no clear idea of the types of problems that were litigated, how they were resolved, what legal doctrines were applied, how the parties represented themselves, how accessible courts were for women, how the judges used social and/or tribal ties to negotiate and solve disputes, and so forth. Thus, none of these issues can be addressed here in a comprehensive fashion, if at all.[40]

What is clear is that during the early years of Islam the processes of legal adjudication were still incipient and thus not entirely formed.

Conclusion

In this chapter, we have attempted to show the nature of decision-making regarding dispute settlement at the time of the Prophet and by the Caliphs succeeding him, when problems were brought to them for their decision. This raises the question of the role of authority in such a society. We must remember that at the time there was no formal, doctrinal hadith or system of prophetic Sunna, and the Qur'an itself was in the process of being revealed to the Prophet. Second, therefore, law-making was fluid and early Muslims were not burdened by history and dogma. It can be said that the Prophet's authority was symbiotic; his authority was based upon assent from his followers who believed in him as the Prophet endowed with not only spiritual and moral but also political and legal authority.

The evolving Qur'an created a cadence of faith. It engaged an aura of sanctity – we must remember that the sacred was a living experience in the pre-Islamic world, hence the centripetal power of the Kaaba.[41] Certain values or virtues were respected at the time and continued to be so even after the establishment of Islam as a revolutionary paradigm whereby the divinity was transcendent and unified (*tawhid*). These heroic virtues included the notions of courage, fidelity, kinship and the finality of each individual's life, which travelled ineluctably towards death. For the pagan, this meant entering the abyss of nothingness, but Islam converted this nothingness into an eternal afterlife of either hell or heaven, and the faithful were now enjoined to make an eschatological choice. In the course of time, the motive for making such a choice became sharia or 'the way' to eternal salvation. Christians and Muslims alike have a millenarian world view, according to which believers will enjoy the eternal light of heavenly bliss, with unbelievers and the wicked consigned to hell.

In this chapter we have also tried to show that Islamic law came into existence over a period as a process of accommodation, acculturation and evolution, and further that the Qur'an, while it embodies some law, is not the exclusive source of law. Muslims inherited pre-existing legal systems, which they drew on over time and adapted to new Qur'anic norms. The first phase was under the Prophet and the Rightly-Guided Caliphs and came to an end in 661 with the assassination of Ali, the fourth Caliph, and the first Shi'i Imam,[42] following a protracted period of internecine struggle. During this period, the caliphate operated mainly in Medina in Arabia but also in Iraq, to where Ali moved in the last years of his life.

In 661 the governor of Syria, Mu'awiya, the first of the Umayyad dynasty, proclaimed himself Caliph, and in his time we see the beginning of sharia taking shape as an organised legal practice. This development took place under the Umayyad dynasty, based in Damascus, which ruled the Muslim world for the next 90 years.

We should note that while we discuss sharia in the context of distinct periods of caliphates, the historical reality was less schematic in that, although the Umayyads took power in 661, there were rival caliphates in Medina and Kufa for a short period until they were vanquished by the Umayyads. The Umayyads were replaced in the Middle East by the Abbasids about 90 years later, and a branch of this dynasty continued to rule in Andalusia well into the 15th century. Similarly, though the Abbasids ruled from Baghdad to 1258, when the Mongols destroyed their rule, there were dynasties who ruled in their name but were not strictly Sunnis, for example the Buyids, and the Idrisids of Morocco. Moreover, the Fatimids, who ruled in Tunisia and Egypt between the 10th and the 12th centuries, were a Shi'i dynasty whose caliphate co-existed with that of the Abbasids.

Chapter 2 will show how legal practice developed in the Umayyad period (661–750), when the Muslim powers made their greatest territorial expansion within a very short space of time and laws had to be adapted to meet the needs of a burgeoning empire made up of diverse peoples with different traditions, histories and laws, stretching from the Oxus in Asia through the Middle East and across North Africa to the Pyrenees in Europe.

It will also show that at no time was sharia the exclusive law used by Muslims. There was a process known as the *siyasat al-sharia*, which enabled laws that were not especially sacred or religious but practically necessary to allow societies to function more efficiently to be promulgated over the course of time.

Legal Practice under the Umayyads (661–750)

Rapid Expansion and Early Development of Law

The year 661 saw the next phase in the development of sharia, with Mu'awiya proclaiming himself as the Caliph of Islam under a new dynastic order known as the Umayyads and ruling from Damascus, which he made his capital.[1] The following map shows how Muslim armies, during the time of the Umayyads and building on earlier conquests, had made major inroads into many lands, including the regions formerly ruled by the Sasanian and Byzantine empires. Muslims had reached the base of the Pyrenees and their empire extended to the Oxus river in Central Asia. The new demography encompassed a mixture of different cultures, races and creeds. All these changes took place within 100 years of the Revelation.

Expansion of Islam within the First Century of the Revelation

The approach to law and its development that had taken place so far in the Medinan oasis had been relatively parochial and ad hoc, shaped in order to meet the burgeoning needs of a rapidly expanding empire. But it now assumed a different approach. Under Umayyad rule the office of the *qadi* began to emerge as a visible, though not immediately influential, feature in the legal landscape.[2] This was by design rather than by default, as

Expansion of Islam within the First Century of the Revelation

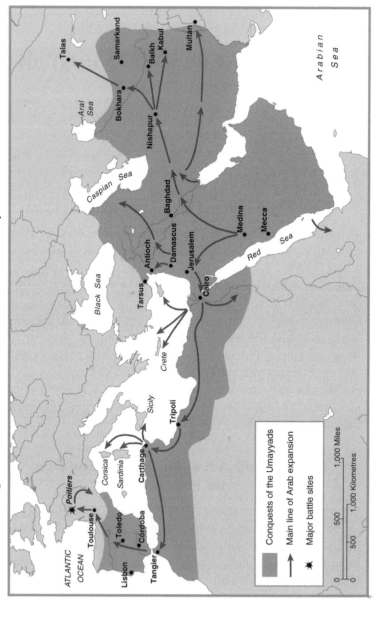

Arabian Sea

Talas
Samarkand
Balkh
Kabul
Multan

Aral Sea

Bokhara

Nishapur

Caspian Sea

Baghdad

Medina
Mecca

Damascus
Jerusalem

Antioch

Red Sea

Tarsus

Cairo

Black Sea

Crete

Sicily

Tripoli

Corsica
Sardinia
Carthage

Poitiers
Toulouse
Toledo
Córdoba

ATLANTIC OCEAN

Lisbon
Tangier

Conquests of the Umayyads
Main line of Arab expansion
Major battle sites

0   500   1,000 Miles
0   500   1,000 Kilometres

the Umayyads were viewed by the rank and file of Muslims as usurpers and it would not have been in their best interests to invest a *qadi*, primarily responsible with the remit of applying religious laws, with too much power and prestige; this could have become a locus of challenge to their authority. Hence, the early *qadi*s operated largely as assistants to provincial governors who were exclusively appointed by, and beholden to, the new Caliph. Unlike his predecessors, Mu'awiya was not prepared to be a servant of the law; rather, he intended to be its master, proclaiming himself Caliph of God (Khalifat Allah, that is to say Deputy of God), as opposed to Caliph of the Messenger of God, the title adopted by his predecessors. Sharia, which was still in the process of being formed, was not regarded by Mu'awiya as the function of God's commands, but more as a tool to secure his own legitimacy.

In the development of sharia, we shall see how this policy ironically had the opposite effect of what Mu'awiya and his successors had intended. By the end of Umayyad rule in the East in 750, the *qadi*s, who started out as subordinate functionaries and servants of the rulers, had acquired more authority, status and experience and became the prototypical practitioners of the law, antecedents of the later classical legal scholars who became the custodians of what came to be regarded by Muslims as the eternal and sovereign system of the law, which consisted of sharia and *fiqh*.

Other Courts and Legal Functionaries

The Umayyads also borrowed concepts from other legal systems and institutions which they modified and adapted for use by a Muslim polity. For example, they adopted from Roman law the notion of *dhimma*, whereby non-Muslims were given protection in exchange for a poll tax (*jizya*) paid to the authorities. From Byzantine law, they adopted the concept of endowment or *waqf*, which became an important legal tool through which trust property could be held. Further, they borrowed the concept of the *agronomus* (market inspector) from Byzantine law and combined it with the Islamic idea of *hisba* (the monitoring of the observance of Islamic principles) and invested the *muhtasib*, a new

functionary, with responsibility for looking after the moral standards of his area, yet still operating within the original marketplace
where the *agronomus* was situated.

There were also *mazalim* courts that were designed to redress
injustices or grievances. Although there was no clearly defined
appellate structure, these courts acted as such. Their remit was
concerned largely with administrative and fiscal regulations.
These rules were subject to a system of appeals which was vested
in the Caliph and the governors. Effectively, this can be argued
to be the beginning of the differentiation between religion and
the state at a very early stage in the evolution of Islam. So *siyasat
al-sharia*, 'government in accordance with the revealed law',
came into existence during this time and, while influenced by
the ethical principles of sharia (see Chapter 12), was not part of
this system of law, which was still in the process of coming into
being. It was, in fact, separate from sharia and *fiqh* which were
consolidated into different legal schools in the centuries after the
death of Muhammad, initially those of Medina and Kufa.

Legal Pluralism

Given the wide geographical scope of the expansion, Muslim
armies, tradesmen and others had interactions with people
from a number of different cultures, faiths and traditions. Legal
interaction must have taken place of the kind that initially faced
the Medinan community, and God's law as outlined in the Qur'an
must have entered the hearts and daily lives of millions of the newly
converted people. Yet very little is known today of the different
court practices in places as diverse as Spain, China, North Africa
and Afghanistan, all of which came under Muslim sovereignty in
the first century of Islam. A factor often overlooked is that the
customary laws of many of these conquered peoples continued
to be practised and, as in the Middle East, legal pluralism became
a fact, with a range of laws co-existing under the broad rubric
of sharia. The focus here is not to dwell on this as much as to
describe the developments that took place in the Middle East and
to extrapolate a number of conclusions in the form of questions,
many of which still remain unanswered today.

Continuation of Legal Development

With the coming to power of the Umayyads, we see the beginnings of a legal structure. Up to this point, and for some time
to come, the law was regarded as a means of maintaining order
and infusing new ethical principles as enunciated in the Qur'an,
but it was not the dominant presence that reigned over Muslim
identity that it later became. The tension had been largely between
pre-Islamic customary laws and the incipient Qur'anic legislation.
The expansion into new territories (such as Kufa and Basra)
governed by pre-existing Sasanian and Byzantine laws gave rise to
different issues, and this is where a sharper distinction took place
between Muslim public and private laws.

The legal systems in operation across the Muslim empire were
not institutionalised. The implementation of legal decisions,
which were made in several places – the mosque, the marketplace, the home of the judge or *qadi*, or those of the early jurists
(*fuqaha*) – was ad hoc in most cases but supported by the political
authorities. Therefore the situation was fluid, open-ended and
diverse, influenced by the particularities of the region where the
decision was taken. Furthermore, the laws were hybrid and shaped
by local customary ordinances that existed before the advent of
Islam. They were also influenced by the fledgling rulings or *sunan*
of the Prophet, his immediate successors, the Caliphs, and by
the traditions of the tribal areas in which a case was being heard
or by the newly developing schools of law located in important
centres such as Medina, Kufa and Basra which, at this time, were
still in an embryonic stage. Indeed, the legal functionaries in the
employment of the Caliph had a degree of interpretative freedom
known as *ra'y*, whereby they used various methods of reasoning
including the process of analogy and interpretation within the
ambit of the text of the Qur'an. This interaction took place across
the vast areas covered by the Islamic empire, which inevitably
meant that the law was influenced by local laws, and customs.
While there was a degree of consistency with regard to *siyasat
al-sharia* or the administrative and financial legal systems, it is
clear that sharia itself was implemented with all sorts of regional
variations, whereby the local *qadi* took note of local customs and

cultural expectations which came under the general heading of
'urf. This practice remains extant to a degree even today. Hence a
problem needing a legal solution may have different outcomes in
a *qadi* court in Morocco and a *qadi* court in Indonesia.[3]

After the End of the Rule of the
Rightly-Guided Caliphs

One of the key problems facing the newly created Muslim
community was to find a way of understanding God's law or
sharia. This process of discovering God's law compelled the
faithful to return to the sources of the law – *usul al-fiqh* – which
meant finding or uncovering and constructing these sources in
various ways. The process of *usul al-fiqh* took some centuries
to mature but often it has been backward projected as having
started with the death of the Prophet. While such reasoning as
embodied in the notion of the *usul al-fiqh* must have taken place,
it has been argued that it does not seem to have been carried out
in any formal sense and, furthermore, the Sunna it referred to,
which was attributed to the Prophet, had not been set down in
its final developed form. Clearly, *usul al-fiqh* was a later construct
that enabled the legal structures of sharia and *fiqh* to develop in an
orderly fashion, thus giving a necessary uniformity and certainty
to later Islamic law.

Theological Discourses

Issues of a theological nature emerged soon after the Prophet's
death and these undeniably had an important influence on how
believers interpreted and understood God's law. Moreover, these
debates were closely linked with struggles for power – political
and cultural, religious and philosophical. The first major debate
was between the Kharijites (Seceders) and the Murji'ites (Post-
poners) around the basic definition of who was a Muslim. The
notion of identity, belonging and group loyalty was central to
this polemic, and affected issues of leadership and authority.
While the Kharijites prescribed certain conditions for being a

Muslim, the Murji'ites held that whether one was a Muslim or not was only for God to decide. This difficult and controversial issue, which had its inception in the war in 657 between Mu'awiya and the last Rightly-Guided Caliph, Ali, remains a perennial debate in the Muslim world with important and in some cases fatal consequences. The cardinal point here is that while sharia was still developing into a more comprehensive system of law and legal practice, other social norms played an essential part in the creation of a legal system. The religious dimension was dynamic and was becoming increasingly central and pivotal to the understanding and implementation of the law.

Some of this dynamic influence can be seen in the passionate debates between those known as the *ahl al-ra'y* – that is, those who believed in the efficacy of personal reason based upon custom and a loosely analogical devolvement from the principles of sharia, which took note of the metaphorical nature of language and thus its role in reasoning – and the *ahl al-hadith* – a group who were essentially literalists, classificatory and traditionalists. This early debate amongst Muslims was an important stage in the development of Islamic law. The classical scholar Ibn Hanbal (780–855), a champion of the *ahl al-hadith*, collected 40,000 hadiths that were understood to be the sayings and reports of the deeds of the Prophet; these later became an essential element of the legal consensus that formed the basis for interpreting sharia. Indeed, this record of prophetic sayings and reports gave rise to a new school of law, the Hanbali school. As a result of these developments, the status of the Prophet was about to be changed posthumously from that of a human interpreter to someone who foresaw the future – a development that was crystallised in the early Abbasid period. The Turkish commentator Mustapha Akyol refers to this when he states:

> Unlike the image of Jesus in Christianity – who, as the Word of God, had existed since eternity and entered into history by becoming flesh – Muhammad was just a human… Interestingly, though, Muslim tradition would later exalt him to a suprahuman figure who, like Jesus, existed before time and universe and performed many miracles on earth … this 'Prophetology' contributed to the rise of an

all-encompassing Sunna (prophetic tradition) as a stagnant force in Islam more than a century after the Prophet's death.[4]

In addition to the intellectual ferment described above, other debates and battles for ideas were taking place. There was a fundamentally important debate between those who argued that the Qur'an was a created book or word of God, who were known as the Mu'tazilites,[5] and the Ash'arites, those who maintained that the Qur'an was coterminous with God and that it contained His speech, which was a part of the deity in existence for all time. According to the Mu'tazilites, the *created* status of the holy text meant that it needed to be constantly interpreted and read in time and in the context *of* the time when it was read. According to the Ash'arites, the *uncreated* book or *mushaf*, had existed and will exist forever and so was out-of-time, an aspect of the divine that was to be read *literally*, without the need of human interpretation, which was regarded as a pernicious form of interference tantamount to disbelief or *bid'a*. Therefore they deemed the holy text to be a monolithic object incapable of interpretation, as if the practice of reading a text consisting of language – in the case of the Qur'an the word of the Divine, which was essentially infinite and mysterious – was not in itself an act of interpretation and an inherent cultural time-bound praxis. This issue is dealt with in more detail in Chapter 3.

This conflict, nonetheless, remains an issue and has crystallised into the bedevilled dichotomy between the notion of *ijtihad* and *taqlid*, and the potentially hazardous conjugations of reason against the unquestioning and purifying submission to the literal holy text, the latter becoming the orthodoxy with consequences for Islam and Muslim culture that we shall see unfolding in Chapter 4. The reasons for the Ash'arites becoming dominant was mainly political, since they served to legitimise the power of the Abbasid caliphate by their insistence on unquestioning submission to authority – that of the Caliph – and their belief in predestination which clearly authenticated the ruler's position since the present state of affairs was inevitably the creation of God's will. This will be further developed in Chapter 3.[6]

One quarrel, which began in the Umayyad era between the groups called the Qadariyya and the Jabriyya,[7] consisted in the former claiming that it was unjust for God to punish human beings if they did not have free will. They developed the idea that human beings were responsible for the choices they made and determined their lives accordingly. The Jabriyya, on the other hand, argued the opposite, stating that people were slaves of the Divine, doing what 'God had written for them'. The Umayyads used this quarrel for their own purposes, and executed one of the leading Qadariyya proponents who opposed their rule. This incident presaged the authoritarian direction that the Muslim political compact was beginning to take at an early stage.

Later in the early 10th century, independent scholars such as al-Maturidi argued in favour of Muʿtazalite philosophy,[8] even though it was dealt a grievous blow in the 8th century, and whose theology was followed by Abu Hanifa, the great founder of the Hanafi school of law. The Hanafis are the major school of Islamic law today.

In the context of theological debates and discourse in the Sunni world, another important school of thought was developing amongst the Shiʿa which would finally be stated as the Jaʿfari school of law after the Shiʿi Imam Jaʿfar al-Sadiq, a direct descendant of the Prophet. He is renowned for his status as a legal expert as is his father, the Imam Muhammad al-Baqir. Later the Zaydi and Fatimid branches of legal discourse developed from this branch of Islamic legal thought.[9] While the Shiʿa are a minority in the Muslim world, they are an important minority both in terms of their numbers – they are the established religious community in Iran and form a majority in Iraq – as well as in their intellectual, theological and cultural influence in the Muslim world. They also form part of the population of Syria, Lebanon, Bahrain, Yemen and Afghanistan. They can also be found in Saudi Arabia, Pakistan and India. The Ismailis, who follow a *tariqa* (persuasion or pathway) of Shiʿi Islam, also have an important presence in the culture and politics of those countries, both Muslim and non-Muslim, in which they live. Shiʿism, therefore, plays an invaluable and important role in the Islamic world, and its historical role in the development of sharia, somewhat understated in the past, must be taken into account and is covered more fully in Chapter 7.

Dictated by the circumstances of the time, the Umayyads wished to preserve the existing administrative structure in the former Byzantine and Sassanian provinces, and so adopted many concepts and institutions that were of 'foreign' origin. They had to deal with very diverse populations whom they had to accommodate in the new polity. Jewish and Christian communities, known as *dhimmis*, were thus allowed their own personal laws administered by their own tribunals. The Umayyads also built on the fiscal principles inaugurated by Umar, the second Caliph. During the Umayyad period, principles and practices of foreign law gradually found their way into the nascent Islamic legal system, so that by the mid-8th century they were taken as an indigenous norm rather than as an import of foreign origin.

The *Qadi*

The office of *qadi*, as a prototypical functionary associated with sharia, was the creation of the Umayyad administration. The *qadi* was the delegate of, and subordinate to, the local governor, entrusted with the task of settling disputes as the new system could no longer sustain the practice of ad hoc arbitrators. In the early days, the chief of police and the master of the treasury acted as *qadis*. In 717 the Egyptian *qadi* was additionally in charge of the state granary. It would appear that it was only towards the end of the Umayyad period that the *qadis* became exclusively concerned with judicial business. As they became more involved in legal affairs, the function of the *qadi* evolved into a position that was less dependent on the political authorities, and in fact Khayr ibn-Nu'aym also held the office of *qass*, or instructor of religious precepts and precedents. This joint position continued for some decades.

As subordinate officials, the *qadis* were beholden to the political authority, but their directives were largely of an administrative nature, although at times there are instances of them seeking and receiving advice from their political superiors on points of law. By and large, the Umayyad administrators were content to leave matters of religious law in the hands of the *qadis*. Given the fact that sharia was not the only law of the land, the result was that there was greater uniformity in the field of public law where the *siyasat al-sharia* applied and was implemented by the central authority. Fiscal law and the treatment of non-Muslim communities, the responsibility of the central authority, were more coherent. In the field of private law, there was greater diversity because the *qadi*'s work was to apply local law, which varied considerably throughout the newly conquered territories, on top of which the *qadi*s enjoyed a great degree of discretion in applying the law in any particular case. This meant that the law was heterogeneous at this level. There was no system of precedent to anchor the application of the law across the dispersed territories. Society in Medina remained loyal to Arabian tribal customs, whereas in Kufa, a town which began life as a military garrison, the existence of diverse ethnic groups operating in an environment of Persian culture gave rise to a more cosmopolitan ethos. This has had a particular impact on women's rights today, especially with regard to a woman's ability to contract or to dissolve her marriage without the intervention of a guardian.[10] It should also be noted that under Article 78 of the *Moudawana* (Personal Status Code) in Morocco a marriage can be dissolved by the husband or by the wife. Far-reaching changes have also taken place in Tunisia with a 2017 change in the Family Law in favour of gender equality.

Another reason for the diversity in legal practice was the power of individual judges to decide cases according to their personal opinion (*ra'y*), which to a large extent was unrestricted. The political authorities were rather lax about this development and there was no hierarchy of superior courts that could create binding precedents in the nature of case law. Laws based directly on Qur'anic injunctions did not provide a strong unifying element because their application was dependent on the knowledge of individual judges, many of whom, apart from applying basic and simple rules, added their own reasoning to decisions. This process was identifiable in family law decisions where specific injunctions from the Qur'an were interpreted according to the cultural practices of different areas of the empire, and according to the variant readings of the Qur'an and diverse opinions of the *qadi*s. One such example was the rights of a finally repudiated wife during her waiting period before she could remarry, or '*idda*; another is the issue of 'fair provision' as enjoined by the Qur'an for such repudiated wives, where the outcomes were different in different parts of the empire.

During the Umayyad era we thus witness the further development of Islamic law even if it remained relatively localised, flexible, provisional in some cases and dependent on the expertise, knowledge and idiosyncrasies of the individual *qadis*. We should note that *fiqh* as we understand it today was not yet in existence during the Umayyad period. As we have seen, by the end of the period *qadis* had become an integral and important part of the administrative machine of the Muslim world. They controlled the customary law, which they adapted to meet the changing circumstances of society. Therefore the basic material of local customary law, as Coulson reminds us, was modified by the elaboration of Qur'anic rules, which were overlaid by administrative regulations and also infiltrated by elements of foreign law. The process of pragmatic application and accommodation of rules and law created a complex universe of legal dispensations in which the purely Qur'anic focus, as was predominant in the early Medinan period, lost its centrality. The Umayyads, who were essentially pragmatists, were mainly concerned about governing a vast and multifarious empire and seemed not to have the drive or the philosophical tools to create a uniform system of law.

While the Umayyad empire expanded at a rapid rate, what is not clear is the extent of the reach of the *qadi* system which they had set up to govern the cosmopolitan demographics that made up the empire. There were many schools of law still in an embryonic stage and a large number of individuals who enjoyed both charismatic appeal coupled with the moral stature to be points of reference for people who wanted to understand how the Almighty intended them to lead a proper life within the bounds of His injunction that enjoined good and forbade evil. These were scholars who belonged to various orientations. Amongst such were Muhammad al-Baqir and Ja'far al-Sadiq, the early Shi'i Imams descended from Ali b. Abi Talib, the first Shi'i Imam and the fourth caliph, and his wife Fatima the daughter of the Prophet. Regarded by their followers as true successors to the Prophet the Shi'i Imams were known for their learning and spirituality. In the field of jurisprudence, Imam al-Baqir and Imam al-Sadiq had a reputation for learning and discernment that was acknowledged throughout the Muslim community.[11] Their thinking on legal issues became known as *madhhab ahl al-bayt* ('the school [of law] of the House of the Prophet'), and individuals turned to them for advice and guidance on various matters. For the faithful, the Imams' guidance constituted the final word in their disputation. However, it is not clear how far their opinions featured in the legal system or in the legal affairs of those who were not the Imams' adherents.

This guidance from the Imam could be a form of what we today refer to as Alternative Dispute Resolution (ADR), although it is not clear how enforcement took place when one of the disputants defaulted on an undertaking. Here it must be remembered that research on legal practice at this time is still not fully developed and that our categorisations and analysis tend to be retrospective. We are not even sure that law-making in that period was the exclusive preserve of the political authority, though we do know that the Umayyads set up the *qadi* system as we know it today.

Of interest is the fact that Muslim jurisprudential thinkers worked together on major issues arising from sharia and that these two Shi'i Imams played a seminal role at a formative period of jurisprudential thinking through their interaction with the eponymous founders of two Sunni schools Abu Hanifa and Malik b. Anas.[12] It must also be noted that the various *fiqh* formulations were not yet consolidated and their contribution was viewed within a broadly ecumenical context, thus contributing to a community of believers known as the *umma*.

Conclusion

In this chapter, we have aimed to set out the early stages of the development of legal practice in the Islamic world, which slowly began to take shape in the essentially volatile and effervescent environment of the growing imperial reach of the new Muslim conquerors. It was not a smooth development or a simple discovery of new worlds. There was internal strife, and external issues, and the nascent community was faced with some of the greatest challenges any society can ever face, and the Muslims of that period met them with great courage.

Most of these dynamic changes were carried out by a dynasty that had usurped power and indeed had killed the Prophet's favourite grandson, Husayn. The members of the dynasty were not particularly friendly to the Prophet or his family, although they belonged to the same Meccan tribal group. Ironically, this dynasty is accredited with laying the foundations of an Islamic legal structure that has existed in some form or other up to the present day. As far as law is concerned, accommodations to the needs of society took place from the very beginning but for different purposes and in different contexts. In the case of the four Rightly-Guided Caliphs, who succeeded the Prophet, the development of the law took place in a relatively confined environment, primarily to accommodate the new dispensation exhorted by the Qur'an with the tribal ethos of a largely Bedouin culture. Subsequently, accommodation was practised by religious functionaries employing *ra'y* and ministering to the needs of a cosmopolitan demography under a more secular type of political authority. In the first case, we see an accommodation of customary practices and, in the latter case, the reception of 'foreign' laws. Islamic law was then administered as an Islamic legal ethic in which behaviour was infused with certain moral principles. In the case of the Rightly-Guided Caliphs, the law developed as it arose. In the case of the Umayyads, it acquired a more formal shape, with administrative and fiscal laws developing side by side with sharia but not administered by the same functionaries or legal institutions.

These accommodations raise questions. How does one define *umma*? Originally, the term applied to all people, but soon after the advent of Islam it connoted only a communal identity of believers. Non-believers were exempt from sharia and they were able to maintain their own tribunals. It is not clear to what extent some of the criminal sanctions that applied under the Byzantine and Sasanian legal systems applied in the new Islamic dispensation in which, for example, murder as such was not (and still is not) a crime. How did sharia laws apply to an expanding world made up of Muslims and non-Muslims? These issues continue to cause problems for many non-Muslim communities living within

Muslim-majority countries and in turn raise the further issue of the sort of obligations a Muslim state owes to non-Muslims and how these differ from its obligations to Muslims. Furthermore, the question also arises as to whether Muslims themselves are sometimes deprived of certain constitutional guarantees on account of being Muslims. These issues raise the question of the validity of the notion of a nation state as understood in its post-Westphalian sense and how it is understood in the Islamic sense. The idea of the *umma* appears to contradict the construct of a nation state which, in any case, has become less stable in the contemporary world.

Many of the important issues that weigh down Islamic law today originated in the era of the Umayyads and have remained unresolved. These include questions such as who has the right to create and promulgate the law. This echoes the problem of the status of faith over the world – or, as Muslims put it, between *din* and *dunya*. Do Sunni legal functionaries, operating under the aegis of the state, or in the case of the Shi'i Muslims the *mujta-hid*s, have the sole right to make and implement the law?[13] Or do the political authorities holding power in the name of the faith have this right? To get a better idea of how these issues played themselves out in the history of Muslim peoples, we turn now to what happened in the time of the Abbasids, the dynasty that ruled Islam from the 7th century for approximately five centuries.

Consolidation of the Schools of Law under the Abbasids (750–1258)

The Abbasids

The Abbasids, who came to power claiming descent through al-Abbas, an uncle of the Prophet, ruled the Islamic Empire from 750 to 1258. After claiming that the dynasty of the Umayyads had degenerated into decadence and injustice, the leaders of this movement seized power through a number of battles in Persia and Syria, promising a return to justice and legitimate rule. The movement ostensibly championed the Family of the Prophet (Ahl al-Bayt). The Shiʿa, whose primary loyalty was to the Prophet and his immediate progeny, welcomed this move, but they became disillusioned since the Abbasids had their own political agenda.[1] With the advent of the new dynasty, Islamic law entered a new phase in its evolution, and the developments that took place during this period have had a lasting impact on the law and its critical role in shaping Muslim identity.

The Abbasid caliphate began its rule by impugning the Umayyads, whom they accused of not being sufficiently true to the evolving Islamic spirit and ethos. Therefore they called upon the pious scholars of the time – the eponymous founders of the fledgling legal schools – to crystallise their grasp of God's law into different schools of legal understanding and prescription known as *madhahib*.[2]

Subsequently, the Abbasid Caliphs sponsored and actively encouraged these embryonic legal formulations, later called *fiqh*, to be consolidated into schools of law. At first, these pious legal scholars were not practitioners. Ostensibly disdaining the previous legal developments of the Umayyad period, their development of legal doctrine took place almost in isolation, while the heterogeneous business of legal practice continued in parallel. Gradually, however, their approach was infused into legal practice as some of the scholars themselves took on the role of *qadis* and legal advisors to the body politic. As a part of this development of sharia, some legal scholars, such as al-Shaybani,[3] wrote treatises on various practical issues such as fiscal and penal regulations, which aimed to be in line with the ethos of Islamic values and Abbasid political needs. Al-Shaybani attributed his work to his teacher, Abu Hanifa, the eponymous founder of the Hanafi school of law. This historical development of sharia in its earlier stages was thus encouraged by the Abbasid rulers, who assigned the task of creating the new Islamic order to the legal scholars based upon their understanding of the Islamic values as expressed by sharia, which acted as a binding force that held together the evolving Muslim community (the *umma*) as a godly and orderly entity. It was under the political sponsorship of the Abbasid Caliphs that the Sunni schools of law were finally formulated into their classical status.[4]

Continuing Theological Discourses

This jurisprudential development has to be viewed against the backdrop of various theological discourses that were taking place in the Muslim regions at the time. There was the crucial debate between the Mu'tazilis and the Ash'aris about the ontological nature of the Qur'an – whether it was the created (leaving it open to interpretation and debate) or the uncreated word of God (and thereby an essential and eternal aspect of the divine, which was transcendent and beyond human interpretation in principle). This issue, as we shall later see, had a profound influence on the nature of Islamic thought and Muslim consciousness which continues to the present day. As we have noted in the previous chapter, there was also a debate between the *ahl al-ra'y*, who based legal opinions on personal reasoning and the *ahl al-hadith* who based them on the Sunna of the Prophet. The former believed that reason had a role in defining faith and legal and moral obligations; the latter, on the other hand, were firm in their espousal of the signal efficacy of Revelation alone. According to them, this was clearly enunciated in the holy texts including the supreme text of the Qur'an and the texts of hadith that represented the sayings and actions of the Prophet.

In brief, the great diversity of thinking and opinion that began at the time of the Revelation continued during Umayyad rule and was prominent during the early years of the Abbasids. This diversity is reflected in the first written compendium of law produced in Islam – the *Muwatta* of Malik ibn Anas (d. 796).[5] Various factors accounted for this diversity, such as the reasoning of individual scholars, particular local contexts, different manifestations of local consensus and the reputed precedents of the Prophet, which in Coulson's words 'lay in uneasy juxtaposition'.[6]

Concern

This open intellectual climate caused great concern amongst many of the jurists and was echoed by those in power, including the Abbasid Caliphs. The bureaucrat Ibn al-Muqaffa,[7] a highly placed state official in around 757, urged the Caliph al-Mansur to take action to codify the law in the interest of order and unification. In effect, he was inviting political power to take an active role in developing and controlling sharia. This move, however, was not possible, since legal authority was by this time beginning to be vested in the body of jurist scholars (known as *fuqaha* and *'ulama*) rather than being an appendage of political power. The relationship between the scholar-jurists and the Caliphs was not clearly delineated and there was a constant and creative tension of power between them which led to the law never being taken over by the Caliphs. The distinction between the law and political power remained – and continues to remain – real and important. This point is well stated by Hallaq, who writes:

> Islamic law did not emerge out of the machinery of the body-politic, but rather arose as a private enterprise initiated and developed by

pious men who embarked on the study and elaboration of law as a religious activity. Never could the Islamic ruling elite, the body politic, determine what the law was.[8]

Hallaq also points out the mutually sustaining relationship between these two groups of power in Muslim societies when he states that

> inasmuch as the legists depended on the financial favors of those holding political power, the latter depended on the legists for accomplishing their own interests. This symbiosis defined the dynamics of the relationship between the two groups; the more the political elite complied with the imperatives of the law, the more legitimising support it received from the legists; and the more these latter cooperated with the former, the more material and political support they received.[9]

Hence the balance of power between those in political authority and those who spoke for sharia was maintained, as it is today insofar as sharia plays a role in modern Muslim states. However, at the time the Abbasids, though they professed to be the servants of the law, in reality tried to become its masters and sought to be called Khalifat Allah (Deputy of God) rather than Khalifat Rasul Allah (Deputy of the Messenger of God).

The *Mihna*

Towards the end of the rule of the seventh Abbasid Caliph al-Mamun (d. 833), an inquisition, or *mihna*, was introduced by the Caliph with the aim of establishing the doctrine of the Mu'tazilis that claimed the Qur'an was a created text rather than being coeval with the divine. This doctrine enabled those in authority to interpret the holy text.[10] For the period of approximately 15 years during which the inquisition was in place, many dissenting scholars (most notably Ibn Hanbal) were persecuted, tortured and imprisoned. However, the very existence of the inquisition actually jeopardised the status of the ruler, because he had broken the implicit seal of approval from the jurists by trying to impose a particular version of sharia and an understanding of the faith as a whole.

This attempt to directly influence the jurists to adopt a particular doctrine failed within a short period, and the inquisition was set aside during the rule of al-Mamun's successor, al-Mutawakkil (r. 847–861), when traditionalism returned with greater force than previously and reinforced the power of the jurists through the notion of *taqlid*, or imitation. This system remains an integral part of Sunni Islam. We shall return in Chapter 4 to this critical aspect of Islamic legal epistemology.

Legal Doctrine and Moral Validation

The early schools of law had been mainly preoccupied with the development of legal doctrine in various parts of the empire. Local institutions and activities were approved or rejected according to their adequacy in terms of the values enshrined in the Qur'an. As an example, one of the ways in which soldiers were paid for their services during the Umayyad period was through receipt of a note that could be used to draw a specified amount of grain from government granaries. This practice gave rise to speculative behaviour in the context of the ever-changing price of the commodity. The scholars disapproved of this practice, as they saw it as falling into the general prohibition of usury (*riba*) as set out in the Qur'an. Moreover, the Qur'anic rejection of gambling or speculative investment (*maysir*) was merged with the prohibition of *riba* or interest, to give it a wider significance. This proscription covered any form of profit or gain that was unearned, and in due course came to form one of the pillars of what is now known as sharia finance, which we shall discuss in Chapter 9. Therefore, the legal rule was formulated that a purchaser of foodstuffs could not resell it until he or she had taken delivery of the product.

A customary contract that was accepted by the early scholars was the barter of unripe dates on the palm against the value of ripe dates, which, although entailing the risk of uncertainty (*gharar*), proved not to be objectionable because they argued that it carried a minor risk. It should be noted that risk per se was not unacceptable since life itself entails risk, but the scholars were intent on ensuring that a transaction was not based on risk alone (which was regarded as gambling) or taken by one party rather than being shared. There was always a threshold when risk became unacceptable. However, this threshold was not mathematically computed; rather, it was assessed in the context of a particular transaction.

Through a piecemeal review of various practices, a body of Islamic doctrine developed, originating in the personal reasoning or *ra'y* of individual scholars. As time passed these pragmatic approaches were endorsed by the firmer legal basis of the consensus, or *ijma'*, of groups of scholars in various legal schools in a region. Once a practice was firmly established in this way, we see the gradual appearance of the Sunna of the particular school which, in the language of the scholars, was the 'ideal doctrine' established in the school and expounded by its current representatives. In jurisprudential methods, two trends emerged: the first of these was that reasoning became more systematic, and arbitrary opinion gave way to analogical reasoning or *qiyas*. However, practical considerations at times necessitated a departure from strict analogical argument with an emphasis on what we refer to today as 'equity'. Public interest, known as *maslaha*, also had a role to play; we discuss this important concept in greater detail in Chapter 5. The second trend was a growing emphasis on the notion of the Sunna, which was portrayed as a historical chain of discovery of ethics, morality, right conduct and religiously legitimated actions that were enacted, established and stated by honoured elders and scholars who were exemplars of legal decision-making. This practice, which was common before the coming of Islam, reflecting the inherently conservative tribal culture of the Arabian peninsula, became 'professionalised' by the jurists. As time passed, they were intent on justifying the results of their thinking by ascribing it to the idealised life and times of the Prophet and his Companions by a process of anachronistic, and often apocryphal, ascriptions or back projections, which, in the case of the sayings and actions of the Prophet, later took on a canonical status.

Diversity

In this way, sharia developed somewhat expediently and circuitously, using the process of analogical reasoning, the customary practice of particular regions, the idealised narratives of the Sunna and the establishment of legal rules by way of *ijma‘* (consensus). However, it also created a situation where the law was not uniform or predictable, and where rulings tended to be based on local predilections and prejudices.

This immense diversity became a cause for concern, since it brought confusion to the outcome of legal decisions. During the Abbasid period, a new legal dispensation was becoming necessary for the multifarious cultures and societies that made up the central parts of the Muslim world where the law was being consolidated, namely in Kufa, Medina, Basra, Damascus and Fustat (which later became subsumed into Cairo). This process, in order to gain traction and legitimacy, had to commence from within the religio-juridical establishment, and was initiated by Muhammad ibn Idris al-Shafi‘i (b. 767), who is referred to by many scholars as 'the Master Architect of Islamic Jurisprudence'. He became the eponymous founder of the Shafi‘i school of law, one of the four main Sunni schools of jurisprudence.

Muhammad b. Idris al-Shafi‘i

Shafi‘i was not an innovator as much as a keen spectator who visited the principal centres of the Middle East where legal discourses were taking place. A Gazan by birth, he claimed to be related to the Prophet. His interest in the law took root when he was a young man and developed into a deep understanding of the legal processes and the foundations of the legal thinking of the time. At first he was a cautious observer of the various, and sometimes stormy, legal debates that were taking place amongst the learned, and he took care not to ally himself to any particular school of thought and thus become mired in partisanship. This scholarly detachment enabled Shafi‘i to develop an overview of the law as a religious-academic discourse, assessing its relative strengths and weaknesses. He was able to 'unravel the tangled threads of multiple controversies and propound a solution creating order out of chaos'.[11] Building on the work of the Hanafi jurist al-Shaybani, he endowed the law with an efficacy which took this discourse beyond the realm of moral evaluation of acts to their legal consequences – something that was required at the time.

In the field of contractual obligations, therefore, his contribution was seminal. What Shafi'i recognised was that the fissiparous nature of the different schools of legal thought endangered the status of the law by allowing too many disparities to prevail, thereby making the law uncertain and heterogeneous. He desired to bring some sort of order to the dispensation of the law, whose purpose was to create a moral and social order in society. His supreme aim was the unification of law, and he attempted to do this by developing a method of neutralising the force of disintegration by establishing the basic constituent elements that underpinned the nature of the law in an Islamic context, building blocks that could be recognised and accepted by all the existing schools of law and which would enable legal thought and practice to be homogenised. He did this by expounding a strong theory setting out the sources of law (known as *usul al-fiqh*), which he identified as made up of four elements, namely the Qur'an, Sunna, *ijma'* and *qiyas*. This was not a novel discovery, since existing schools of law had worked on this framework for some time, but Shafi'i strengthened and, in a sense, enfranchised it by 'giving existing ideas a new orientation, emphasis and balance, and [by] forging them together, for the first time, into a systematic scheme of the "roots" of law'.[12]

Usul al-Fiqh – the Sources or Roots of Islamic Jurisprudence

For Shafi'i, the Qur'an was the primary source of law, since he argued it embodied a deeper legal significance than his predecessors had hitherto recognised, beyond its substantive and clearly stated precepts. He maintained that the Qur'an indicated the means whereby it could be subsequently interpreted through the repeated injunction in it that the faithful should 'obey God and His Prophet'. This injunction made clear, according to Shafi'i, that not only was the text of the holy book to be read with care and due submission, but that the Prophet was the exclusive arbiter of the meaning of the text through what he subsequently said and did – his Sunna – thus establishing the precedents of the Prophet as a source of law second only to the word of God. As to the authority of the Prophet as a lawgiver, Shafi'i went beyond the Traditionalists by positing the Prophet not only as first among equals, but by expounding for the first time the principle that the Prophet's legal decisions were divinely inspired. His arguments proved difficult to refute, and once the Prophet's sayings and actions were accepted as the crucial Tradition that fortified and embellished the law, they could no longer be rejected by objective criticism of their content. Thus their authority became binding, unless the authenticity of the report itself could be denied. The notion of Sunna, which had different connotations in the various schools that were still in their formative stages of development, hence acquired a more unified meaning stemming from one single origin endorsed by that key phrase in the Qur'an. Therefore Muhammad, the holy Prophet, Messenger and man, became a quasi-divine figure whose Sunna was a fundamental element of the law.

Shafi'i had initiated a revolution in the conceptual understanding of Islamic law by privileging the Tradition which, if not equal to the Qur'an, certainly became its exclusive legitimate mode of interpretation and commentary, upon which legal decisions were crafted by way of transmission (*isnads*) that created a causal chain of authentic precursors who it was believed had related the sayings and actions of the Prophet. Shafi'i did not invent a new process of thinking but he cleverly leveraged the tendency of the various schools of law to project their ideas, as the Prophet's Sunna, backwards to an origin in the Prophet's life and thoughts.[13]

His doctrine 'achieves a subtle synthesis of the apparently contradictory attitudes of "the Establishment" in the early schools and the opposition groups'.[14] Shafi'i's work did not immediately resolve all the potential conflicts that could arise between the various sources of law, which needed a process acceptable to all Muslim legal scholars in order to establish their priority when a conflict arose. Shafi'i recognised that if his aim was to bring a degree of universality and coherence to Islamic law, he would have to establish an acceptable process that could resolve such tensions by providing responses to issues such as whether the Qur'an could abrogate the Sunna and vice versa. Shafi'i also turned his acute legal mind to the third source of law, *ijma'*, which he finessed by propagating the notion that the consensus that it entailed was

not to be ascribed to localities where the law was being actively
discussed and developed in the Middle East – Damascus, Medina,
Kufa, Fustat and so on – but that its efficacy was only maintained
and legitimated if the consensus reflected the opinion of the *entire*
Muslim community thus it was not achievable. This notion may
have been possible when the Muslim community was small and
centred in Medina, but it soon became impracticable after Islam
acquired a vast imperial geographical realm. This apparently
magisterial status in effect neutered the role of *ijma'* as envisaged
by Shafi'i, since the Muslim world was no longer a homogeneous
society like that of Medina but a great conglomeration of people
and cultures who claimed to be Muslims. *Ijma'* as a source of law
remains problematic since what constitutes it is uncertain.

The fourth and final source of law, *qiyas*, Shafi'i maintained,
had to be subordinated to the dictates of Revelation and could not
be used to achieve a result that contradicted a rule established by
the other three pillars of the law, namely the Qur'an, the Sunna
and *ijma'*. His predecessors had employed analogical reasoning
but without such prescriptions, thus creating a variety of potentially diverse doctrines. Shafi'i reduced the risk of uncertainty and
conflict in the law by imposing such a limitation, which aimed to
achieve uniformity. Thus he argued that 'on points on which there
exists an explicit decision of God or a Sunna of the Prophet or
a consensus of the Muslims, no disagreement is allowed; on the
other points scholars must exert their own judgment in search
of an indication in one of these three sources... If a problem is
capable of two solutions, either opinion may be held as a result
of systematic reasoning; but this occurs only rarely.'[15] *Qiyas* had a
role, but it was circumscribed and disciplined and very much the
junior pillar of the law. It was a world apart from *ra'y* or personal
reasoning, which had not been uncommon amongst legal scholars
of the previous generation.

Shafi'i's Legacy

Islamic legal scholarship has recognised Shafi'i as the 'Master
Architect of Muslim Jurisprudence', though his contribution, as
we noted earlier, was not an innovation so much as a consolidation

that granted existing notions and judicial lines of thought a new orientation, and forged for the first time a systematic scheme of the so-called 'roots' of law. His theory set the authority of law on a firmer footing by arresting the forces of disintegration that existed during his time. He is attributed with achieving a reconciliation between the two opposing viewpoints of reason versus revelation. Though he was not successful in everything he posited, most of the principles he enunciated were accepted over time and were not contested over the following few centuries. Their impact had an important influence on the development of law, both for good, in that they brought a degree of cohesion to the law and predictability, but also for bad in that they also created an atmosphere of stagnation and unbending conservatism, which stifled creativity and innovative modalities and deeply affected the methods of legal thinking in the Islamic world.

In the century that followed al-Shafiʿiʾs death, the Sunna of the Prophet became the focal point of legal development and attention, and within some decades Muslim jurisprudence had absorbed Shafiʿiʾs teachings, which led to the growth of a separate science of hadith with a literature of its own based on the collection, documentation and classifying of the Prophetic hadiths by scholars who were not jurists as such but rather law reporters who provided raw material, which lawyers used to evaluate and integrate the hadiths into the larger scheme of jurisprudence. Muslim scholars were conscious of the fabrications that had taken place, but now that the hadiths were recognised as divinely inspired they could not be challenged on the basis of content but only on the validity of their chain of transmission.[16] The reliability of hadiths was based on the same criteria as the validity of accepting evidence in a court of law, though in the case of the former the rules were not as stringent. Once the trustworthiness of the reporters was established, hadiths were classified in varying grades of authority according to the *isnad*s or chain of transmission.

During the 9th century, scholarship in this field produced several compilations of Traditions which claimed to sift the genuine from the fabricated. Two such compilations, that of Bukhari (d. 870) and that of Muslim (d. 875), enjoy high credibility among Sunni Muslims as containing authentic accounts of the practice of the Prophet. The Shi'a added to their corpus of hadith the sayings of their Imams and these also included reports (*akhbar*) of the Prophet authenticated by their Imams. Important compilations of Shi'i Islam include those of al-Kulayni (d. 941), Ibn Babawayh (d. 991) and Muhammad al-Tusi. (d. 1067).[17] These compilations were made after the Occultation of the Twelfth Imam, the last of the Imams in the Ithna 'ashari tradition, in 874.

The Effect of Shafi'i's Legal Theory on the Development of Muslim Law

Shafi'i aimed to introduce uniformity to Islamic jurisprudence, but varying reactions to his work produced three other schools, including one named after him. His school represented a middle position between the two extremes of interpretation. Amongst the other groups was the Hanbali school, founded by Ahmed b. Hanbal (d. 855), which took the literal status of the Traditions to their extreme: Ibn Hanbal himself refused to eat watermelon because he could not detect any Prophetic hadith in his compilation of 40,000 hadiths that stated one might enjoy this fruit. The Zahiri school of Dawud b. Khalaf al-Zahiri (d. 883), by contrast, strongly reacted against the increasing subtlety of legal reasoning which it thought frustrated the spirit of the law.[18] One of the adherents of this school was Ibn Hazm (d. 1064), who denounced the use of analogical reasoning as a perversion and heresy.

Within the established schools, the Malikis and the Hanafis were reluctant to revise their corpus in keeping with Shafi'i's theory, though they accepted the authority of the Traditions in a qualified form. However, by the end of the 9th century the controversy had died down and the privileged place of the Sunna of the Prophet was established in Muslim jurisprudence. Over-enthusiastic support for the Traditions was tempered by the recognition that, in the elaboration of law, human reason could be utilised in the form of analogical deduction (*qiyas*).[19] This was the case with the Hanbalis. The Zahiris, on the other hand, refused to accept any compromise and consequently their school faded into oblivion. The established schools, having formally succeeded in justifying their respective doctrines, were prepared to accept the authority of the Traditions as a matter of principle. With the spread of the area of law covered by divine Revelation came an increasing rigidity of doctrine. The scope for independent activity was restricted as particular terms of the law through the Traditions became identified with the command of God.

> The spring of juristic speculation, which had supplied the rapidly moving stream of Islamic jurisprudence in its early stages, gradually ceased to flow; the current slowed, until eventually and inevitably, it reached the point of stagnation.[20]

The question of whether stagnation set in or whether sharia adapted to changing circumstances largely through necessity will be explored in the following chapters.

Developments after Shafi'i

The four elements that made up the *usul al-fiqh* evolved, as we have seen, in the early centuries of Islamic history and were focused by the work of Shafi'i. This took the form of law that aimed at establishing a pristine Islamic society – that is, a recreation of the religious society prevailing in the Medina of the Prophet's time. The Qur'an, the revealed and uncreated word of God, was therefore the core of faith and practice, followed by the Sunna of the Prophet, which took on canonical status and became the exclusive mode of understanding the text of the Qur'an as illuminated by the hadith, reports of the words and deeds of the Prophet. The hadith may be regarded as an authorised system of hearsay with its intricate formulae of verification and valorisation – *isnad*s, chains of reports from the Prophet – that form a causeway to a quasi-divine discourse of truth, persuasion and commandment that flows from the sayings and actions of the Prophet and forms a pillar of the law. Where gaps or a hiatus in the prescriptions of the Qur'an or the Sunna were observed, and consequent hadiths ascribed to the Prophet, the jurists used a process of reasoning underpinned by the ethical values expressed in the Qur'an and on the needs (sing. *darura*) of the wider Muslim society – determined by public interest known as *maslaha*. The aim was to ensure that the law retained a degree of flexibility and remained relevant to the context and time of its application. Though not fully developed, the notion of *maqasid al-sharia* (purpose of the law) found its expression in early Islamic history and in a more focused articulation through the work of later jurists such as the 14th-century Andalusian Maliki jurist al-Shatibi.[1]

However, this potentially freewheeling application of the law was tempered by the authority of recognised scholars, who offered legitimate solutions to particular problems. Furthermore, the final and important part of the *usul al-fiqh* was the concept of *ijma'*, or consensus among Muslims, which acted both as a brake to potentially overweening and divisive decisions by the courts and scholars and as a cement that ensured the legal system remained true to the ethos of Islam, as legitimised by the community's acceptance ultimately of the scholars of the accepted schools of law who oversaw legal rulings and the status of the law in general. Hence *ijma'*, which, initially had a dialogical relationship with *ijtihad*, or the exercise of independent judgement on a legal or theological issue, ensured that the identity and purity of the faith was maintained by proper recognition of the holy texts and also, in accordance with Sunni tradition, of ancient Arabian customs which were not specifically excluded by such texts. *Ijma'* also forbade innovatory and eccentric readings of the holy texts, thus eventually establishing a considerable degree of homogeneity in the practice of the faith and the ordering of Islamic society and thought in the desire and pursuit of the imagined ideal of the early Medinan society of the Prophet.

Shafi'i held that *ijma'* was the product of the entire Muslim community, which by his time made it impractical if not impossible for it to be enacted, given that the Abbasid empire was large and heterogeneous. The *ijma'* of the Prophet's time, reflecting the consensus of a small and close-knit group of people who knew each other and had a level of common understanding and trust, could never subsist in the great multicultural entities that were now ruled by Muslims. A parallel could be made between the original Medinan practice of *ijma'* and Athenian democracy, where every citizen had a direct voice in the running of that great city-state. However, *ijma'* was saved from becoming entirely theoretical by being made into a highly practical and pragmatic device for legitimising *fiqh* and aligning it to the corpus of hadith and Sunna after the death of Shafi'i in 820, when it became the sole province of the scholars, or *'ulama*, who became the recognised legal authorities in the Islamic world. When all or most of these recognised scholars were in agreement on a particular ruling, it was therefore considered as being permanently binding. This was the positive aspect of *ijmaʻ*; but there was a darker negative side which could already be seen developing during Shafiʻi's time and took hold of *fiqh* by the 10th century, when, as the contemporary scholar of Islamic Studies, John Esposito, explains:

> the agreed doctrines of the schools [of Islamic law] were considered fixed, unchangeable. Henceforth jurists were to practice *taqlid*, to follow the established principles of their individual schools. Thus the 'closing of the gates of *ijtihad*' in the medieval period, which had its authoritative basis in the consensus of the scholars of the time, became the prime cause for the general loss of dynamism.[2]

The *usul al-fiqh* became highly circumscribed, and the authority and efficacy of the law were held to come from the Qurʾan, the Sunna, *ijmaʻ* and *qiyas*, or analogical reasoning, which was essentially conservative. The last aspect, *qiyas*, was tied to the jurists' understanding of the other three pillars of the law, which acted as a control mechanism on independent reasoning. Thus *ijmaʻ* now assumed a circular self-validating role that enforced imitation or *taqlid* and forbade innovation (*bidʻa*).

Hitherto reason, sensitive to the contemporary demands and needs of society, which had formed part of Islamic legal thinking, was now circumscribed. These reason- and sense-based elements of the Islamic legal structure were further enforced by the normative influence of the practice of *ijmaʻ*, as mentioned above. The principle of *maqasid al-sharia*, identified as early as the 10th century by the Persian scholar al-Tirmidhi, was further elaborated by great Islamic scholars such as al-Juwayni (d. 1085) and al-Ghazali, (d. 1111).[3] But now form predominated over substance and purpose. Modern Muslim exegetes are endeavouring to re-create a *maqasid/maslaha*-based theory of law which, it is argued, provides a strong base for the reform of Islamic law from within the Islamic tradition.[4]

The sources of legitimacy and foundational sovereignty of secular law are notoriously difficult to pin down, and cannot exist as points of certain knowledge and overriding instrumental

purpose that justify a rules-based polity whereby we may lead
safely ordered lives in accordance with generally accepted norms
of good behaviour. Compromises are made and secured by
continuous intellectual debate, both philosophical and political, to
ensure that an acceptable level of order exists in a secular society.
However, Islamic law short-circuits this conundrum by positing
that sharia is the expression of God's command and the exemplar
of the divine imperative: 'For Islam ... Law is the command of
God; the acknowledged function of Muslim Jurisprudence, from
the beginning, was simply the discovery of the terms of that
command.'[5] Clearly, the central notion of 'discovery' is not as
simple as it appears and, in itself, is open to further debate, which
will be pursued later in this chapter under the heading 'The Role
of Customary Law'.

The role of the jurists, therefore, was to discover what is set
out in the Qur'an and to interpret and explain the inherent law.
However, this primal basis of the law was embellished and diluted
to a degree not openly acknowledged by religious scholars through
a system that evolved in the early years of Islam and crystallised
into a generally accepted mode of recognition, at least in the Sunni
community, in Shafi'i's doctrine of *usul al-fiqh*. This necessary
construct for recognising and establishing legal edicts is made
up of four elements that permeate and support each other, and
indeed at times are in a dialectical, if not competitive, relationship
with each other, whereby potential conflicts are ironed out by a
process of acceptance agreed by jurists over a period of time.

Clash between Revelation and Reason

We begin to witness, with the passage of time, the emergence of
what the scholar and historian Maxime Rodinson referred to as
'post-Qur'anic ideology'.[6] Qur'anic values were overshadowed by
normative interpretations of the text but also by later interested
readings whereby the practice of reasoning, which the Qur'an
encourages, is ignored for a more ossified process of exegesis and
the formulation of rules, something that was inimical to the spirit
of enquiry that is an essential part of the Qur'anic ethos. Sharia
therefore became a rigid set of rules with a tendency towards

a rigour that fails to take into account the context and wider significance of social needs as it becomes increasingly introspective and rule-bound. For the interest of the reader, it is worth noting that there was, after the advent of Shafi'i, a proliferation of hadith. This was because hadith became an important factor in law-making, being claimed to be a process of discovering God's law through the acts and statements attributed to the Prophet, who then became a figurehead rather than an actual person. As the scholar Suleiman Ali Mourad has pointed out, it is clear that many of these so-called sayings and acts attributed to the Prophet were legal fictions expressed in narrative form, since they were anachronistic and of doubtful provenance.[7]

We also begin to see the Prophet of the Qur'an, a modest man who said 'I am a mortal like you' (Q 18:110), becoming, in Akyol's words, '[a]n omniscient prognosticator who knew everything about the future'.[8] The proliferation of hadith was in danger of running out of control. And so, in order to give the process of legitimisation order and authenticity, as has been seen, the new science or system of recognising hadith was developed in the 9th century, beginning with Ahmad ibn Hanbal – the arch-traditionalist and eponymous founder of the Hanbali school of law, one of the four Sunni schools of law – and ending with the collection and canonisation of hadith by various scholars over a period of time. The most prominent of these scholars, al-Bukhari, of Central Asian origin, is said to have chosen 2,602 hadiths from a pool of more than 300,000. As time passed, some scholars began to attribute such a standing to these hadith that some of them held that a hadith could abrogate a Qur'anic verse. This notion of abrogation was one of Shafi'i's constructions.[9] The traditionalist-minded jurists opposed rationality and any change to the law which they termed *bid'a*, yet unconsciously they engendered a fundamental change by introducing their own innovation and thought into sharia by creating a process of law-making through a system of divinising the Sunna and hadith, which enabled them to create laws that were neither contained in the Qur'an nor in line with the values and ethos of the supreme holy text. Thus, for instance, it is argued that 'the original message of Islam [improving the rights of women as provided by the

Qur'an and the Prophet] lost its impetus and was modified under the influence of pre-existing attitudes and customs'.[10] Therefore, world views of the time, and even those of the pre-Islamic period, entered into the ethos of sharia.

Consequently, sharia was never the only law in Muslim societies, and *fiqh* was never a pure product of sharia through the agreed processes of law creation – the *usul al-fiqh*. The Islamic message was influenced from the beginning and continued to be influenced by pre-existing attitudes. Customary law, as Chapter 5 will show, was also a real presence in various Muslim jurisdictions, in some areas, such as the Maghreb, and later in places such as Indonesia, India and northern Nigeria, more than others. But in all cases, attitudes and customs that existed before the arrival of Islam were influential. Much of this type of law, known as '*urf*, had a negative impact on what we would regard today as Human Rights. Marshall Hodgson, in his magisterial work *The Venture of Islam*, shows this point in the way Muslim women are placed into a subservient and occluded position in society through 'the influence of pre-existing attitudes and customs'.[11]

Apropos the practice of veiling, for example 'the Qur'ânic injunctions to propriety were stretched, by way of hadith, to cover the fashionable latter-day seclusion'.[12] This latter-day seclusion referred to by Hodgson is the infiltration of Byzantine and Persian cultures that secluded upper-class women from all men but their own. The Qur'an exhorts modesty for both men and women but does not prescribe a particular dress code. However, there is a range of apparel deemed by believers to fulfil this Qur'anic requirement, which is influenced by local culture, climate and social status. In recent times, the issue of veiling has acquired a more strident significance due to identity politics. Furthermore, there are a number of hadiths relating to dress and these appear to be the predominant point of legitimisation. In practice, there is a range of clothing which comes under the rubric of *hijab* which means screen or curtain. Across the Muslim world this is interpreted from the full *niqab* where only the eyes are visible, to partial covering of the hair. In recent times, the *hijab* has become both an identity marker as well as an item of fashion now being appropriated by fashion houses both in Muslim countries and the Western world. There is no clear-cut position on this issue in Sharia. It should be noted that the Qurʼan only ordered seclusion for the wives of the Prophet on account of their status as his wives. This practice could raise the counterargument that what is good for the Prophet is good for all Muslims, and also why, in the first place, were the Prophet's wives secluded?

Islamic interpretation or exegesis, which claimed to ascertain or elicit the 'true' meaning of the holy texts – that is the Qurʼan and hadith as established by *ijmaʻ* and adduced by *qiyas* or analogical reasoning – at times departed from what was actually stated in the Qurʼan and even contradicted it. For example, the Qurʼan speaks of Adam and Eve's fall from grace without cursing Eve, as was the case in the Hebrew Bible.[13] In the Qurʼan, Adam alone is the recipient of divine reproach.[14] However, interpretations and commentaries from Islamic scholars from the beginning of the 9th century begin to blame Eve for the original infraction of God's command. This misogynistic trend infected views about women generally among Muslims. Women therefore began to be regarded as deceitful, sly, untrustworthy and immoral. This attitude was contrary to that of the Qurʼan and is highly unlikely to have been the attitude of the Prophet, who was known to respect his wives and enjoy their company, some of whom, such as Aisha, were famed for their courage and social confidence. He championed the rights of women in the context of his time. Modern Muslim women writers such as Fatema Mernissi, Asma Barlas and Amina Wudud Muhsin have returned to the Qurʼanic text to challenge the anti-female hadiths that have been prevalent for several centuries, as a result of what Mernissi calls a male-domination ideology.

This regressive approach not only affected attitudes towards women but infiltrated other areas of law and society. Therefore, we see a tendentious and negative disregard of representational art, for example, and even such abstract forms as music. According to Albert Hourani, a respected scholar of Islam, 'most jurists basing themselves on *hadith*, held that [representational art] was the infringement of the sole power of God to create life'.[15] Thus the literal was conflated with the metaphorical by these scholars.[16]

In the perennial debate between free will and predestination, hadith also played an important role in forming the Muslim consciousness. Most hadith supported predestination, reflecting, in Montgomery Watt's words, 'ancient Arab beliefs'.[17]

The role and perception of interest in Islamic finance were also heavily influenced by hadith which, in this case, extended the limited remit, set in the Qur'an as usury (*riba*), to all forms of interest.[18] This phenomenon, according to Timur Kuran, a Turkish-American professor of Economics and Political Science, drained the economic dynamism of the early Muslim centuries and acted as a 'drag on development by slowing or blocking the emergence of central features of modern economic life – including private capital accumulation, corporations, large-scale production and impersonal exchange'.[19]

Jihad, another complex notion, has been simplified into a metaphor for terrorism in the modern-day media and mindset of the Western world. However, its origin is to be found in the notion of self-improvement or the greater jihad, as the Prophet called it, which calls for the individual to struggle to attain mastery of his/her basic selfishness and acquire wisdom and compassion. While the earlier scholars focused on religious obligations such as prayer and mosque attendance and did not regard jihad as involving physical action.[20] The same process can be seen with regard to issues such as apostasy, which we shall discuss in Chapter 8 as an actual case-study, and stoning for adultery, neither of which features in the Qur'an but entered Islamic law through hadith.

Another example of the jurists' complex relationship to the source text of their faith, the Qur'an, is to be found in Shafi'i's arguments for using the process of abrogation which he championed and which was later adopted by the legal scholars. Shafi'i argued that the earlier pacific verses of the Qur'an, which promulgated peace and understanding amongst people, were discounted and, indeed, cancelled or abrogated by the later 'sword verses' that advocated more belligerent actions. Additionally, Shafi'i argued that the world should be divided into the abode of Islam (*dar al-Islam*) and the abode of war (*dar al-harb*), and that these were in constant conflict with each other. Shafi'i's viewpoint may be described as one reading of a divine text whose verses were revealed within a context that called out for them. Shafi'i categorised certain verses as a universal acclamation by God rather than being applicable only to the time of the Revelation.[21] We touch on this point in the critique in Chapter 13.

Taqlid Gains Primacy

The history of Islam and the development of sharia during the 9th century is crucial to the subsequent development of the law, which slowed down considerably, and to the standard practices of the Muslim world, which in fact ossified most significantly during the 11th century under the influence of al-Ghazali. New thinking in the Islamic world only began much later, in the 18th and 19th centuries, in the wake of the invasion of Egypt by Napoleon Bonaparte and the greater interaction between the colonialising European powers and the Ottomans in the 19th century which gave rise to the Ottoman *Tanzimat* reforms – a forerunner to important legal developments in Muslim countries that took place in the 20th century. We discuss this new thinking in Chapter 6.

With the closure of the gate of *ijtihad* in the early 10th century – caused by the adoption of *taqlid* or imitation of the opinions of previously idealised and respected legal scholars to the exclusion of *ijtihad*, which was regarded as an obligation rather than mere jurisprudential reasoning – Muslim legal discourse, as opposed to legal practice that existed in the courts, was dominated by a remarkably convoluted degree of casuistry. This practice was assisted by the use of *qiyas* or analogical reasoning, which was often a marker of pedantic excess that led to obsessive debates between jurists that sometimes spilled over into surreal and specious solutions to imagined problems far from the practical issues addressed by the courts and from the issues faced by Muslims in their day-to-day lives.

Scholars would therefore exercise their capacity for futile argument on the most arcane topics to ensure that Muslims retained the purity of their faith. Metaphor was replaced by an obsessive metonymic type of thinking. In order to arrive at the cause (*illa*) of any given law, for example, scholars would debate the situation of a mouse drowning in melted butter, where it was posited that the butter was deemed unacceptable as a fuel because the air would become polluted by the impurity of the dead mouse. Or again, was it permissible to ride a camel that had drunk wine when the rider was in danger of being polluted by the sweat of the inebriated animal? Abu Al-Walid Muhammad (d. 1126), chief judge of Cordoba under the Almoravids and grandfather of the philosopher Averroes, refers to this last rule without irony as 'the final word in godliness and the ultimate degree of piety'.[22] This attitude was not uncommon amongst legal scholars. Jurisprudence was generally dominated by what Coulson calls 'a spirit of altruistic idealism, where law was studied and elaborated for its own sake'.[23]

As stated at the beginning of this chapter, Islamic law was created and curtailed by God's commands, with these being elaborated by the rigid interpretations and rulings of subsequent legal scholars intent on control, predictability and the purity of the faith as they perceived it. They regarded themselves as the gatekeepers of the final truth, and their truth was reinforced by the power of the caliphal state, thus truth became the product of a symbiotic relationship of power between scholars and their political masters, who were also their supporters as long as they served the needs of the state. Sharia was conceived as an ahistorical entity apart from Muslim society, which it claimed to control. At least that was, and is, the theory, while in practice both Sharia and non-Sharia law grew, and grow, out of the society in which it is established as the law of that society, and responds to contemporary needs.

Different Courts and Different Laws

Sharia law, as shown above, came into being as a doctrinal system binding on an individual's conscience with greater focus on what can be termed private law at the neglect of what we today refer to as public law. Once the doctrine had been developed, the issue arose as to the obligation of the de facto political authority to support and implement God's law. The Umayyads, as we have seen, had a number of legal functionaries who conducted certain public law functions, and while the *qadi* was nominally the central organ of the administration of justice, in reality the

Caliph was in overall command. The classical doctrine was lacking in substantive law and was burdened by a procedural and evidentiary process that was cumbersome and impractical, so much so that in the field of fiscal law and criminal law sharia was inadequate to meet the needs of an increasingly complex Muslim political entity and society.

Invoking his right to legislate for the public good, the Caliph turned to *siyasa shar'iyya*, 'a system of government in accordance with revealed law', and developed a system of public laws that were administered in a number of different courts that sat alongside sharia courts. Though the *de jure* position of the *qadi* was not limited, in practice his decisions were subject to review by the *mazalim* court. Fiscal matters in time came under the jurisdiction of a functionary called the *sahib al-radd*, while criminal matters were handled by a *wali al-jara'im*. Legal scholarship on public law first articulated itself in the work of the Hanafi jurist and legal practitioner Abu Yusuf in the 8th century in his book *Kitab al-Kharaj*.[24] This was followed by the treatise *al-Akham al-sultaniyya* in the 11th century, by al-Mawardi,[25] who drew precedents from the Rightly-Guided Caliphs and cited the Caliph Ali's ruling, making a case for the principle of what we call today contributory negligence in a case for damages for personal injury.

Further developments took place in this area of law in the 14th century with the work of the Hanbali jurist Ibn Taymiyya,[26] and the Maliki jurist Ibn Farhun.[27] These early scholars took a highly idealistic approach to the law, seeing themselves in the role of 'spiritual advisors to the conscience of Islam … rather than practical administrators of its affairs'.[28] The former became spokesmen for God's law, while the latter administered laws made in the shadow of God's law. We see a dichotomy here between faith and politics, with the scholars attending to matters of faith and administrators to matters of the world. Courts and their various functionaries exemplified this distinction. Though there was a great degree of overlap, it is clear that neither the scholars nor Islamic government ever envisaged sharia and its courts to have exclusive jurisdiction of the Islamic juridical landscape. Over time, this position was transformed into the configuration we see today, whereby a panoply of laws occupy the same juridical space, many of them broadly operating under the rubric of Islamic law.

The Role of Customary Law (*'Urf*)

As there was a division or dichotomy between the political authorities and classical doctrine with regard to the apportioning of legal duties and obligations, there was also tension between the classical doctrine and customary law (*'urf*) in the so-called peripheral domains of the Islamic world. This apparent deviation from sharia and its consequent *fiqh* was to be found not only in non-Arab Muslim populations but also in Yemen, where certain Arab tribes have never relinquished their native customary law even to this day. We should note that, in some cases, customary law was less developed and enlightened in terms of rights concerning individuals, for example women, than was *fiqh*. With the passage of time, as Chapter 5 will endeavour to show, the division between *fiqh* and customary law in the newly converted domains became more porous and new accommodations were arrived at whereby *fiqh* and customary law adapted their rules towards each other. This fusion became noticeable in matters such as the return of the dowry upon the dissolution of a marriage, inheritance issues and matters of custody regarding the children of a dissolved marriage.

Fiqh was thus diluted by an infusion of customary law, and customary law in turn took on the guise of *fiqh* in many instances, thereby giving it more respectability in terms of religious legitimacy. Certainly with regard to family law, *fiqh* was deemed the pure ideal of Islamic law as a doctrine, even though its accommodation with local law was a practical solution to this inherent division. Despite the classical scholars of the law regarding locally implemented sharia as inferior to the ideal standards posited by the doctrine as they understood it, compromise enabled by regional *qadi* courts ensured that a system of law was put in place that was responsive to the needs of, and acceptable to, the local population.

The sense of superiority of the classical legal scholars was not entirely justified, since the classical law itself had its own implicit contradictions and complex processes that were necessary in order

to allow the law to be implemented in areas where a pure interpretation was simply impractical. Therefore a process of implementation came into being that introduced legal devices such as
the concept of *hiyal* (legal devices, for the purposes of expediency
or contrivance), first in the central Muslim regions and also in
the peripheral areas, where it helped to enable customary laws to
be used in more acceptable guises. This concept is discussed at
greater length in Chapter 5.

What we see are various factors at play. First, the apparatus
for the discovery of God's law was already in place and various
accommodations were developed, for example between religious
scholars and the political authority, with regard to both the law
and its implementation through the various judicial and administrative institutions. Second, new centres of power were emerging
as Muslim influence expanded into new areas of the world, where
further accommodations had to take place given varying environmental conditions. In al-Andalus between the 8th and 15th centuries, for example, Muslims were in greater contact with Christians
and Jews, which gave rise to new issues and thus to new ways of
understanding the law. Third, an important new centre of power
was emerging in the Islamic world as the Fatimids, a Shiʿi dynasty
from the family of the Prophet, emerged from Syria, established
a foothold in Tunisia in the early 10th century and then, having
expanded across North Africa, founded the city of Cairo as their
new capital. The Fatimids began to codify their law, based on the
Shiʿi theory of law with a living Imam who also held the position
of Caliph. The classical doctrine had developed within a narrow
geographical context and largely in an Arab cultural milieu, while
the reality of the Muslim world was far-ranging and multifarious.
This demanded significant adaptation. The classical doctrine thus
had to negotiate with customary law, and after the 15th century
also had to contend with the influence of European powers who
were making major encroachments in areas settled by Muslim
peoples. Muslims, like any other group, had to negotiate with
changing circumstances, and sharia, despite its portrayal as an
immutable system, also had to adjust to new circumstances.

As one looks more deeply into the role of Islamic law from its
inception to the present day, one finds that there is no system of

law that is complete, fixed and sacrosanct, notwithstanding the rhetoric that surrounds the notion of sharia and *fiqh*. Even after the settling of the legal process by the adoption by the various Sunni schools of law of Shafi'i's construction of the *usul al-fiqh*, we should keep in mind that *fiqh* did not cover all the needs of society in terms of legal regulation but that, in essence, *fiqh* covered elements of private law such as family law where it was technically regarded as the sole legal dispensation. It did not have such a role in public law. While the law was being ideally fixed by scholars, therefore, in practice it was never a comprehensive system and other courts, which were not governed by sharia or *fiqh*, took care of the legal needs of Islamic society under the aegis of the political power of the time.

Chapter 5 will examine how customary law played an essential role, especially in the so-called peripheral regions, and how *fiqh* had to work with it in order to enable the law to be relevant to local needs and expectations. In addition to this injection of other legal systems, *fiqh* was further developed by the practice of the provision of legal opinions, known as fatwas, by legal scholars, called *mufti*s, who bridged practice and doctrine. Their opinions took into account public interest, or *maslaha*, which enabled them to adapt the classical law to ensure it was relevant to the time when an opinion was sought. The *mufti*s were not making revolutionary changes to the law. Their work ensured that the law did not become entirely moribund but remained a living process to reach solutions deemed fair and just for the time. Their work was not confined to civil transactions but encompassed many other areas of law where sharia-based rulings were called for. Their opinions also covered matters of faith known as 'ibadat and of the ethics concerning everyday problems encountered by individuals. We shall now describe how theory and practice were merged in the so-called peripheral areas of the Islamic world and more particularly in the Maliki courts of North-West Africa.

Further Geographical Expansion and Cultural Accommodation

A Move from Theory to Practice

Sharia law, as we have seen, was not fully formulated *ab initio*. God's commands were indeed contained in the Qur'an, but the development of positive law came about later. The Qur'anic edicts were few and did not cover the entire life of a believer or his or her life within society. There were clear obligations regarding the individual's submission to the faith and to God – for example, it challenged and generally replaced the pre-Islamic notion of obligation, which was essentially a group or communal duty, mainly the duty of the tribe. Muhammad's revolutionary message was to devolve this notion of duty to the individual, whose responsibility was to God alone and for whom none could deputise. This was the theoretical position. In practice, the tribe and communal obligations subsisted and continue to do so even today, and are mainly reflected in the role that customary laws play in the lives of Muslims across the world.

However, it is fair to say that sharia was at first a system of law derived from a number of verses in the Qur'an that were concerned with limited subjects such as family law, the law of succession and certain offences – apostasy, the false imputation of unchastity against a woman, theft, the imbibing of alcohol and illicit sexual relations – which were regarded as offences against the social group. As time passed and the Muslim world expanded from the small community of Medina, where the

Muslims had personal knowledge of each other and shared a homogeneous culture, revived and reformed by the Revelation of the Qur'an, sharia evolved to take on a greater role in society and lives of Muslims.

This expansion, as shown earlier, took place over a century or so, culminating in the doctrinal construct of Shafi'i, whose process of identifying, formulating and implementing sharia by way of *usul al-fiqh* became accepted in due course by all the Sunni schools of law. The recognition of law and its formation was thus generally accepted, and the multitude of competing schools of law that were extant during the Umayyad period, between 661 and 750, thereby making sharia unstable and to a degree arbitrary, were trained, tamed and reduced to a systematic and more or less predictable legal system acceptable in principle to all Muslims and to the various Sunni schools of law themselves. The situation was more complex, however; more interesting, more hybrid, more flexible and more realistic. Coulson describes the jurists as being idealists, and, like all idealists, their vision of justice was liable to be constraining and even dogmatic. However, the Umayyads and their successors, the Abbasids, were more intent on establishing rule than an ideal religious polity. Hence, from the start, sharia and its consequent *fiqh*, or positive law, had to share the stage of legal discourse and imperium with other non-religious systems of law, and in fact sharia law at this time remained a doctrine developed by legal jurists who were not practical lawyers taking part in the business of the courts.

Modus Vivendi

The jurists and the *qadi*s accepted that their remit, as representatives of God's law, was going to be limited; that the Caliph had supreme political power. In the time of the Umayyads the *qadi*s, who actually dispensed justice in accordance with sharia, were initially administrators. Their position improved under the Abbasid empire, but they remained employees of the caliphal government even though their remit, albeit limited, was deemed in theory to be sacrosanct. In practice, they were generally subject to the Caliph's oversight, and their decisions could be overturned by the Caliphs through the implementation of *ta'zir* (discretionary punishments) and through the *mazalim* courts. Therefore, although sharia allowed for the payment of blood money in lieu of capital punishment in a case of homicide, if the family of the victim accepted this lesser punishment, the Caliph could still exercise *ta'zir* on the grounds of protecting public order – known as *maslaha*, which denotes public interest – and have the defendant executed. It could be argued that while sharia did not envisage a system of criminal justice beyond the *hadd* offences (see Chapter 11), *ta'zir* was in fact an instrument through which a more practical criminal justice system was introduced.

A *qadi*'s remit was, therefore, limited and constrained. At one time, it was so precarious that the *qadi*s felt constantly vulnerable and many did not wish to take up the position. This fragile status of sharia not only affected the *qadi*s but also the legal scholars or jurists who initially did not participate in actual court cases or proceedings. Coulson writes about this sense of dependency of both *qadi*s and legal jurists, who he says were concerned with the 'vulnerability of the decisions given by the *qadi*s, but not against the extent of their jurisdiction'.[1]

There was an apparent modus vivendi between the legal scholars, the practitioners of sharia and the ruler who had his own legal fora and rules as exemplified by the *siyasa shar'iyya* rules dispensed by the *mazalim* courts. Other government administrators also had a legal remit, such as the police or *shurta*, the *muhtasib* who was the official whose job was to ensure fair trading in the markets, and even officials in charge of the water supply. Sharia was reserved for the laws that were elicited by *usul al-fiqh*, essentially in the domain of private law and a limited number of criminal offences defined as *hadd*, which the jurists expected the Caliph to implement through the appropriate officers of government. The jurists were quite happy with this division of labour, which they found to be convenient. It suited their self-imposed terms of reference.

Public versus Private Law

Public law remained and still generally remains outside the remit of sharia, which did not have the substantive law to deal

with issues in this domain; nor did it have adequate court procedures to carry out the work of implementing the necessary rules
to satisfy individual cases. For example, the procedure of sharia
courts involved the swearing of oaths by the parties in a case, and
there was no cross-examination, no provision of what would be
recognised under Common Law as types of evidence that enable
a proper judgement to be reached, and nor was there evaluation
of the balance of probabilities. Sharia's innate idealism is clearly
demonstrated by the procedure adopted by sharia courts based on
the belief that the parties to a case would not lie or swear fraudu-
lently out of fear of eternal punishment by God. This is similar to
compurgation (oath-taking) in medieval English Common Law,
where the defendant could establish their innocence by taking an
oath. However, in modern Muslim-majority states the assumption that a defendant would not lie is no longer valid and modern
criminal legislation has superseded this approach. Although
under sharia law a person is innocent until proved guilty, as in
English Common Law, most Middle-Eastern Muslim countries
have developed their criminal codes on the basis of the French
system, where a person is presumed guilty until they can prove
their innocence.

Sharia as Marker of Identity

Sharia, therefore, played only a limited role in the legal universe of
Muslim societies from the earliest times, but it was nevertheless a
respected and growing area of the law which provided a necessary
element of Muslim identity. Both these facts remain in place today
in Islamic jurisprudence. The accommodations in law mentioned
in the previous chapter enabled Muslims in the 10th century to
manage their lives, and enabled sharia, as formulated, to take
into account various practices of customary and other laws, and
provided cohesiveness to a widely dispersed community. This
community of Muslims, known as the *umma*, stretched from the
Oxus river in Central Asia to the Pyrenees in Western Europe and
shared a common identity based on the notion of brotherhood
and a common belief in one deity. Interaction with other cultures
and traditions took place and Islam continued to experience a

cultural efflorescence. New dynasties, known as the 'gunpowder empires', came into power in the early modern era.² And on the subcontinent of India the Mughals, descendants of the Mongols of Central Asia, established their empire, which lasted until the 19th century. In 1453, the Ottomans took Constantinople from the Byzantine Empire and established a foothold in eastern Europe for Islam, proselytising many in the Balkans who, over time, came under their suzerainty. Also, in the early 16th century, the Safavids, originally a Sufi brotherhood or *tariqa*, established an empire in Iran and subsequently made Twelver Shi'ism the official religion of their state.

Classical Sharia Undergoes Modification and Acculturation

As Islam expanded into the newer geographical and cultural domains during the centuries that followed the closure of the gate of *ijtihad*, Muslim rulers expected their new subjects to adopt the faith and its evolving legal system in place of their pre-Islamic ways of life and values. However, the sway of the faith was not pre-eminent in many parts of the growing Muslim domains. The identities of the new Muslims were remoulded by varying degrees of adherence to the tenets of Islam, and many tensions arose not only in the further reaches of the empire but to some extent also in the Arab heartlands. The social values of the early Arab converts to the faith were often quite alien to later, non-Arab converts, and hence disparities and conflicts became apparent in areas of legal application such as family and civil law. This problem continues to this day.

As we have pointed out above, tensions were apparent even in some Arab areas, such as Yemen, which were not prepared to jettison their pre-Islamic customary practices.³ Such dissent and eventual accommodation gradually established itself in many parts of the empire. Thus, in North Africa with the Berbers and in Western Nigeria with the Yoruba, for instance, a compromise between sharia and customary law came into existence. A similar process took place in parts of Indonesia such as Sumatra and on the Indian subcontinent with the Gujarati and Cutchi Muslims (both Shi'i and Sunni), who, at one time, followed Hindu customary law with regard to inheritance. The compromises made by the authorities over the application of the law varied in nature and extent in different regions. In some places there was a sharp demarcation between sharia and customary laws with their own separate domains and discourses that were applied alongside sharia-based rulings of the *qadi* courts; in other places, the principles of sharia informed or infused customary law; in yet other regions of the Muslim domains, sharia was textured with customary law without violating the underlying values of the Islamic ethos. Over time, we witness what Coulson called the 'gradations of fusion' with sharia and customary law, which vied and balanced each other in order to create a legal system that was recognised and accepted by the local populations.[4] One of the areas of the law that remained resistant to this dilution and diffusion of sharia was family law, where sharia retained its 'purity' with the doctrine of the classical texts being held to be sacrosanct; and from an Islamic perspective this approach assumed a superior standard of legal dispensation and justice to those of customary laws.

Further Evolution

Thus, albeit theoretically, sharia was deemed the pure command of God. As we have seen, it was systematised and set by a human process called *usul al-fiqh* which expanded the Islamic legal remit from the small number of 'legal' verses in the Qur'an into a more ample and practical system that was meant to provide guidance to the wider areas of social needs prevailing in the different cultures and areas of the expanding Muslim world. After the settling of the *usul al-fiqh*, initially by Shafi'i, the law in theory became a fixed point of reference and application. However, in practice it continued to evolve during the subsequent centuries in response to the changing conditions of society. Sharia and its *fiqh* were never a closed corpus of law as the classical legal jurists may have wanted it to be. In the field of civil transactions, therefore, the classical doctrine that had been formed by scholars who were not generally practitioners of the law like their counterparts the *qadis* merged over a period of time with legal practice as dispensed in the courts of the different regions of the Muslim world. In this way, legal practice was gradually modified by the introduction of legal fictions or devices to meet the changing economic needs of the time. This process of pragmatic response to developing social needs is exemplified by the fiction known as *hiyal*, whereby transactions were designed to circumvent the impractical demands of the law. This provided a solution to particular problems, but at the price of undermining the law's essential purpose. We see its influence with regard to the status of *riba* and *gharar*, which can be defined respectively as the incurring of interest and the existence of risk or uncertainty meant to deceive – situations where sharia principles and *fiqh* formulations prohibited the taking of interest or the making of contracts with this misleading element of uncertainty.

Another example is found in the 15th-century fatwas in North Africa that used the device of *tawlij*, which the legal scholar David Powers describes as 'an attempt by a proprietor to circumvent the Islamic inheritance rules by transferring wealth to one or more of his children by means of a gift, sale, or acknowledgement of a debt'.[5] Like all these legal fictions, this device came into being, according to Ahmed Fakhri, a professor of linguistics who has worked on the rhetorical forms of fatwas, as a result of attempting to avoid 'the fragmentation of family wealth and to favor certain relatives'.[6] The rationale of using these fictions, which inevitably vitiated the essence of sharia in one way or another, was mainly economic.

Another example from property law is the practice of gifting a narrow strip of land that divides a property from that of a neighbour. By legalising the gift, the vendor of the land could ignore the right of pre-emption that was built into sharia whereby, before one sold one's property, one had to give one's neighbour the first option to purchase it. A gift of property did not incur the right of pre-emption, so a prior gift of a bordering strip of land to a potential purchaser simply destroyed the neighbour's pre-emptive right. Predictably, these fictions created a backlash and resistance. We see, therefore, that the Hanafi school of law, with its focus more on formalism, accepted the notion and the later Shafi'i scholars, despite the earlier objections of the eponymous founder of the school, also condoned it. However, the Maliki school, on the other hand, which looked to the real intentions behind overt acts, rejected *hiyal* and took counteraction by creating the principle known as *sadd al-dhara'i'* or 'the stopping of the means', thus ensuring that legal means were not used to achieve illegal ends forbidden by sharia and *fiqh*. The Hanbali school was more intransigent and rejected it outright with a lengthy treatise written by one of its famous scholars, Ibn Taymiyya. A more benign and moralistic way in which doctrine accommodated itself was through the formulation of novel rules such as *bay' al-wafa* and *bay' al-hawa*, commercial transactions largely to facilitate the alienation of property and its financing. These were modifications of the classical law, 'and not [necessarily] the veiling of an illegal activity behind a facade of existing legal machinery'.[7]

The Role of the *Muftis*

The development of law on the basis of accommodation as outlined above was largely facilitated by the *mufti*, a legal scholar who gave his formal opinion (fatwa) on the factual situation provided to him, regarding himself to be bound by existing doctrine and claiming to be developing its inherent principles on the basis of necessity, while still professing to be very much within the prescribed creed of *taqlid* or strict imitation as posited by classical doctrine. Fatwas came into existence in the form of questions and answers – the *muftis* were asked questions concerning sharia and *fiqh* by various parties, by ordinary Muslims concerned about issues involving family law, by government officials who wanted to know whether a particular public policy was in accord with sharia, and even by judges, who consulted *muftis* over difficult points of the law. The practice of issuing fatwas was formalised and given an institutional standing, known as *ifta*. There were, and still are, institutions known as *dar al-ifta* whose main task was and is to proffer opinions.

A body of judicial opinions developed that enjoyed a status complementary to sharia manuals. In the 17th century a comprehensive and subsequently well-known collection of fatwas was established in India known as *Fatawi-e 'Alamgiri*.[8] Earlier important collections were made by Ibn Taymiyya, whose collection was named *The Great Fatwa Compilation*. By the 15th century the Maliki *mufti* Ahmad al-Wansharisi had compiled a collection called *The Clear Standard* (*al-Mi'yar al-murib*) which consisted of thousands of fatwas written by hundreds of *mufti*s operating in the Maghreb and Andalusia.

Fatwas, while they were not in themselves legally binding, became a key instrument for the promulgation of sharia, and important fatwas have contributed to the development of substantive law and acted as precedents to subsequent legal cases in the *qadi* courts. While they reflect the style of the particular *mufti* who gives a fatwa, and are produced within the socio-cultural context of the time, they have their own particular rhetorical and linguistic features which make them a distinguishable genre of legal discourse within the remit of *usul al-fiqh*. As one would expect, the content, style and form of fatwas have changed over the centuries. Modern fatwas reflect the changes in legal education in various Islamic countries following the introduction of secular law mainly through the influence of colonialism. This had a material and cultural effect in many countries with Muslim populations, and subsequent teaching methods and curricula influenced judicial points of view in those countries and over time challenged traditional thinking.

Progressively, these opinions grew in stature and volume, as works of reference complementing the standard sharia treatises became an established corpus of legal direction and reference. The law thus remained alive to the various demands of society. What we see is that the gate of *ijtihad* was never quite closed but remained ajar to enable the law to make incremental changes to reflect the needs of societies (*darura*) and to cover areas where *fiqh* was wanting. These opinions themselves had gradations, ranging from dominant (*mashhur*), preferable in certain circumstances (*rajih*) or weak (*da'if*), which in due course were used by the courts to reach a decision. While in theory the *qadi* was supposed to choose the dominant opinion, in practice he could choose the less favourable opinion if he considered this to be warranted by public interest (*maslaha*). This was not an arbitrary choice but one that slowly developed in order to provide realistic legal decisions that made sense to the community. This new development took place, as we have noted, largely in north-west Africa. It exemplifies the first instance of a practice-based development of Islamic law that was more pragmatic and realistic than the idealised notions of law as conceived by the legal scholars.

The role of the *mufti* remains central in many areas of Islamic life today, but new sources of information, including that of the internet and social media, which the *mufti*s use readily, are opening up for the Muslim world; new issues are arising that often have grave socio-political consequences, not to mention ramifications for the essential religious requirements for Muslims. Up to the 1990s, fatwas were the main form of religious discourse, disputation and advice; however, 'today's leading clerics have gone virtual, using Twitter, Facebook and other forms of social media as their main platforms'.[9] These novel factors are affecting the style and content of fatwas, and the notion of religious authority amongst Muslims in the modern world.[10] The profession of the *mufti* itself has been formalised by various governments such as those of Saudi Arabia, Yemen and Lebanon, which thus maintain control over legal scholars while ensuring their own legitimacy in terms of religion, as did the Caliphs during the Abbasid period. A final initiative, though not part of the official doctrine, was under-taken by *qadi* tribunals and mainly in the Maghreb, whereby 'certain customary contracts succeeded in becoming an integral part of the *corpus juris* applied by the Maliki Sharia Courts'.[11] Whereas in classical legal doctrine *'urf*, or customary law, had a subsidiary value, certain practices, even though not squarely within sharia, were nevertheless accepted by most jurists as valid under customary law and became tolerated by sharia.

Malik b. Anas had countenanced these practices and Maliki legal writings laid great stress on the notion of *maslaha*, and through the maxim 'necessity makes prohibited things permitted' we find the judiciary in Maliki areas, in North and West Africa for instance, adopting a more tolerant and pragmatic attitude to customary practices. These customs became accepted on the broad ground of public necessity. In the case of a contract called a *khamessa*, for example, which dealt with agricultural produce, though the contract was not fully in keeping with sharia principles, commercial necessity in due course made such *khamessa* contracts licit and thus acceptable by sharia courts in those areas where such contracts were part of the customary law.[12]

Pragmatic Accommodation of Sharia to Local Conditions

The Maliki courts in the Maghreb reflected a novel approach to the dispensation of justice, and while doctrine posited a reliance on the dominant opinion of a school, later Maliki courts in the 19th century even accepted, on the basis of dispensing justice, weaker opinions of the same school even if these were of a subordinate nature and not the preference of the eponymous founder. Changes also took place over the administration of justice through the activities of a class of functionaries known as the *'udul*, a body of professional witnesses whose moral probity (*'adala*) was established through a process of screening known as *tazkiyya* and whose witnessing of contracts relieved the parties from undue and cumbersome court procedures stipulated by classical doctrine.

These witnesses became the official notaries public and produced deeds known as *watha'iq*. Therefore the introduction of the *'udul* became an influential instrument in strengthening the notion of the authority of *'amal* (practice). Through this process we see the development, particularly in north-west Africa, of a relationship between practice and doctrine unique in the Islamic world as Maliki jurists recognised the practice of the courts as the supreme criterion of legal authority. This was the first 'realist' form of Islamic jurisprudence to show a concern with the law as it is actually administered, rather than with law as a theoretical concept.

Conclusion

In summary, legal practice, which was never fully in line with strict legal doctrine, diverged from it even more during the medieval period as the claims of *'urf* and the socio-economic pressures of a developing society took hold of the law. However, classical standards prevailed in family law, which had been given a special status in Arab society since the birth of Islam. Hence, obligations regarding family law – many of which were actually set out in the Qur'an – were deemed distilled from God's words and thus were not open to dilution or detraction by other rules or laws. They were perceived as an integral part of religious duties as promulgated by the divine, and any variations or vitiating processes that reduced their proper status were unacceptable and illegal. In this case, the distinction between sharia and customary law was clear. In public law, on the other hand, no such firm line could be, or was ever, drawn.

The theoretical purity of sharia was thus not consistently maintained in public law, since to do so would have meant the law becoming impractical in many societies where customary law had a strong presence, and the changing and complex demands of urban societies in the Muslim domains required a more sophisticated mode of legal redress. The public doctrine of *siyasat al-sharia* also took into account the requirements of political, cultural and economic interests, which enabled rulers to create laws – always under the general ethical values of sharia – that were regarded as supplementing the work of sharia courts; and in the field of civil transactions these pressures from these various interests led to considerable modifications. In both family and public law, the *mufti*s played an important role in making the law relevant to the needs of the times by adapting public law with their fatwas, and they also added a degree of realism, still accountable to sharia, by acting as advisory counsellors who provided religious legitimacy by validating the activities of the *mazalim* tribunals.

While in theory Islamic law provided the basis for Muslims to lead a life according to God's commands, in practice the divine edict was tempered by the ethos and needs of the societies in which sharia and *fiqh* were in place and administered. The law, therefore, in many cases followed the demands of the social structures in which it was administered. It provided a backbone of orderly conduct and stability and was conservative, as is all law, by nature. It did not mould Muslim societies even if it influenced their ethos, and it was not a dynamic element in the Muslim world, which remained somewhat hide-bound to traditions that over time became outdated and even regressive.

From the above, we can see that the predominance of classical doctrines formed one particular stage in the development of Islamic law but it was never the sole point of jurisdiction in the Islamic world. Though accorded great respect as portraying the ideal religious doctrine, from a realistic standpoint 'the classical doctrine never formed a complete or exclusively authoritative expression of Islamic law'.[13] The situation was far too complex to admit such a position.

With these modes of accommodation between the political authority and the religious establishment on the one hand and the religious establishment and customary practice in newly conquered areas on the other hand, sharia met the needs of Muslim communities as they developed over the course of history. This state of affairs represented an adequate system of law that met the needs of the time until the modern period when the Western world became dominant and challenged Muslim power, norms and expectations. As Europe started to break loose from the hegemony of the Christian Church during the 16th century, a new secular world was coming into being that brought about major social, philosophical and political changes, including the development of new ways of thinking. It became apparent to Muslims that their laws, as formulated, could no longer meet their needs as they began to interact with Western powers and deal with the new problems of living in a fast-changing world. The situation was not caused, we believe, by sharia or *fiqh* alone, even though it is generally stated that the gate of *ijtihad* was closed. This attitude of regarding the law as a closed corpus immune to further development played a part in supporting the stasis that afflicted the Islamic world, and we may recall that legal scholars were against any form of innovation, or *bid'a*, which was regarded as being contrary to leading a godly life. However, there were many other complex factors that caused the Muslim world to follow a more conservative approach and to which space does not allow us to do justice in this book. The need for reform was acutely felt in the Ottoman Empire because of its geographical contiguity and thus its contact with European states. We shall discuss how the Ottomans responded to this new existential challenge and how this affected the entire Muslim world and sharia, a process that began in the 19th century with the *Tanzimat* and continues to this day.

Call for Reform – from the *Tanzimat* to the Arab Spring

Beginnings of Modernity

Until about the 16th century, the Muslim world and what we call the West were more or less on equal terms intellectually, economically and politically.[1] Changes occurred in both worlds that were largely comparable. However, from the late 16th century the West began to change and the beginnings of modernity took shape in Europe, thus leaving behind and challenging the Muslim world in crucial areas – economic, intellectual, social and existential. Thus we see the inception of the scientific revolution in the 17th century, the agrarian revolution in the 18th and the industrialisation of Western Europe in the 19th century, which not only increased the economic power of the West but also brought with it widespread social upheaval and consequent changes in politics and values.

The Industrial Revolution, for instance, created a surge in productivity, new capital formation and accumulation, which enabled further technical improvements that demanded a new focus of energy and time to be invested in order to produce more efficiently and to consume more; and this in turn enhanced the economic power of the Western world. Scientific innovation by the 19th century had became a norm in the West, creating a matrix of interconnecting specialisations and scientific discoveries that fed the new practice of intellectual autonomy, which no longer existed in fear of transgressing traditional custom and belief. Simultaneously, the countries of Western Europe further extended their colonial reach through trade, war and annexation, and a series of treaties with non-Western countries such as Persia and Morocco.

Consequently, by the beginning of the 19th century we see the establishment of European hegemony across the world. This overriding influence took the shape not only of military power, but also of economic efficiency and intellectual pre-eminence. A new world-wide system of dominance was being created by Europe, which was able to influence other societies for better or for worse. This revolutionary change affected all parts of the globe; and other cultures, including the Islamic world, had to take cognisance of the shift in power and respond to the new political and economic reality that was coming into being. A step change between Europe and the rest of the world was taking shape. Suddenly, the Muslim world could no longer take for granted the civilisational and moral superiority of its institutions, faith and culture.

Therefore, by the 19th century the world of Islam had encountered the full impact of the European world, including European colonialism. Muslim rulers and elites realised that there was an urgent need, if not to copy the Western model of society, then to examine seriously the elements of its growing power and influence, if only to resist it. The need to modernise its laws and customs was felt directly by the ailing Ottoman Empire. With its defeat at the Second Siege of Vienna in 1683, which clearly marked the beginning of the supremacy of European power, the Ottomans began slowly to realise that their empire's own weakness was due not only to internal corruption and disorder but also to its failure to innovate, in contrast to the Western world. As a consequence, the Ottomans dispatched senior members of their establishment to France to examine and understand the new and threatening phenomenon of European power. In the 1770s an Ottoman bureaucrat, Ahmed Resmi Efendi (1700–1783), recommended that the Ottomans should pursue the path of diplomacy and reform.[2] Various delegations were sent to Western Europe, including one to France, which led to the creation of new schools, curricula and translations of Western scientific works. Sultan Mahmud II (r. 1808–1839) initiated further reforms, including the concept of equal citizenship for all, regardless of faith. This edict extended to the Balkans where the population was becoming increasingly influenced by the notion of nationalism. The expansion of this new idea of equality was introduced in order to counter the divisive forces of nationalism.

The *Tanzimat* Reforms

In 1839, Sultan Mahmud II's newly enthroned son, Sultan Abdulmecid I (r. 1839–1861), announced the edict of *Tanzimat*, a document that has been described by some as the Magna Carta of the Muslim world. This document (known in Turkish as the *Gülhane Hatt-ı Şerif*), which means Supreme Edict of the Rosehouse and which legislated for the reorganisation of the Ottoman Empire, heralded a period of reformation that lasted for 37 years and culminated in 1876 with the ending of the first Constitutional Era. Interestingly, the changes that it posited were projected as 'Islamic' and embedded in the Muslim ethos, while their primary thrust was based on European thought, culture and inventions. The edict included limiting the Sultan's powers, so that they were no longer arbitrary, which was viewed by the Ottoman elite as a reaffirmation of the primal values of Islam. The retraction of the Sultan's previous right to confiscate private property arbitrarily and the protection of private property owned by individuals were seen as sharia principles that had been eroded by the patrimonial power structures of the older Islamic empires. One of the architects of the *Tanzimat*, Sadiq Rifat Pasha (1807–1857), articulated these new ideas within a religious framework so as to win for them general acceptance in a still traditional society.[3]

In 1856, the Ottoman government proclaimed another edict, called *Islahat*, which removed all remaining distinctions between Muslims and non-Muslims, thereby securing rights for the latter. In practice, this amounted to the abandonment of the classical Islamic legal system which contained a division of rights between Muslims and others. Ironically, these changes were seen as too little too late: the non-Muslim territories of the Ottoman Empire such as Serbia, Romania and Albania were motivated by the new ideology of nationalism that was permeating the Balkans in the aftermath of the Greek War of Independence (1821–1832), and were now intent on being separate from Muslim rule.

One of the effects of the *Tanzimat* reforms, however, was broader religious freedom, and although the sharia laws on apostasy were not rescinded they were in effect ignored. In 1857 a government commission investigating the conversion of an individual from Islam to Christianity regarded this change of faith as legitimate. This was even applied in 1860 in Damascus where the Ottoman central power supported the Christians, who had been compelled by the local authorities to convert to Islam, to revert to Christianity on the basis of the Qur'anic verse (2:256) that states: 'There is no compulsion in religion.' It is clear that the Ottomans were intent on the reform and modernisation of the state and its legal structures. This meant that new thinking about politics and society began to percolate into the wider community.

Capitulations

Given the fact that in the mid-19th century the Ottomans were beginning to entertain liberal thinking, in some cases even before many countries in Europe, which had their own later histories of development towards modernity, the ruling class in the Ottoman Empire began to look at using the Capitulations[4] as the basis for reforming their existing legal system.[5] As the term suggests, the Capitulations were an admission of weakness by the Ottomans since they allowed a separate system of legal dispensation to be enforced in the Ottoman Empire at the insistence of Western powers, whereby subjects of European countries living in the empire would be governed by their own private laws,[6] even where Muslims were involved in cases that affected Westerners. The Ottomans, with their usual pragmatic approach, saw the Capitulations as a useful tool for introducing Western laws which they regarded as being fit for a modern society in an increasingly interconnected world. At the same time, they detected a political advantage in keeping control of Westerners living in their domain and forestalling the encroachment by foreign powers on the sovereignty of their state at a time of increasing nationalism in the Balkans. In this way, European laws – mainly French – began to become part of the Ottoman legal landscape. It should be noted that most of the changes affected the public laws of the empire, while issues related to the Muslim family, which were considered a part of private law, continued to be governed by sharia.

Therefore Western subjects who lived and traded in the Ottoman Empire were not totally subordinated to Ottoman laws, many of which were based on classical sharia formulations, albeit adapted, but by the laws of the Western countries whose citizens they were. This gave them an edge in so far as cases between them and a local Muslim trader were concerned, since the dispositive laws in such a situation were those of European countries and not of the Middle East. The Ottomans felt that by adopting European laws they might provide an incentive for Western countries to acquiesce in the abolition of Capitulations, which were proving irksome in the light of a growing national consciousness. It must not be forgotten that the Napoleonic invasion of Egypt at the end of the 18th century also had an impact on the local laws in that Ottoman *pashalik*, or territory ruled by an Ottoman-appointed pasha.

As we have seen, between 1839 and 1876 a series of reforms (*Tanzimat*) were introduced whereby a number of legal codes from the Western world were imported and enacted in the Ottoman Empire. These included, inter alia, the Commercial Code in 1850. This was in part a translation of the French Commercial Code, which embodied a provision for the payment of interest. The Penal Code of 1858 (again a translation of the French Penal Code) resulted in the abolition of the *hadd* punishments, though the death penalty for apostasy remained. There followed a Code of Commercial Procedure in 1861 and a Code of Maritime Commerce in 1863, both of French origin. The basic law of obligations was also codified in 1869 and 1876 followed by a new system of secular courts called the *Nizamiyya*, which had jurisdiction on all civil matters in the empire. These new courts were to implement the codes, while the *Mecelle*, the basic law of civil obligations derived largely from Hanafi law, provided a guide as the courts were not able to ascertain clearly the law and its procedures from the authoritative manuals that were inherently incomplete and piecemeal. Codification also led to unification, which was deemed necessary in the light of the wide divergences fostered by sharia texts and legal practice.

Changes in Egypt

Egypt, which had been invaded by Napoleon Bonaparte in 1798 and had come into contact with Western systems and thought, also promulgated reforms in the penal, commercial and maritime codes.[7] This occurred under the government of Muhammad Ali Pasha, the semi-independent governor of the province. Egypt set up secular courts to implement them and enacted Civil Codes, modelled on French law, which contained little that was based upon sharia. Consequently, laws and legal processes of European origin form a part of the legal systems of most Middle Eastern countries to this day, as they were influenced by both the Ottoman Empire and Egypt. However, in the middle of the 20th century there was a trend to move away from French laws, while remaining within the influence of other European laws (e.g. Italian and German) whose sway was felt in Egypt, Lebanon and Libya. As for the law of civil transactions, this was also almost Westernised.

Over time the *Mecelle*, which was a code of civil obligations based on Hanafi jurisprudence, applied to many Middle Eastern countries as well as to the *vilayet* or province of Palestine (later Israel), where it was later superseded in 1923 by the British Mandate for Palestine. Syria and Libya promulgated Civil Codes derived from the 1949 Civil Code of Egypt. This last code was a departure from indiscriminate importation of foreign laws and can be regarded as a compromise between sharia and Western laws, although, despite all protestations to the contrary on the part of the chief architect of the Code, Abd al-Razzaq al-Sanhuri,[8] almost three-quarters of the Code resembled the Westernised Egyptian codes of 1875 and 1883. Article 1 of the Code, for example, made a gesture to sharia by providing that on matters not covered by the Code the courts should follow 'customary law, the principles of Islamic law, or the principles of natural justice'.[9] This left the door open for sharia law to be incorporated in theory, but in practice it became difficult to continue using sharia given its rigid philosophy of immutability and its simplistic procedural rules. From the latter part of the 19th century, pure sharia law in the Middle East was largely confined to family law. Changes took place in most areas of the Muslim world except for the Arabian peninsula where, in places such as Saudi Arabia, Yemen, and the Aden Protectorate, as well as in the Trucial States in the Gulf, traditional Islamic law remained the fundamental law (as far as it was applied) well into the 1960s and 1970s. Important changes were made in the Gulf States and Kuwait when they achieved their independence in the 1970s, a period which coincided with the Arab oil boom.

Muslims Outside the Middle East

Outside the Middle East, the reception of Western laws was determined through Western colonial policies, with each colonial power imposing its own laws. Here again, sharia was relegated mainly to matters of personal import. In Indonesia, Dutch public and penal laws were introduced, though customary law in the form of *adat* continued to govern the general field of private law, even if sharia received only limited recognition despite Dutch attempts to impose it as the appropriate law for Muslim populations. This happened because customary law in the region was already established and accepted by the population.

In India, by contrast, British policy was to preserve the existing system, which was traditional Hanafi law sponsored by the Mughuls and administered by the *kazis* (the local pronunciation of *qadi*) or local judges. However, after the 1772 reorganisation of the courts by the first de facto Governor General of India, Warren Hastings, English law was specifically applied in the Presidencies, as the principal trading settlements of Bengal, Madras and Bombay were known, while elsewhere in India Islamic criminal law was applied by Muslim judges across the board.[10] In civil matters, sharia law was applied to Muslims in accordance with advice from clerical specialists, called *maulvi*s,

attached to the courts. In 1862, the Indian Penal Code and the
Code of Criminal Procedure, based directly on English law, were
promulgated, superseding what remained of Islamic criminal law.
Civil laws became increasingly Anglicised by virtue of the adoption of the principle of deciding cases in accordance with 'justice,
equity and good conscience'.[11] British and Indian judges, trained
in legal thinking as practised in England and Wales, found this
convenient in terms of the uniformity it engendered for a mixed
population but also for its certainty, something that they could
not draw from the Arabic manuals. Codification took place on a
massive scale, and from the 19th century onwards Islamic law on
the subcontinent, as elsewhere, was limited generally to family
law for Muslims.

New Nation States

During the 19th century, the nation states, while they were intent
on maintaining sovereignty and increasing their power, were
becoming more and more intertwined in terms of trade, political
involvement and economic growth. This development brought
with it new alliances, new antagonisms and increasing turmoil
throughout the world, so much so that by the beginning of the
20th century Europe and its allies stumbled into a devastating
world war that destroyed the old world in a final catastrophe. The
Muslim world was mostly not directly involved in this war apart
from the Ottomans who joined the Axis powers. With the 1919
Treaty of Versailles, the Ottoman Empire was carved up into a
number of new states under the protectorate of the victorious
Western powers, and the Middle East, now even more under
the influence of Western economic, political and cultural sway if
not actual direct control, was in dire need of a new dispensation.
The Ottomans, as mentioned above, had begun a process of
modernisation with the *Tanzimat* reforms which, in effect, meant
modernisation through adopting many Western institutions,
educational systems and laws. But in the aftermath of the First
World War the empire was dissolved on 1 November 1922 and
the Turks lost influence in the Muslim world owing to their loss
of power and of the secularism enshrined in the 1928 amendment

of the Turkish Constitution of 1924, which removed the provision declaring that 'the Religion of the State is Islam'. The Muslim world recognised the need to reform and to adopt new ways of thinking and acting in order to play a role in the modern world. Muslims therefore looked to another reforming country, namely Egypt: while claiming to be aligned with its Islamic heritage, in fact it had adopted laws and a legal system based mainly on the French model.

Egypt Becomes the Compass for Reform

Legal reform after the 1920s came mainly through newly independent Egypt and not the newly formed Republic of Turkey. The new laws were projected by Egypt as being based on sharia or laws that were consonant with sharia principles and ethos, though here again, as mentioned, there were few similarities with sharia in actual fact. Abd al-Razzaq al-Sanhuri,[12] who championed these reforms, was educated in France and was the architect of most of the Arab countries' constitutions and commercial and civil codes, which were mainly fashioned on the French model. These developments continue to give rise to tensions owing to the discrepancies today between the foundational documents. For example, while the civil codes preclude the charging of interest, the commercial codes allow for it, which brings under legal scrutiny the very nature of the state whenever Islamisation is discussed. It was therefore questioned in the 1980s whether Egypt was a Muslim country or a country with a Muslim population. If it is the former, then the question arises as to what the source of the law is. If sharia, is this then *the* source of law or *a* source of law, for if it is the former then all subsequent legislation that conflicts with sharia principles is *ultra vires* the constitution which is based on sharia.[13] If sharia is *a* source of law, then the country can resort to a number of laws, including sharia. In such a situation, sharia is not the exclusive source of the country's laws. This thorny issue has arisen in cases in Egypt, the United Arab Emirates, Pakistan and most recently Iraq,[14] and potentially can arise in any country calling itself a Muslim republic or an Islamic political entity.

The issue of the identity of a modern Muslim nation state is recurrent and emerges each time a piece of legislation is tested in a court of law either through a court case in a Muslim country or through a foreign legal decision that has to be enforced in a Muslim country and may be challenged for being *contra bonos mores* or against public morality. At the political level, given the need for revising national constitutions to accommodate different demographic needs in post-conflict situations, the position becomes more complex and even intractable. Iraq is a case in point. Following a nationwide referendum held in October 2006, the new constitution was approved with a provision stating that all Iraqis are equal before the law 'without discrimination due to sex'. Yet the same constitution also states that no law can be passed that contradicts 'the established rulings of Islam'. Concern was voiced by many women's groups as well as by politicians and religious leaders, as it is not clear to which version of Islam this refers. For women's groups, there was a legitimate fear that the 1959 Personal Law, which was secular and which was now being abolished, would be replaced by sharia whose implications, with regard to which interpretation was to apply, were not clear.

Resolution 137, which abolished the 1959 Iraqi Personal Law, was vague about this issue though it spoke broadly about each Muslim community's right to impose its own rules concerning their Personal Law. Interesting dimensions that emerge from the debate show that the majority of the population voted for sharia, and after lengthy discussions and debates Article 2 of the constitution was promulgated – making Islam the official religion of the state and citing the faith as a basic source of legislation and emphasising that no law can be passed that contradicts its 'undisputed rulings'. The Article states that the Supreme Court of Iraq is the final judicial arbiter on this issue. From this it appears to be clear that sharia is supreme in Iraq and that any citizens who wish to implement any change will have to work within an Islamic framework. Though the country lacks strong institutions to protect the rights of women, religious minorities and others, recent developments in some Muslim countries show that change is possible within such a paradigm.

Morocco, with its *mudawana*,[15] and Indonesia with the Fatayat, a women's wing of the Nahdlatul Ulama,[16] attest to this possibility. According to Isobel Coleman, a US foreign policy specialist, greater collaboration with Islamic feminists from within Iraq's mainstream religious parties coupled with greater training of functionaries in modern Islamic legal thinking and the promotion of judicial reform provide the greatest hope for change taking place. While Coleman makes the point emphatically that in many Islamic countries 'reformers have largely abandoned attempts to replace sharia with secular law, a route that has proved mostly futile, instead they are trying to promote women's rights within an Islamic framework', we are not sure that training women in Islamic jurisprudence alone is a guaranteed method to effect change. Training in the basic elements of the law would give these women the necessary language to withstand the largely patriarchal structures and notions of sharia. However, new thinking on jurisprudence would be required if more effective changes that respect Human Rights and the rights of women are to be implemented.[17]

Further Need for Reform

As the post-First World War world evolved with the dissolution and break-up of the Ottoman Empire, new needs for reform arose in territories that had been ruled previously by the Ottomans. The European colonial powers worked closely with Muslim leaders to bring about new dispensations of power and institutions. Egypt, as mentioned, played an important role in drafting the necessary laws that, in the case of public laws, were largely based on Western laws. These reforms gave the impression that they were more Islamic than the Ottoman-inspired changes of the *Tanzimat*. While Western influence was more or less acceptable in public law, the same was not true in the realm of private law (which affected the family), where reform was also needed. The main focus was thus on family law and more particularly on a woman's right to divorce and a man's so-called right to polygamy, and particularly his unilateral right to repudiate his wife. Here, in order to gain the necessary traction, reformers were compelled to consult the authoritative manuals and use all the existing 'sharia' tools for this purpose. They carried out this process instrumentally but in the most unconventional manner. Appearance trumped reality in order to allow the reformed laws to gain acceptance amongst the Muslim population. A multiplicity of methods were used. Court jurisdictions were utilised to restrict substantive sharia laws based on the sultan's inherent *siyasa* powers limiting the jurisdiction of his court. This was known as *Takhsis al-Qada*. A similar expedient of using the court structure to restrict sharia jurisdiction had been used in India for over two centuries, and the paradigm was exported by the British to their other colonies.

In the Middle East, however, Family Law Codes were introduced after the Ottoman Law of Family Rights of 1917 had been enacted, which gave an impetus to carry out reform in this part of the law in all those territories which had been under Ottoman rule. These Codes sought Islamic justification for reform on the basis of *taqlid* – a contradiction in terms, since the word is supposed to signify imitation of the authorised manuals of law. The ruling powers, nevertheless, had to use traditional notions to make reform acceptable to the population at large as something that was mandated or acceptable to the faith of Islam and not necessarily imposed from outside.

What were the Sharia Tools?

To start with, there was the overall notion of *taqlid* under the umbrella of which all modifications were taking place. This served to assure people that nothing new was being done and, if principles were borrowed from other schools, there was a precedent for this practice as the shared orthodoxy of all Sunni schools was accepted by *ijma'* – and hence we find wholesale borrowing from other schools. To an extent, this was possible to do, as Hanafi laws and courts with Hanafi judges were a known phenomenon in many areas with a Maliki and Shafi'i population such as prevailed in Egypt, as the Ottomans had made Hanafi law the law of the empire. Muslims generally accepted this approach and there are legal precedents in British Indian courts for this internal *ijma'*-mandated legal pluralism. To initiate this process, the tool of *takhayyur*, or selection, was used, which was a classical technique of drawing principles and legal solutions from other schools. This process of selection took place in three stages.

1) The first consisted of taking on board the dominant views of different schools in order to meet new issues. This was important as the grounds for divorce for women were not identical in all the schools of law. In some schools, failure to maintain a spouse or inability to consummate a marriage could be a ground for divorce, whereas in other schools there were different reasons. The Hanbali school, for example, which was generally the most conservative and literal-minded system of law, provided in this case the best solution for overcoming the archaic provisions of divorce generally extant in sharia. It respected and upheld the principle of the sanctity of contract – we must remember that marriage in Islam is regarded as a contract – which states *al-'aqd shari'at al-muta'āqidayn* ('the contract is the law of the two parties').[18] This principle corresponds with the Common Law, *pacta sunt servanda,* which emphasises the sanctity of contract. Maliki followers incorporated Hanafi rules allowing women to marry without the permission of a guardian, as Maliki rules on this point were restrictive. These modernising rules were rationalised on the historical basis of *ijma'* operating under the broad umbrella of *taqlid* and supported by a hadith of the Prophet that extolled diversity (*ikhtilaf*) as a blessing of God.[19]

2) The next stage of modernisation did not entail the use of dominant opinions but, rather, of the subordinate views of different schools, and here the views of scholars that pre-dated the consolidation of the various legal schools in Abbasid times were taken on board, such as those of the judge Ibn Shubruma (d. 761) and others. This gave the reforms a colouration of *taqlid* and thus legitimacy, but the connection became more tenuous.

3) As reforms were taking place, *takhayyur* entered its third stage known as *talfiq*, which amounts to patching together or combining the views of different schools and jurists, or elements therefrom, to form a single rule. The resemblance to *taqlid* or obeying the rules, according to Coulson 'had become nothing more than a thin veil of pretence',[20] which

was purely formal and superficial and masked the reality of an attempt to meet the needs of modern society. Explanatory notes accompanying various codes emphasised the changing needs of society. In line with all historical devices and fictions, the role of *taqlid* had been played out and its status was in fact otiose, although its reputation with the pious continued to exert rhetorical influence. Whereas *ijtihad*, or new legal thinking, remained notionally taboo, in practice it was returning to invest modern Muslim legal scholars with tools and processes to reform and in effect to dilute sharia to make it fit for purpose in the modern world. These changes were created largely by way of jurisprudential opportunism which took the form of neo-*ijtihad*, and they brought about further changes to the private laws of most Muslim states. The changes, however, have only created some limited reform. Thus, for example, legal violations are proscribed but are not followed up by sanctions beyond fines for certain infringements. A major rethink, in our opinion, is still required.

New Challenges

The First World War and the break-up of the Ottoman Empire gave rise to new challenges, with once-colonised Muslim peoples coming under new spheres of influence that were largely dominated by European powers. The United Kingdom and France carved out the Arab Middle East into the new nation states of Iraq, Syria, Transjordan and Lebanon, and the Zionist movement in Palestine succeeded in creating the state of Israel. In Africa and Asia, Western colonial powers had to contend with nationalist movements aspiring for self-determination. All these developments called for changes in the field of education, economics, political institutions, government and law. In the latter case, great care was taken to ensure that any changes made were acceptable culturally to the majority of the people. Receptivity to change varied throughout the Muslim world. Generally there was a recognition that sharia, as formulated from medieval times, was no longer able to serve the needs of new nation states where there was a diversity of people. Some countries resisted change, including Saudi Arabia, Yemen, northern Nigeria, Afghanistan and Oman.[21]

As countries gained their political independence, new constitutions came into being, new civil and commercial codes were enacted and new personal legal statutes, incorporating sharia principles and drawing as much as possible from different schools of Islamic law (mainly Sunni), were passed. The changes were gradual and statutory legislation was not the only method of change, but in areas such as the Indian subcontinent judges, both Muslim and non-Muslim, who had been trained in the English Common Law tradition, carried out changes through judicial activism which effectively adapted sharia principles to fit into the national mood of the time.[22] In the 1970s, some of the newly independent nation states witnessed political revolutions and the institution of military dictatorships calling for a return of sharia, which led to a drive for the 'Islamisation' of laws in the field of commerce, criminal and family matters, especially in Pakistan and Sudan. Iran also made similar changes in its laws.

In 1973, some oil-producing Arab countries witnessed an upsurge in their earnings through the increase in revenues following the Arab-Israeli war when the Organization of Petroleum Exporting Countries (OPEC), the major oil cartel, decided to raise the price of oil significantly. This gave rise to major increases in earning power both on the part of governments as well as individuals from various Muslim countries who worked in these areas. This development provided further impetus to the Islamisation of laws particularly in the field of economics, giving rise to the phenomenon known as Islamic banking that today has morphed into sharia-compliant financing. This, though still small compared with conventional banking, is witnessing exponential growth, with major centres of Islamic finance emerging in countries such as Turkey, Bahrain, Malaysia, the United Arab Emirates and the United Kingdom – which has passed enabling legislation to facilitate the utilisation of Middle East and South-East Asian finances and to develop infrastructural programmes in the United Kingdom in accordance with sharia principles.

All these changes, it must be noted, coincided with the challenges faced by the civil and criminal justice systems globally and the emergence of ADR as an alternative to litigation, leading diasporic Muslims, mainly in the United Kingdom, to establish sharia councils to deal with family disputes, a phenomenon that has given rise to much controversy in both the United Kingdom and Canada.[23]

In the next chapter we discuss the Shi'i legal understanding and theory of law, which we believe has been largely overlooked or sidelined in most discussions on Islamic jurisprudence, and the possible reasons for this neglect.

Shi'i Legal Understanding and Theory of Law

Islamic Law Seen as Sunni Law

Islamic law, as it is generally understood today, is portrayed largely as Sunni law or law as it evolved within the interpretation of what later became known as Sunni Islam, with little or no reference to the Shi'i interpretation of God's law as it subsequently developed from the Shi'i theory of law. As noted above, the Shi'a are those who regard Ali as the rightful successor to the Prophet both in his temporal and spiritual aspects. The reasons for this division are many, including limited access to original sources upon which researchers, mainly orientalists, relied. According to Mohyddin Yahia in *The Study of Shi'i Islam: History, Theology and Law*: 'the situation is even less favourable, because the experts still often tend to be over-dependent on the discourse of the heresiographers whose direct information remains questionable'.[1] Another reason could be that immediately after the death of the Prophet Muhammad the evolution of the law took place within the context of what could be referred to today as a Muslim state, and the development of the state was dominated by Sunni doctrine.

The head of such a state was the Caliph, whose mandate vis-à-vis God's law was not clear at the time or indeed, for centuries later.[2] However, this initial period contained within it the germ of notions of legitimacy, authority and power that later became predominant identity markers for both branches of Islam in their respective formulations of Shi'i and Sunni ideologies.

Fiqh as Identity

Before the formulation of the different legal schools, both Sunni and Shi'i, *fiqh* was not the decisive criterion for the identity of Muslims. In fact, there were a large number of schools, some of which atrophied and died out in the course of time. The situation during this early period of Islamic history was changing and taking on new shapes which only later solidified into the major division between the Sunnis and the Shi'is.

Sufism

An important current of thought and faith in Muslim history which was from the first associated with inner or esoteric knowledge arising from the Prophet, his cousin and son-in-law Imam Ali, and the Prophet's father-in-law Abu Bakr, the first Caliph – is Sufism or the mystical dimension of the faith. Sufism has strong associations with Shi'ism but also lies at the heart of Sunni experience and awareness, deepening it and opening new perspectives alongside the overt, textual and legalistic apparel of the faith. Sufism did not eschew sharia, but nor did it make it an icon of Islamic identity.

History with the Sufis becomes subsumed into the pursuit of a spiritual understanding of holy texts and into a generous practice of the tenets of the faith. This does not emphasise division but rather seeks to harmonise and pull together different strands into an elemental and core consciousness of Islam brought alive as prayer, meditation and the inner search for the final truth, or *haqq*, which itself is one of the 99 attributes of God. Sufism spread across the entire Muslim world in various stages and guises. Sufism is a process that regards knowledge as a function of being. Through it one may discover a spiritual consanguinity with the mystical traditions of Judaism and Christianity, not to mention with other non-Abrahamic religions. Over time, it became a bridge between the two major strands of Islam, as well as between Islam and other major faiths. It remains the practice of millions of Muslims today and is generally respected across the world by Muslims and non-Muslims.

Over the course of time, both the Sunnis, and to a lesser extent the Shi'is,[3] built a formal legal system. Sufism, while it also became formalised into *tariqa*s, or brotherhoods, continued the search to acquire knowledge of the spiritual dimension of the faith. In some cases, this took a formal shape, but retained the ethical dimension that all conduct was a necessary element of being a Muslim.

Maqasid al-Sharia

In the legal domain, *maqasid* is reflected in giving greater primacy to the purpose of the law based upon public necessity as encompassed by the notions of sharia, *al-maslaha al-mursala*,[4] and *al-mashlaha al-daruriyya*.[5] These notions were recognised not only by Sufis but also by some of the established schools of law such as the Hanafis, who followed the teachings of al-Maturidi in laying great emphasis on the purpose behind the law. All this helped to retain a degree of flexible, open-ended and reflective consideration of the social good and its contro-versial antitheses, which is at the heart of an understanding of the open science of ethics. Therefore Sufism and Shi'ism, as well as the less rigid Sunni formulations of sharia, have the potential of retrieving for sharia its higher ethical purpose, its *maqasid*, something originally discussed by the eminent jurists and theo-logians such as Ghazali, Juwayni and Tirmidhi, as well as by the 14th-century Maliki jurist al-Shatibi. This process of renewal was the preoccupation of many modern Muslim thinkers of the late 19th and early 20th centuries, such as the Egyptian *mufti/jurist* Mohamed Abduh who lived in the early 20th century and Jamal al-Din al-Afghani, an Islamic intellectual who was an earlier contemporary in the Arab world, Sir Muhammad Iqbal, a leading Muslim thinker, and Sayed Ahmed Khan, an education-alist, both of whom lived in the Indian subcontinent, and Imam Shamil in Central Asia, who wrote about Islam and its interface with modernity in the late 19th century. In the present day, this process of renewal could also be achieved through the practice of ADR, which already exists in the Western world and is being progressively embraced by Muslims in the diaspora,[6] as well as in many Muslim countries.[7]

The Shi'i Theory of Law

We examine below certain basic notions that have had an impact on the development of law from a Shi'a perspective, and we aim to show how this historical dimension can help us to examine the evolution of sharia from a different perspective, one that is complementary to the Sunni notion of law and shows that sharia is not monolithic since, for the Shi'is, it is predicated on different principles. The Shi'i version of sharia is based on the authority of the Imam who, for the majority of the Shi'is, went into occultation in 874.[8] The authentic basis of the law is thus derived not only from the Qur'an and the Sunna as transmitted through the Shi'i Imams, but also from the rulings and precepts handed down by the Imams, who are descended from the Prophet through his daughter Fatima and his son-in-law and cousin Ali, the fourth Caliph and the first Shi'a Imam.

Hence, the doctrine of Imamate dominates the Shi'is' jurisprudence and produces a concept of law that fundamentally differs from that of the Sunnis in that whatever administrative powers belong to the Sunni Caliphs must always be exercised within certain circumscribed limits set by sharia. The Caliph, therefore, is theoretically as much bound by the religious law as are his subjects. However, legal sovereignty in Islam, contrary to the Sunni notion, vests for the Shi'a in the Imam, who speaks as an agent of the Divine Lawgiver. According to Coulson, 'Legally, it [the difference] is between a system which is basically immutable and represents the attempt by human reason to discern the divine command and one which purports to be the direct and living expression of that command.'[9]

The Imamate

To understand the concept of Imamate better, one needs to recognise the role played by the Prophet during his lifetime and the role the Imams took on after his death. The Prophet, through whom the Qur'an was revealed, not only set out the message of the faith but also interpreted it for the newly formed Muslim community in Medina. For Muslims, therefore, the Prophet was both the medium and the interpreter of the Revelation. Following his death, Muslims believed that Revelation per se came to an end, but the need for guidance continued. For this some of the faithful turned to Ali, the Prophet's cousin and son-in-law, whom they believed was designated as Imam to provide this significant interpretative function. While Abu Bakr (d. 634), Umar (d. 644), Uthman (d. 656) and Ali (d. 661) are all recognised as having acquired the temporal mantle of the Prophet, Shi'is (*Shi'at 'Ali*) believe that in addition to acquiring this temporal position of leader Ali also was the first spiritual leader after the Prophet. This core belief is disputed by Sunnis, who maintain that the Prophet made no such designation and that his successors were selected by the Muslim community according to right, by a process known as *shura*.[10] This difference of opinion about the successor to the Prophet eventually led to the division of Islam into its two main branches, the majority Sunnis and the minority Shi'is.[11] This debate concerning authority, legitimacy and power remains alive today, and fuels much of the present turmoil in the Islamic world where geopolitical tensions exacerbate it.

It should also be noted that in Shi'i Islam there were splits based on differing views as to who was the rightful Imam. Following the death of Ja'far al-Sadiq in 765, the first major split amongst the Shi'a took place. The majority followed Ja'far al-Sadiq's son, Musa al-Kazim, as the rightful Imam; the minority paid their allegiance to Musa's brother Ismail, and became known as Ismailis. They later established the Fatimid Caliphate and in the time of the Imam-Caliph al-Mustansir (r. 1036–1094), the Ismailis themselves split when one group followed his son Nizar while the other took another son, al-Musta'li, as their Imam, they are known today as the Musta'lis or Bohras. The Ismailis are the only Shi'i group to have a living hereditary Imam, who is called the Aga Khan, a direct descendant of the Prophet. The Ithna' asharis (generally known as Shi'a) are also known as Twelvers, as opposed to the Ismailis who are referred to as Seveners.

From the perspective of jurisprudential theory, both the Sunnis and the Shi'is represent a similar schema with regard to the sources that form the foundation of sharia. This theory is 'a systematically idealised rather than a historically factual account of the sources of law'.[12] Both branches of Islam regard the Qur'an and the Sunna as the basic material of divine Revelation, although their versions of the Sunna differ. As distinct from the standard corpus of Traditions recognised as authoritative by the Sunnis, the Shi'is developed their own collection of hadith, based on their own standards of authentication which were a key criterion for validating the transmission of a particular Tradition by one or other of their recognised Imams. Two important Shi'i collections of hadith were compiled by legal exegetes, namely al-Kulayni (d. 941) and al-Qummi (d. 940) after the Occultation of the Twelfth Imam of that line.[13] Like the Sunni hadith authorities, they attempted to refine the bulk of the hadiths and purge them of fabrications. They also relied heavily on a study of the credibility of the narrators. Al-Kulayni's famous book, *al-Kafi*, covered all sayings relating to all parts of the faith (dogma, practical rulings and so on). Al-Qummi, on the other hand, both compiled one of the major Shi'i hadith collections and wrote various books on Shi'i *fiqh* such as *al-Hidaya* and *al-Muqni'*.

Other Differences

In addition to the doctrine of the Imamate, which is a fundamental issue that impacts on the theoretical basis of law in Shi'i Islam, there are other important differences that have also influenced the law's development over the course of time. First, the Shi'i approach to the understanding of pre-Islamic legal norms is conceptually different from that of the Sunnis. The Shi'a consider the pre-Islamic dispensations as being superseded by the advent of the Qur'an, whereas Sunni legal thinking maintains that there was a continuity between the norms of the pre-Islamic world and those of the new world brought in by Islam. The earlier norms, according to Sunni Islam, continued to be legitimate, except where they were specifically and overtly abrogated by new Qur'anic values and particular injunctions set out therein.

Therefore, we see a contrast between the idealism of the Shi'is as against the pragmatism of the Sunni interpretation of the law as they understood it. It can be argued that this understanding was inevitably political on account of the Sunnis having a state and government in which positive law had to be provided and implemented. The question thus revolves around the juristic inter-pretations of the Qur'an. Existing customary law for the Sunnis is endorsed by implication in the Qur'an unless it expressly rejects it. For the Shi'is, it is the opposite: customary law is abrogated unless expressly confirmed by the Qur'an. There is therefore a fusion in the scheme of inheritance in Sunni law between the old agnatic heirs of customary law and the new heirs specified in the Qur'an. For the Shi'is, by contrast, the law of inheritance is viewed differ-ently. The express Qur'anic norms are no more subject to modifi-cation by subsequent practices than they are by pre-Islamic ones. In brief, Sunnis view Qur'anic regulations as piecemeal changes while Shi'is regard them as providing an outright paradigmatic break with past practices, thus laying down the first principles for the elaboration of a 'new' legal system. We provide three examples of these changes – inheritance, *talaq* or divorce, and *mut'a* – to show how these two versions of sharia are applied in these two different branches of Islam.

Inheritance

An area of sharia that remains controversial, certainly in modern Western notions of law, concerns the rules relating to inheritance in which females do not inherit equally with males. However, this is not true of Islamic law as a whole, as the Shi'i Ithna 'ashari law of inheritance is substantially different from Sunni law, where entitlement on intestacy is based on three specific grounds that create three separate groups of heirs, namely those who share under Qur'anic principles; in other words the surviving spouse, the male agnate relatives of the deceased (*'asaba*) and, failing these two primary groups, female and cognate relatives.[14] Sunni law, on the other hand, recognises only one basis of entitlement, which depends on the relationship of the deceased with those entitled to inherit. Therefore, while the Ithna 'ashari law divides all relatives (except the surviving spouse) into three classes – which, in order of priority, are lineal descendants and parents of the deceased, brothers, sisters and their issue and grandparents of the deceased, and uncles and aunts and their issue – Sunni law does not. Entitlement under Shi'i law thus does not accord a special place to the male agnate relatives (*'asaba*), who merely fall into the three classes listed above. While female and cognate relatives only succeed in the last resort in Sunni law, they are integrated within the general framework of Shi'i law.

In Sunni law, if the father has pre-deceased the son the paternal grandfather has a favoured position. Ranking in the place of the father, he takes the Qur'anic share of one-sixth of the estate when any child of the deceased is alive. By virtue of his agnate relationship, he is entitled additionally to any residue where the only surviving child of the deceased is a daughter. In this case, he takes twice as much as the deceased's mother when in competition with her alone or in company with the surviving spouse. Finally, this division of assets totally excludes any children of the deceased's daughter. These convoluted rules enable the paternal grandfather to occupy a privileged position, whereby he is granted an additional value to the existing one-sixth of the estate when the only other heir is the deceased's daughter.

In the Ithna 'ashari system on the other hand, the existence of any one of the relatives mentioned above, child, grandchild or mother of the deceased, precludes the paternal grandfather from any succession rights at all. This shows that Shi'i law gives preference to the child, grandchild or mother of the deceased, and the paternal grandfather has no rights. If the deceased has lineal descendants or parents living at the time of his death, his siblings are equally excluded from succession under Ithna 'ashari law. In Sunni law, siblings are excluded only by the deceased's father or male agnatic descendant. Germane or consanguine brothers and sisters inherit as residuary heirs when in competition with the deceased's daughter. In competition with the deceased's mother, sisters – in the absence of brothers – take a collective Qur'anic share of two-thirds of the estate. While a brother, with or without sisters, inherits as a residuary, two or more brothers restrict the mother to her minimum share of one-sixth, while any brother or sister will totally supplant the issue of the deceased's daughter. Overall, we can see that the law of the Shi'a conceives of the family as a narrower unit consisting of the father, mother and direct issue, whereas Sunni law regards the family as made up of a wider constellation of relatives including grandparents, brothers, uncles and so on.

Divorce, or *Talaq*

Moving on to divorce, we note that *talaq*, or divorce by repudiation, is another example where Shi'i legal provisions differ radically from Sunni law. While both branches concur on the basic right of a husband to repudiate his wife unilaterally when he so chooses, these two systems of law differ substantially in the way the rules operate. Sunni law has minimal formalities with regard to the process of repudiation, which can be any words that signify a husband's repudiation of his wife, either orally or in writing. Furthermore, witnesses are not necessary for the repudiation to come into effect. On the other hand, Ithna 'ashari provisions have a strong formal structure which must be observed. The pronouncement therefore has to be made orally and must use the precise term *talaq*, or some form thereof, in the presence of two witnesses. Additionally, there has to be evidence of a definite intention to repudiate by the husband. Ithna 'ashari law is thus more formal. Generally, in the case of the Sunnis, repudiation can be pronounced as a jest or a threat, and for the Hanafi school, repudiation uttered under duress or by a husband in a state of inebriation remains valid, and divorce is brought into effect.

Depending on the circumstances, repudiation is classified by the Sunnis as being either approved (*talaq al-sunna*) or disapproved (*talaq al-bid'a*). Even so, the latter form of divorce remains effective for Sunnis, although not approved as such and morally doubtful. Shi'is, on the other hand, refuse to recognise *talaq al-bid'a* and insist that divorce must follow the process of *talaq al-sunna*, otherwise the divorce is regarded as null and void.

Mut'a Marriage

The third significant difference in sharia as understood between Sunnis and Shi'is is the practice of *mut'a* marriage – a temporary relationship between a man and a woman

for a specific period and for a specified remuneration (*ujra*) –
which is recognised by some Shi'is but not by Sunnis. Owing to
constraints of space, we do not go into this controversial practice
in detail.[15]

Ibadis

We should also take note that another branch of Islam, namely
the Ibadi Muslims, who are considered as being neither Shi'i nor
Sunni, have their own interpretation of the theories of law and
thus their own version of jurisprudence. Their school of law is
followed today in regions such as Zanzibar, Oman and parts of
North Africa, largely among the Kabyle people who live in the
Atlas Mountains in the north of Algeria.[16]

Muhammad al-Baqir and Ja'far al-Sadiq

Although history has preserved few details about the relationship
between the early Shi'i Imams, such as Muhammad al-Baqir
(d. 733) and Ja'far al-Sadiq (d. 765) and their influence on Sunni
jurisprudential thinkers such as Abu Hanifa and Malik b. Anas,[17]
they are included in Sunni *isnad*s (transmissions of hadith) in
works such as Malik's (d. 795) *al-Muwatta*, al-Tabari's (d. 923)
Tarikh al-Tafsir, Ibn Hanbal's (d. 955) *Musnad* and Shafi'i's (d. 820)
Risala.[18] Imam Muhammad al-Baqir is unanimously considered
in non-Shi'i circles to be one of the most credible authorities on
the Traditions of the Prophet bearing the quality of *thiqa* – the
highest degree of trust bestowed by Muslim scholars on those
whom they considered reliable, trustworthy and accurate in trans-
mitting the Traditions. Muhammad al-Baqir was a contemporary
of some famous Medinan jurists with whom he worked closely.[19]
To some scholars of law on the subject of hadith, al-Baqir excelled
and stood above these eminent scholars in learning. His prestige
was generally recognised by both Sunnis and Shi'is.[20]

In addition to this influence, Shi'i Imams gave rulings on ethical
issues that shaped Shi'i jurisprudential understanding throughout
Islamic history. More importantly, in today's world where the
practice of ADR is beginning to gain greater recognition, these
teachings could be of great value in helping bridge law and ethics

in the resolution of disputes which ADR encourages and actually calls for. These teachings could also help illuminate the discourse on the *maqasid al-sharia* mentioned above, which remains an important task for Muslim jurists to explore if Islamic law is to play any meaningful role in addressing the contemporary issues concerning Muslim societies today.[21] Additionally, the Shi'is regard the sayings of the Imams as a source of law. While all Shi'is follow these principles, the Occultation of their Imam does give rise to various issues concerning authority which, for the Ithna' asharis vests with those scholars whom they call *mujtahids*. On the other hand the Ismailis have a living hereditary Imam to guide the process of understanding ethical behaviour, good governance and law which is provided to them on a regular basis by the Imam of the time. Shi'i law developed within Shi'i communities in the Muslim world according to their notions of authority given the fact that there were splinter groups that broke away on the basis of who was the legitimate Imam at any particular time. Shia legal tradition and the Ismaili *fiqh* in particular strongly emphasises the practice of *ta'wil* or the search for the original and inner hidden meaning of the Qur'anic text. It was used extensively by the Ismailis for allegorical, esoteric and symbolic interpretation of the Qur'an and other important texts including sharia, recorded historical events and the world of nature. It stands comfortably side-by-side not only with the *maqasid al-sharia* but with the poetry of great Sufi saints such as Rumi, Attar and indeed, the spiritual fables of the Ikhwan al-Safa – a group of intellectuals in Basra generally dated to the 10th century. *Ta'wil* is distinct from *tafsir* which is the philological exegesis of the Qur'an and other texts. In accordance with Ismaili belief and tradition this process is guided by the Imam of the time through his *firmans* and other pronouncements. This basic principle of Ismailism is mentioned in the preamble to the global Ismaili Constitution that governs the entire community.

The Ismaili Version of Shi'i Law that Gained Prominence during the Fatimid Caliphate (909–1171)[22]

A discrete Ismaili *fiqh* was founded only after the establishment of the Fatimid state in 909 when the Ismaili version of Shi'i law was codified by al-Qadi al-Nu'man (d. 974),[23] culminating in his monumental work *Da'a'im al-Islam*, which was undertaken with the approval of the fourth Fatimid Imam-Caliph al-Mu'izz and endorsed by him as the official legal code of the Fatimid state.[24] Al-Nu'man compiled several legal treatises based on legal hadith transmitted from the *ahl al-bayt* (the Family of the Prophet) which are set out in various Shi'i compilations. The *Da'a'im*, consisting of two volumes, follows the pattern of legal manuals current at the time. The first volume covers religious observances (*'ibadat*), while the second is mainly concerned with worldly transactions (*mu'amalat*).

Fatimid Ismaili law integrates Shi'i beliefs as articulated in the doctrine of the Imamate with general legal concepts accepted by all Muslims. Like all other Muslims, Ismailis accept the Qur'an and the Sunna of the Prophet as the primary sources of law, but, in line with other Shi'is, they depart from the norms of the Sunni schools in acknowledging only those hadiths reported by the Imams from the *ahl al-bayt* and the hadiths transmitted from their own Imams. As a consequence, the authority of their Imam and his teachings become the third and most decisive principal source of law for the Ismailis.

The *Da'a'im* continues to remain the main legal text for the Tayyibi Musta'li Ismailis, including the Daudi Bohras of South Asia,[25] while the Nizari Ismailis have followed the guidance of their living and hereditary Imams in their legal affairs, as well as in the normative and ritual practices of their communities.[26]

Shi'i jurisprudence, as we have shown, embodies principles that appear more equitable to women's rights particularly in the field of inheritance and the way in which unilateral repudiation by a husband can take place. Given the fact that the Ithna 'ashari Imam went into occultation in the 9th century, legal functionaries have subsequently undertaken the task of interpreting the law in the name of an ever-present Imam.[27] In the context of the application of a religious law, occultation raises issues concerning the notion of authority and legitimacy. There are tendencies for the law to become fixed and ossified, with the introduction of certain time-marked legal dispensations that can conflict with contemporary notions of justice. This issue of occultation and its impact upon the interpretation of law poses for the majority of the Shi'is a problem not dissimilar to that faced by the Sunnis, namely the legitimate basis of legal reasoning. This issue is obviated in the case of the Ismailis as they have a living, hereditary Imam.

The situation of the Ismailis raises an interesting point as their living, hereditary Imam has the authority to interpret sharia according to the demands of the time. However, Ismailis, who are scattered across the world, have no state of their own and hence no temporal power. In keeping with a cardinal principle of sharia, Ismailis accept and adhere to the law of the land in which they live. In addition, they have developed a sophisticated, transnational dispute resolution system that gives primacy to the ethical principles that underpin sharia (the *maqasid*), helping disputants to settle their legal problems in keeping with the notion of *sulh* or negotiated settlement as mentioned in the Qur'an 4:35. Moreover, Ismailis apply reason in understanding and practising their faith as directed in the Imam's *firmans* (guidance). The *firmans* are themselves influenced by contemporary society and its needs, thus ensuring that the law, for them, remains relevant to the problems and issues encountered by them at any particular time. The Ismailis' classical position with regard to sharia was reiterated at the Amman conference in 2005 by Aga Khan IV when he stated: 'Our historical adherence is to the Ja'fari *madhhab* and other *madhahib* of close affinity, and it continues, under the leadership of the hereditary Ismaili Imam of the time. This adherence is in harmony also with our acceptance of Sufi principles of personal search and balance between the *zahir* and the spirit or the intellect which the *zahir* signifies.'[28]

Conclusion

We have endeavoured in this chapter to show the outlines of sharia as understood by Shi'is, and we note that while the actual principles between the two systems of law are not incompatible in many instances, the foundation of the law for Shi'is has a distinct dimension in that it is continually interpreted and mediated through Shi'i Imams who act as special conduits for the expression of God's will.

Summary

The narrative so far related is necessarily brief but we hope that it gives a sense of the context of Islamic law, how it came into being during the first centuries of Islam, how it was then codified in order to give it shape, uniformity and predictability, and how it became a tool of power for the ruling elite while retaining the legacy of the Revelation, the basis of Muslim identity. Inevitably, as the gate of *ijtihad* was reputed to be closed – changes in the law were incremental and hence sharia became less open to change and consequently less capable of adapting to new circumstances with the passage of time.

Sharia – which was originally based upon the Qur'an whose legal verses are sparse in comparison to the total body of the Revelation – was never a system of law that covered all aspects of the society in which it was situated. There has always been a part of the legal system which, in practice, was outside its ambit, and which was controlled by the political power of the Caliphs and later by rulers of the various parts of the Islamic world; and where sharia did prevail there were places where its domain was mixed or combined with the demands of customary law. In these cases, it held a place as part of the local laws of regions, such as north-west Africa, sub-Saharan Africa and Indonesia.

With the passage of time, Muslim peoples had to learn to accommodate themselves to new conditions and to new power relationships where they were no longer the dominant force but were in fact having to keep up with the scientific, technological, military and concomitant cultural, political and intellectual changes that were revolutionising Western societies. Sharia was accordingly challenged, and efforts were made in the Ottoman Empire, including Egypt and further afield in the Muslim world, to adapt it to the demanding new circumstances of the modern, rapidly globalising world.

In this chapter, we have discussed the Shi'i legal understanding of law, the doctrine of the Imamate as a cornerstone of authority in Shi'i Islam and the different Shi'i schools of law. This was followed by our discussion for the need for changes brought about by greater contact with the Western world.

The Multiple Manifestations of Sharia

Background

One often hears in the media of so-called sharia rulings that are offensive and unethical. These rulings are unacceptable, and many Muslims themselves are offended by them, especially since they are made in the name of their faith. Moreover, there are media reports of punishments meted out based on summary justice, showing victims being lashed or people calling for this type of retribution. However, there is a real tension here in that there are many lawyers, both male and female, in those countries where sharia is being used for repressive and cruel purposes who are actively and overtly struggling against this phenomenon at the risk of their lives. There are also customary practices followed by some diasporic Muslims that are not accepted by sharia but are perceived to be part of it, largely because Muslims are involved in many of these cultural practices, such as female genital mutilation (FGM), forced marriage and crimes of honour. Finally, there are isolated incidents that emerge due to individual interpretations of Muslim lifestyle that people confuse with sharia but are again often largely based on cultural norms. These include issues such as dress codes, the wearing of beards and whether one can work in a business whose activities include the sale of alcohol or pork products.

In this chapter, we discuss all the above with a view to exploring the forces at play, the emotions they unleash, how they become resolved and what they say about Muslim self-understanding and self-presentation in an increasingly globalising world.

These practices often tend to offend liberal thought, natural justice, broad ethical principles and basic Human Rights. We also wish to explore the reasons for the negative responses towards certain aspects of sharia, while in other cases – such as sharia finance which is covered more comprehensively in Chapter 9 – principles of Islamic law are not only recognised but welcomed in many Western countries, a reality which is helping to enable the development of this branch of sharia through supporting legislation to fit into the international financial system.

We shall first discuss the cases by providing a brief set of facts, followed by the outcome, then show the forces at work by highlighting the call for sharia punishments; and we shall then attempt an analysis of what we believe is the rationale. We shall touch on the customary practices among some Muslims, including diasporic Muslim communities, show how they are not a part of sharia and discuss how this issue is being addressed. Finally, we shall discuss the idiosyncratic interpretations of individual Muslims, mainly in diasporic contexts, which other Muslims find either abhorrent or erroneous. Some of these are episodic: they appear in the newspapers fleetingly and attention often fizzles out following a clarificatory letter by a Muslim writer or someone who has a proper understanding of the issue. On occasion there is confusion. Frequently, Muslims in diasporic contexts do not have a realistic idea of what sharia is in actuality. This is often compounded by the judicial opinions or fatwas of self-styled clerics, some of whom operate online and without the supporting argumentation that would lend them at least a degree of respectability. Outside specialised academic circles, Western understanding of these issues is at best superficial. Media coverage is often sensational and feeds into the phenomenon of Islamophobia, which at times reaches spectacular proportions.[1]

If one analyses the points of conflict between sharia and the modern world, one will notice only a few areas of fundamental variance.[2] In many instances, there are convergences between sharia principles and Common Law values. However, fundamental differences exist in a few areas such as apostasy, adultery, blasphemy, a range of lack of rights for women and minorities, and certain criminal punishments in some Muslim countries that create conflict with national and international laws, impinging on the fundamental rights of the individual. These attacks on the freedom of individual conscience and rights assumed greater significance in the Western world when, in 1989, the writer Salman Rushdie was deemed an apostate by a fatwa given by Ayatollah Khomeini in Iran.[3] The fatwa was issued on account of Rushdie's book *The Satanic Verses*, which used a report by the medieval Islamic scholar al-Tabari suggesting that the Qur'an contained verses that were a diabolical incursion into its narrative. This legal opinion went viral, and there were calls in Muslim countries and elsewhere for the execution of Rushdie for apostasy. It was pointed out by some that Khomeini's opinion was that alone, and that no court had actually tried Rushdie and found him guilty; sharia is not lynch law but requires due process. However, this argument did not have much traction in the widespread hysterical outcry for the author to be punished for this alleged crime. Rushdie's case led to a new level of politicisation of Islam both in the Islamic world and indeed in the West, which continues to reverberate to this day. Apostasy, as we point out below, is a real issue in the Muslim world.[4]

Apostasy

Apostasy remains a capital offence or one punishable by long-term imprisonment in many countries of the Islamic world. It represents a deep fissure between modern Western culture on the one hand and certain manifestations of Muslim consciousness on the other, and comes into direct conflict with the International Bill of Rights and associated conventions and protocols that all Muslim countries in principle have signed but to which many are not always able to adhere. The case of Abdul Rahman in Afghanistan exemplifies some of the issues at stake.[5]

Abdul Rahman was born in 1965 and is an Afghan citizen. During the 1990s, while working with a Christian aid organisation providing medical assistance to Afghan refugees in Pakistan, he came in contact with Catholicism, was baptised into the faith and adopted the biblical name Joel. In 1993, he moved to Germany, subsequently applied for asylum in Belgium but, being unsuccessful, was deported to his native Afghanistan, where, upon his return, he was divorced by his wife as a result of his conversion. In his battle for custody of his two infant daughters, his wife's mother raised the issue of his religion as a ground to deny him custody. He was disowned by his parents and even his children turned against him.

In February 2006, his wife reported him to the police, who, on finding a Bible in his possession, charged him with apostasy. He was unable to secure a lawyer in Kabul willing to act on his behalf. Legal experts say that Abdul Rahman's case arose as a result of contradictory laws in the Afghan Constitution, which theoretically recognises both freedom of religion and the Hanafi school of Islamic jurisprudence. Article 130 of the Afghan Constitution states that, while processing a case, courts must apply provisions of Hanafi jurisprudence if there is no provision in the Constitution or other laws regarding a specific case.[6] Prevailing Hanafi jurisprudence, as applied in Afghanistan, prescribes the death penalty for the crime of apostasy.[7]

Prosecutors called Abdul Rahman a 'microbe'. One stated: 'he should be cut off and removed from the rest of Muslim society and should be killed'. The chief judge in the case, however, did mention that Abdul Rahman would be asked to reconsider his conversion. 'We will ask him if he has changed his mind. If so, we will forgive him.' This underlines a hadith where the Prophet is reputed to have said several times that those who convert from Islam should be killed only if they refuse to come back to Islam. The chief judge stated – without apparent irony – that 'Islam is a religion of peace, tolerance, kindness and integrity, but if he does not repent ... you will all be witness to the sort of punishment he will face.'[8]

Afghan clerics had their own views on this controversial issue. They denounced what they regarded as interference by other countries and indeed by the Afghan president in the autonomy of the Afghan courts. A chief cleric addressing more than a thousand other clerics and young people in Kabul stated: 'Afghanistan does not have any obligations under international laws.' He added that the Prophet said: 'when someone changes his religion, he must be killed'. Another cleric announced at a mosque: 'if he is allowed to live in the West, then others will claim to be Christian so they too can do so. We must set an example … he must be hanged.' It was felt that there was unanimous agreement by all religious scholars in the country that Abdul Rahman should be executed, with one cleric even going as far as to state that he did not mind if the West withdrew their support for Afghanistan because of this as God would take care of the country.

As far as the public was concerned, according to the BBC, many people were vocal in support of Abdul Rahman's execution, though there was no clear indication whether they made up the majority. A religious scholar speaking about the conversion opined that 'he will have to be executed … if somebody at one point affirms the truth and then rejects or denies it, it would jeopardise the whole paradigm of truth. This is such a big offence that the penalty can only be death. At the very most some scholars argue that the person should be given time to re-think and if he embraces Islam again, he will be forgiven.'[9]

International Reaction

International reaction varied. A White House spokesman said that Abdul Rahman's arrest and trial 'clearly violates the universal freedoms that democracies around the world hold dear.'[10] The Canadian government expressed especial concern as Canadian armed forces had recently taken command of the coalition force in Kandahar Province and the government was under pressure to ensure that the Canadian mission would lead to an open and democratic Afghanistan.

Pope Benedict XVI urged the President of Afghanistan to pardon Abdul Rahman out of 'respect for human rights sanctioned in the preamble of the new Afghan Constitution.'[11] Germany, which then headed the International Security Assistance Force in Afghanistan, mandated by the United Nations (UN), suggested that Afghanistan could potentially lose aid or technical support for reconstruction efforts depending on the outcome of the case. The German Interior Minister stated: 'we contribute a lot to re-building Afghanistan and towards its stability, so I truly believe that Afghanistan must realise that we insist upon the freedom of religion. You cannot punish people because they change their religion.'[12] In response, a minister from the Afghan government accused politicians of the West of reacting very emotionally, stating that the situation was not yet resolved and a decision had not yet been made, and that statements of the kind made by the German government amounted to blackmail. The government also stated that Afghanistan was still attempting to build a democracy following the ousting of the Taliban in 2001 and that accepting the right to convert from Islam to Christianity – thereby opposing the Islamic view that apostasy should be punished – was too extreme for what remained a traditional Islamic society. He stated that 'Afghanistan cannot switch suddenly from one extreme to the other.'[13]

As it transpired after certain legal and political developments, Abdul Rahman submitted to a psychiatric test, the results of which were controversial. However, he was found unfit to stand trial and was acquitted on the basis of 'investigative gaps'. On 29 March 2006, the Prime Minister of Italy announced that his cabinet had approved Abdul Rahman's asylum plea and that he had already arrived in Italy.

An Islamic Perspective

Since Hanafi law figured so prominently in the resolution of this case, we should mention the two Qur'anic verses that refer to apostasy. These are:

> As for those who believe, then reject the faith, then believe again, then reject the faith again and become increasingly defiant, God will not forgive them, nor will He guide them on any path. Q 4:137

> Say, 'Now the truth has come from your Lord: let those who wish to believe in it do so, and let those who wish to reject it do so.' We have prepared a Fire for the wrongdoers that will envelop them from all sides. If they call for relief, they will be relieved with water like a molten metal, scalding their faces. What a terrible drink! What a painful resting place! Q 18:29

It should be noted that neither verse actually ordains a death penalty for apostasy. Indeed, there is another Qur'anic verse that makes it clear there is no compulsion in religion. However, it would appear that, according to many Islamic scholars, apostasy, contrary to what is stated in the Qur'an, does indeed merit the death penalty. They support their position by citing a hadith where the Prophet is reported to have called for the killing of an apostate. By its very nature, such a hadith is not as verifiable as a Qur'anic verse, and so is not universally accepted in the Muslim world. This awkward disjuncture between the cardinal text of the faith and a subsidiary text, which was noted down after the death of the Prophet and circulated with a degree of unquestioning acceptance, remains an ethical and intellectual challenge to Muslims.

Two newspaper editorials published in the United States brought up a salient issue. The *Washington Times* of 22 March 2006, with reference to the mental test that led to the non-prosecution of Abdul Rahman, described it as a 'manufactured loophole to enable the [Afghan] government to back down to avoid a disastrous internal and diplomatic crisis'. This convenient solution, the editorial points out, shows the underlying discrepancy in Afghanistan's constitution. Americans, it argued, who defined faith differently from those who must employ executioners to force believers to be devout, are naturally disdainful of such a culture of fear and intimidation. However, the editorial recognised that if this type of manipulation is the only way to save the life of a man who is following his faith, then we must be surely grateful.

In addition, a *New York Times* editorial on 23 March 2006 stated on the same issue, with heavy-handed irony, that perhaps Afghanistan should also return to stoning women to death for adultery. It called upon the United States, the United Kingdom and every other country helping the Afghan government to take a hard look at that country's legal institutions. It also urged Muslim leaders to criticise and reflect upon the Afghan case; those who continued to hold the teachings of Islam hostage to intolerance, argued the editorial, were doing grievous harm to their faith. The move to declare Abdul Rahman mentally incompetent was called 'a cheap trick', since the law on apostasy continued to remain on the country's books.

There are interesting undercurrents in these editorials from a country that had suffered from McCarthyism only a few decades earlier, when freedom of expression and ideological choice was being threatened. The writers urged Muslim countries to state their own position regarding apostasy: this was met with deadly silence from such countries, Muslim scholars, the media in Muslim-majority countries and Muslim institutions.

It can be argued that this case is fissured with contradictions, false construals, bad faith and fatal ambiguities. The rule of law was challenged and in fact ignored, the legal process was jeopardised and the accused was found guilty before a case was put to the court. The clerics were prodigal with their certainties: they claimed to know the outcome of the classical position of Hanafi law before first searching the range of legal discussions and discourses that took place in Muslim countries over centuries.

The Afghan government was in a dilemma. It was dependent on, and accountable to, foreign support – from the United States, the United Kingdom and other European countries – during a period of civil war and could not ignore the Human Rights objections of these countries. It was also compelled to respond to the faith of the general populace, which was essentially orthodox and conservative and was in thrall to the opinions of the legal scholars who were intent on imposing capital punishment.[14] All these pressures led to an attempt to apply sharia ahistorically; to deal with a dangerous and explosive political situation subjected to the superficial opinions of the media coverage that did not actually examine the underlying issues of culture, politics and power, and to the failure of a proper response from sections of the Islamic world, where a bolder political stance – which took into account the ostensible obligations of Human Rights that most Muslim countries signed up to in order to be members of the UN – would have been more appropriate and ethical in an Islamic context.

To summarise, what we witnessed here was a government in turmoil, beleaguered by political uncertainties and military threats; a judiciary obsessed with its own sense of autonomy, even though it failed to follow the judicial process required by natural justice; a group of clerics intent on imposing superficial notions of what they regarded as the proper law; and the necessary but overbearing demands of Western governments and the panoply of their supporting groups, such as non-governmental organisations and media agencies.

Blasphemy

Another area of great contention is the crime of blasphemy. The English word 'blasphemy' is made up of two words from ancient Greek, namely *blapto*, which signifies 'to harm', and *pheme*, which means 'speech'. Hence, 'blasphemy' literally means saying something that harms.[15] In the case of Islam, it constitutes any words or actions that intend to harm or abuse God, His Prophet Muhammad and other certain related sacred entities, including the good reputation of Aisha, wife of the Prophet. This is claimed to be affirmed by verse 24:11 of the Qur'an, which some inter-preters believe was revealed in response to an accusation levelled at her. The Qur'an itself, as the uncreated word of God, is liable to be blasphemed against by an individual. However, the notion of blasphemy in practice is cloudy and overlaps with other criminal acts such as unbelief, apostasy and heresy. The *Encyclopedia of Religion* refers to the prevailing uncertainty between these various offences when it states:

> From the viewpoint of Islamic law, blasphemy may be defined as any verbal expression that gives grounds for suspicion of apostasy (*riddah*). In theological terms, blasphemy often overlaps with infi-delity (*kufr*) which is the deliberate rejection of God and revelation. In this sense, expressing religious opinions at variance with standard Islamic views could easily be looked upon as blasphemous. Blas-phemy can also be seen as the equivalent of heresy (*zandaqah*)... Thus, in describing the Islamic concept of blasphemy, it is necessary to include not only insulting language directed to God, the Prophet and the revelation, but also theological positions and even mystical aphorisms that have come under suspicion.[16]

This vagueness of the concept, which entails words and the meaning of words that are actively affected by their context, and also by the sensibilities of the communities in which they are stated, is further complicated by the different outcomes that the various schools of Islamic law append to the offence, which generally carries the death penalty.

All of this, too detailed to examine here, opens up a Pandora's box of indecision and confusion. For this reason, blasphemy can become a tool of oppression in the hands of governments who wish to keep tight control of opinions and also in the hands of those who are concerned about keeping their hold over the faithful. The toxicity of an accusation of blasphemy is made more palpable by its being used to incite mass hysteria and violence, which can lead to great injustice against minorities such as Christians, Yezidis, Shi'i Muslims in Sunni-majority countries, and indeed against Sunnis as well. The vagueness of the law, coupled with the arbitrary processes used by courts not always with legitimate credentials, can create a travesty of justice where, in some cases, the accused is not even sure of the offence that is alleged to have been committed.

We should note that the Qur'an indicates no clear worldly punishment for blasphemy: even this has been taken up and argued over by the schools of law by way of *fiqh* to prescribe various punishments, including death. Muslim clerics may call for the punishment of a blasphemer by issuing a fatwa, or legal opinion (as in the case of Salman Rushdie).[17] We can see some of the effects of the status of blasphemy being played out in Pakistan today. Thus, for example, the hanging of the murderer of the Governor of Punjab, Salman Taseer, has given rise to a number of issues in Pakistan. Taseer took a public stand on the iniquity of the blasphemy law and recommended that the law be repealed. He stated: 'The blasphemy law is not a God-made law. It's a man-made law.'[18] As a result of this statement he was murdered, and the crime was supported by many in Pakistan – in fact, a shrine has been built for his murderer. The blasphemy law, which has been extended over the past two decades under Islamising governments, now has a provision whereby individuals can be executed for 'using derogatory words in respect of the Holy Prophet'. This law, while it did not save a privileged person such as Salman Taseer, can operate to the detriment of minority groups such as Christians, Hindus, Ahmadis or Shi'i Muslims.[19] What is more alarming is the fact that nearly two-thirds of Pakistan's Muslims support the death penalty for the crime of leaving the faith. Equally alarming is the fact that such a situation evokes allegiance in Muslim diasporas, even those living in the United Kingdom, where in March 2016 prayers were offered at one of the largest mosques in Birmingham for Salman Taseer's assailant as a martyr. Influential preachers in Bradford and Dewsbury held similar meetings. While this extreme response to the hanging of Taseer's murderer is not reflected in the majority of Muslim opinion in the United Kingdom, it does give rise to concern about the attitudes shown by some Muslims in the diaspora.[20]

The blasphemy law, as conceived and practised in many Muslim countries, is in effect a bar to any critical thought, no matter how benign or well meaning. It thus becomes a potent form of censorship. On 9 May 2017, Basuki Tjahaja Purnama, the first Christian governor of Jakarta in decades, was sentenced to two years in prison for the crime of blasphemy. He had stated that Jakarta's imams were misusing Qur'anic verses to discriminate against Christian candidates. His remarks were ill received in the Muslim-majority country of Indonesia, which led to massive rallies against him and, as a result, he was defeated electorally. According to Usman Hamid, Amnesty International's Indonesia Director, Purnama may have been tough talking but he did not deserve to be imprisoned. Amnesty International and other civil rights organisations have called for the blasphemy laws to be repealed. This case reflects the 'growing influence of Islamists – on the streets and in the state bureaucracy – on Indonesia's politics'.[21]

The Case of Asia Bibi

Asia Bibi, a Pakistani Christian, was found guilty of blasphemy for allegedly making derogatory comments about the Prophet Muhammad during an argument with Muslim women.[22] Even though Asia Bibi denied the charge of blasphemy and stated that it was brought against her by Muslim women to settle an old score, the Lahore High Court rejected her appeal against a sentence of death by hanging that had been passed by a lower court. As we show below, from an evidentiary point of view this case was fundamentally flawed from the outset.[23]

Asia Bibi's defence lawyers then took the case to the Supreme Court of Pakistan in 2009, where it still remains at the time of writing (2018) to be considered and decided upon. The defence maintains that the judgement against Asia was flawed on account of the evidence against her being fabricated and that she did not have legal representation at key points during the court process. In any event, the entire case against the defendant was based on hearsay and contradictory evidence presented by the witnesses, two of whom did not even appear in court despite being allegedly involved in the incident. A Muslim prayer leader, who did appear, stated that he did not witness the original altercation, but he further averred that Asia Bibi confessed to the alleged crime before him. The legal situation is uncertain and imperfect, since the law does not sufficiently define the offence and evidence cannot be reproduced in court for fear of committing a fresh offence. Additionally, the officials of the court are constantly in fear of their lives if a judgement is made in favour of the defendants. Intimidation of victims of the blasphemy laws and those who defend these victims and support a move to reform the laws is widespread, and while there has been no official execution for blasphemy in Pakistan, there have been a number of extra-judicial killings by mobs and individuals intent on carrying out what they regard as their religious duty by implementing a form of lynch law.

Two prominent politicians, the above-mentioned Punjab Governor Salman Taseer and Minorities Minister Shabaz Bhatti, were murdered in 2011 for having called for a reform of the laws of blasphemy in the wake of the trial at the Lahore High Court. Members of Asia Bibi's family have gone into hiding since they too have received death threats. Her defence lawyer argues that the blasphemy laws as presently enacted in Pakistan violate the country's Human Rights obligations to ensure freedom of expression, thought and religion.

This case has become a focus of debate all over the Muslim and non-Muslim worlds. As mentioned, the murder of the Governor of Punjab and the fact that the Supreme Court of Pakistan dismissed an appeal by his assassin gave the Asia Bibi case international prominence. The court hearings have been fraught with security issues concerning not only the defendant but also the judges, legal representatives and the media, all of whom operated in the shadow of potential violence by the religious lobby, ready to invoke street power should the laws on blasphemy be changed.

This jeopardised the administration of justice, with clerics present and religious extremists reciting Qur'anic verses in close proximity to the court. The same points of law that were taken on appeal were addressed again in the Supreme Court, the highest judicial forum in the country. This court, even though it was under acute religious and mob pressure, upheld the death penalty against Taseer's assassin. According to the defence counsel, Naeem Shakir, to its credit the court's judgement recorded that 'citizens have a right to contend, debate or maintain that a law has not been correctly framed by the State in terms of the mischief sought to be suppressed or that the law promulgated by the State ought to contain adequate safeguards against its misapplication or misuse by motivated persons'. The court stated further that 'seeking improvement of a man-made law in respect of a religious matter for better or proper enforcement of such law, does not ipso facto amount to criticising the religious aspect of such law'. It held that 'if the asserted motivation of the appellant for the murder committed by him by taking the law in his own hands, is to be accepted as a valid mitigating circumstance in this case, then a door shall become open for religious vigilantism which may deal a mortal blow to the rule of law in this country where divergent religious interpretations abound and tolerance stands depleted to an alarming level'.[24]

Writing in *Lapidomedia*, Shakir states that 'the cases of vigilante justice that wreaked havoc on society in general and religious minorities in particular, have significantly decreased after these rulings. Yet, alarmingly, blasphemy cases against religious minorities have increased.'[25] Shakir continued that the High Court judgement removed much of the debris surrounding the case with testimonies, including that of the complainant – the Imam Masjid (a local cleric) – being rejected as hearsay. The defendant's alleged confession, according to the judges, 'lacked legal requirements'. Instead, the High Court relied on the testimony of two sisters who had quarrelled with Asia Bibi for drinking from the cup at the well despite being a Christian and therefore 'unclean'. Asia Bibi denied the allegation of having uttered blasphemous words against the Prophet Muhammad. An important point raised before the High Court remains to be resolved by the Supreme Court. The defence urged that, since the offence of blasphemy against the Prophet carried the *hadd* – Islamic corporal penalty requirement (and the only offence to carry a mandatory sentence) – the principles of Islamic legal thinking required of witnesses a particularly high standard of Islamic probity. Therefore, the court was under an obligation to conduct an inquiry into the Islamic status of the witnesses. It was therefore held to be an incurable omission by the trial court not to have held a mandatory investigation to determine the Islamic character of the witnesses, so vitiating the trial and hence the conviction. The High Court judges, however, instead of deciding this point of Islamic justice, referred the matter to the federal government to reframe legal procedure in blasphemy cases carrying *hadd* penalties. According to Shakir, it is unclear whether any official memorandum was issued to the federal government, and if so what action has been taken.

We have outlined the bare bones of the case, which revolves around three sets of laws, namely British colonial laws against blasphemy,[26] which aimed to keep the various faiths in line with law and order; second, Islamic law as it obtains in the Hanafi school of Islamic jurisprudence; and finally, the later statutory law on the crime enacted in Pakistan during the rule of Zia-ul-Haq between 1980 and 1986, who wanted to Islamise the state and its legal system. These statutes include capital punishment as part of the penalty for blasphemy, and unfortunately the status of this law remains unclear.[27]

Adultery

Another dilemma for Islamic law is the varying treatment of adultery in different Muslim countries. In this case, we shall examine the problem of adultery in Nigeria, which, although a predominantly Muslim country, has a cultural environment that differs widely from that of Afghanistan. In Nigeria, we find that the sharia court itself acquitted the defendant on the basis of the lack of sufficient evidence.

The Case of Amina Lawal

In March 2002, Amina Lawal Kurama, a Nigerian peasant woman born in 1972, was sentenced to death by a sharia court in Funtua, in the northern Nigerian state of Katsina. The penalty was death by stoning, for adultery and for conceiving a child out of wedlock on the basis of a confession she had made and the fact that she had become pregnant outside marriage.[28] The putative father of the child was not prosecuted, owing to a lack of evidence, and he was deemed innocent without undergoing a DNA test, while his sworn oath on the Qur'an that he was innocent was considered, as is usual in sharia procedure, to be sufficient to prove his innocence. Nigeria, a country of 182 million people speaking over 200 languages, has a federal system of government whereby the 36 states that make up the federation have the constitutional authority to impose their particular system of laws in their own territories. The state of Katsina adopted sharia as its legal system covering those areas of jurisdiction that are not covered by the federal legal system. It should be noted that the legal system in the country as a whole is complex, with four different systems of law prevailing, namely the Common Law inherited from the English legal system, codified customary law, uncodified traditional (African) law and, for the Muslim-majority states, Islamic law.

The court of first instance ruled that Lawal should be stoned to death after she had weaned her baby, who was at the time of the appeal only 20 months old. Later, the death sentence was confirmed by an upper sharia court. This led to a further appeal to the Katsina State Sharia Court of Appeals, which acquitted her on the basis of technicalities in the application of sharia.

The case was dismissed because Lawal was not given 'ample opportunity to defend herself'. Lawal's case, as it happened, attracted international attention, since the 2002 Miss World contest was to be held in Nigeria. As a consequence of the case, several contestants pulled out of the competition and the Oprah Winfrey show in the United States held a special report on the case, encouraging viewers to send protest emails to the Nigerian ambassador to the United States – over 1.2 million emails were sent, and they had an effect. The President of Nigeria, Olesegun Obasanjo, condemned the application of sharia punishments on the grounds that they contravened Nigeria's constitution, emphasising that the country would not allow a sentence of stoning to be carried out, and that whatever the ruling it could still be challenged by the appellate structure of the federal government's courts of law.

The introduction of strict sharia law in 12 of Nigeria's 36 states from 1999 onwards had increased tensions between the country's Muslim North and the Christian South, which led to sectarian violence and the death of thousands of people. Lawal's conviction was overturned by a four to one majority in the Sharia Court of Appeal, which took cognisance of strict legal arguments rather than being directly influenced by the Miss World contest demonstrations and the email campaign launched by the Oprah Winfrey show. Although it should be acknowledged that these events must have had some tacit influence on the court's decision, the legal arguments revolved around a mixture of secular law and sharia as applicable under the Maliki school of law.

The first argument was based upon the fact that Nigeria was a signatory to the Universal Declaration of Human Rights, which proscribes torture or punishment that is degrading to human dignity, and it was argued that stoning for adultery fell under this principle. Second, sharia tenets were also called upon to defend Lawal's case. It was thus argued by the defence team that the court that originally convicted Lawal did not explain the offence for which she was being prosecuted and its penalty. Under sharia, four witnesses have to be present to attest the physical act of adultery, but in Lawal's case no such evidence was produced. Furthermore, it was argued that her confession of adultery was not admissible as she was not given the opportunity to fully comprehend the offence and its legal significance, which is a necessary part of sharia process. The defence further argued that under Islamic law the notion of the sleeping foetus, whereby a foetus could be in gestation for up to five years, was not taken into consideration in the earlier court hearings. The majority of the Sharia Court of Appeal accepted this argument, with only one judge disagreeing with the submission that the confession was faulty. The court, however, rejected the argument that to consider pregnancy per se as evidence of a crime inherently discriminates against women.

The defence lawyer, Hauwa Ebrahim, the daughter of an imam, understood the cultural context of the case against Lawal. Therefore, she did not regard the prosecution's case against Lawal as some sort of unreasoned antagonism against the defendant's rights. She championed Lawal's rights but also realised that sharia could not be simply set aside. Islamic law, with all its shortcomings, remained an integral part of the community's self-definition and self-understanding, and this community was one to which she also belonged. Therefore, she approached the issue with a degree of cultural sensitivity. She asked to meet the elders of the community, who had accused her of being impervious to its culture. They agreed to see her and were pleasantly reassured by her respectful demeanour, especially when she preferred to sit on the ground rather than on a chair before them. This apparently small concession indicated in their eyes her respect for their status as elders, and they remarked to her that she had not abandoned her culture, in which respect played a central part. They were therefore persuaded of her good intentions and subsequently dismissed the case for lack of evidence. We are compelled to ask what the outcome of the case would have been had the elders regarded Hauwa Ebrahim as less than deferential and whether law can justifiably be based upon such extra-legal considerations. What is often not taken into account is the fact that it was the Sharia Appellate Court that acquitted Lawal on the basis of sharia evidentiary principles.

After Amina Lawal's acquittal, according to Aminu Adamu Bello, Professor of Law at the University of Abuja, it appeared that there was unanimity in the conclusion that women and women's organisations have acquired significant knowledge of Islam and Islamic law to marshal an appreciable arsenal in the defence of women living under sharia or Islamic law. Hitherto, knowledge of sharia and Islamic law was confined to the privileged masculine domain, but there existed the opinion that aspects of sharia were biased and prejudiced against women, and the amount of literature supporting this position was staggering. As civil society organisations, non-governmental organisations (NGOs) have added their weight to the discussion of the sharia gender bias against women and are championing a move to ensure that women are granted adequate protection under the new Sharia Criminal Justice system in Nigeria. NGOs at the time of the Abdul Rahman case were regarded more negatively in Afghanistan. In that country, the courts and religious authorities looked upon them with deep suspicion as agents of Western countries that are trying to undermine the basis of the Islamic state.

Sexuality and Informal Justice –
the Case of Mukhtaran Mai

Sexuality plays a large part in the implementation and understanding of sharia criminal offences. The Mukhtaran Mai case, which was heard in Pakistan in 2002, is a significant example.[29] This case was based upon a tribal dispute resolution process in which Mukhtaran Mai, a young Pakistani woman from the village of Meerwalla in the rural county of Jatoi in the Muzaffar Garh district, was the victim of a gang rape carried out as a form of honour revenge on the orders of the local *jirga* (the tribal council) of the Mastoi tribe, still the dominant tribal group in the area. The reason given for this action was that Shakur, the 12-year-old brother of Mukhtaran Mai, was alleged to have sexually violated a girl, Salma, from the Jatoi clan. This act was deemed to have besmirched the honour of the tribe and of the girl and required to be satisfied by an equal sexual act of vengeance ascribed to the law of talion (retaliation). Therefore the *jirga* requested that Mukhtaran appear before it to publicly apologise for her brother's alleged act, which was affirmed by the head of the *jirga*. She was inveigled into believing that her attendance would allow some form of negotiated settlement.

However, two members of the *jirga* insisted that the principle of talion be maintained and the original sexual act by Shakur be 'balanced' by his sister being raped. When she arrived at the *jirga* to apologise, she was taken by a group of men, including Salma's brother, Abdul Khaliq, who was armed with a pistol, to a stable where she was gang raped. After this act, on the orders of the *jirga* she was paraded naked through the village until her father draped her with a shawl and took her back home. Although she was expected to commit suicide, which was the custom after being raped in the culture of the region, Mukhtaran did not do so and decided to pursue her rapists by reporting the appalling incident to the police station. It should be noted that an imam of a local mosque in Meerwalla, Abdul Razzaq, was deeply offended by this heinous act in the name of customary law, and he condemned the rape in his *khutba* or sermon on the Friday following the event. He drew it to the attention of a local journalist, who then met Mukhtaran's father and persuaded the family to report the rape to the police. Over the following days the story became headline news in Pakistan and in July 2002 it was picked up by the BBC, followed by the American *Time* magazine. The *New York Times* journalist Michael Kristoff played a key role in the dissemination of the story, particularly in the United States.

In September 2002, an anti-terrorism court sentenced the four rapists plus two others to death. In 2005, the Lahore High Court acquitted five of the six convicted men, because of 'insufficient evidence', and commuted the sixth defendant to a life sentence. Mukhtaran and the Pakistani government appealed this decision to the Supreme Court of Pakistan, which suspended the acquittal and held appeal hearings. The case was mired in the labyrinthine processes of the appellate structure, including Pakistan's Federal Sharia Court's procedures, and it was only in 2011 that a decision to acquit all the accused was arrived at by the Supreme Court.

Although Mukhtaran's case was supported in part by the Pakistan government and by civil rights lawyers in Pakistan, the legal process reached a cul-de-sac and nothing more has occurred to date with regard to further litigation. However, the case was broadcast internationally, and Mukhtaran visited the United States, France and Norway, where she was hailed as a pioneer in defending women's right to justice and education in Pakistan. Her case has been discussed in documentaries, made into a feature film and has been written about in her autobiography, *In the Name of Honour: A Memoir*, published in 23 languages, and indeed in books by other journalists and activists. While the legal result of the case has been unsatisfactory, it has raised public awareness, including obtaining support from various NGOs which have helped to fund a school for 600 pupils, mostly girls, and a women's shelter in the village. One of the positive outcomes of this dreadful case has been the raising of public awareness across the world of the fundamental importance of education, especially that of girls.[30]

Issues Arising from the Mukhtaran Case

The case raises a number of interesting issues both relating to sharia and the role of customary law and informal processes which, under the guise of sharia, mete out a primitive form of dispute resolution based on a notion of vengeance as a balancing mechanism. Sharia is used as a form of corroboration by such groups without a proper understanding of its workings. This is why the local imam in this case, who was clearly appalled by the abuse of justice, saw fit to intervene publicly and assist Mukhtaran's family to take action and seek proper remedy by the state. The case illustrates that negotiations always take place in the shadow of the law, but the law itself has to have a degree of communal acceptance and respect. In this case the law was diluted as, in the realm of informal justice, the power dynamics of the society went unchecked. Law was therefore influenced by the politics of the stronger clan.[31]

This matter demonstrates a fatal weakness in the process of informal justice: the failure to resist the implicit power imbalances represented by tribal or clan influences in Muslim traditional societies that protect the interests of the clan members. It should be noted that the government of Pakistan helped Mukhtaran initially, but when she was given the opportunity to take the case and its issues to the international stage, it took countervailing measures to prevent her from doing so. Civil society organisations, both local and international, played an important role in bringing the case to the public arena. In the United States, Muslim civil society organisations were actively involved in bringing the issue to the attention of the people.

Constitutional Law – the Case of Lina Joy

In the realm of constitutional law, a great deal of ambiguity exists as to the rights and obligations of a Muslim even in a Muslim country, since there is a discrepancy in the idea of a nation state and the belief in sovereignty which, for Muslims, lies exclusively with God. According to Article 11 of the Malaysian Constitution, 'Every person has the right to profess and practise his religion.' However, Lina Joy, a former Muslim born as Azlina Jailani to

Muslim parents of Javanese descent in Malaysia, was informed that she could not convert to Christianity.[32] Nevertheless, Lina Joy did convert to Christianity and was baptised in 1998. She wanted her conversion to be legally recognised by the Malaysian courts, but although her change of name was accepted in 1999, and was noted in her identity card, her change of religion was not recorded for lack of a *mahkama syariah*, or sharia court, confirmation document. For this reason, she filed a suit at the High Court in 1999, thereby bypassing the sharia court. In 2006, she continued her battle by filing suit in the Federal Court for this confirmation. In a majority verdict, the Federal Court rejected her appeal on a two-to-one basis. The ruling stated that 'a person who wanted to renounce his/her religion, must do so according to existing laws or practices of the particular religion. Only after the person has complied with the requirements and authorities are satisfied that the person has apostatised, can she embrace Christianity... In other words, a person cannot, at one's whims and fancies renounce or embrace a religion.'

The dissenting Chief Judge of Sabah and Sarawak, Datuk Richard Malangjum, wrote: 'in my view this is tantamount to unequal treatment under the law, in other words, it is discriminatory and unconstitutional and should therefore be struck down. For this reason alone, the relief sought for by the appellant should be granted, namely for a declaration that she is entitled to have an identity card in which the word "Islam" does not appear.'[33]

Legal recognition would have allowed Lina Joy to have this change noted on her national ID card. In Malaysia, the sharia court alone has the power to deal with Islamic issues, including recognition for conversion to and from Islam. This apparently transparent process has at its heart a fatal ambiguity. The sharia court can only deal with cases concerning Muslims and does not have any jurisdiction over non-Muslims. Lina Joy had ceased being a Muslim by dint of her conversion to Christianity, therefore at one level she was no longer under the jurisdiction of the sharia court. However, it is also mandated that the sharia court must decide on both conversion to Islam and from Islam. Therefore, the legal system was faced with an impasse. Conversion is not unknown in Malaysia, and indeed in the state of Negeri Sembilan the sharia

courts earlier had allowed 16 people to renounce Islam. The
country's National Registration Department (NRD) took the view
that to change her religion on her ID card would mean that the
NRD would be officially declaring Lina Joy as an apostate, which
falls under the exclusive jurisdiction of the sharia court. In recent
years, this issue has been causing much public consternation in
Malaysia and has been reported closely by the media. Article 11 of
the Constitution has been part of the enabling document since the
independence of the country. However, by a 1988 amendment,
the issue became unclear as the change denied the regular courts
jurisdiction over matters dealt with by the sharia courts. Until
the Lina Joy case, it was unclear whether the sharia judges had
the right to overrule Article 11 for those persons who were born
Muslims and whether to order them to remain so. Now the case
appears to suggest that the sharia court indeed has this (exclusive)
right, which contradicts the right enshrined in Article 11.[34]

The ruling caused consternation, not only among the ethnic
Chinese and Indians but also among many Malays, about the
increasing Islamisation of the state. With the increasing reach of
the sharia courts' jurisdiction along with the powers of the state
authorities dealing with Islamic issues, concern has arisen about
the encroachment on the freedoms enjoyed by non-Muslims.
Muslims, who constitute 60 per cent of Malaysia's 27 million
people, are also affected negatively. This factor is dividing families
and causing discord amongst many people where one parent
is deemed a Muslim, despite that person's claim to have ceased
being so. The Lina Joy case has highlighted the lack of clarity
in Malaysia's legal system and the ambiguous role played by the
implementation of Islamic law as classically formulated, with
tension having been created in the country where Muslims,
though a majority, are not guaranteed the equality provisions
of the Constitution, thus perversely making them in this case
second-class citizens.[35]

Issues Not Specific to Malaysia

This lack of clarity in constitutional law gives rise to difficulties
in the modern Muslim state, particularly when the sources of law

are defined in the founding document. If the state is projected as being a Muslim one, then sharia has to play a role in the laws of the country. If the constitution states that sharia is *the* source of law, then all the laws of the country theoretically have to conform to sharia. If it is described as only *a* source of the law, then sharia is not the exclusive determining factor.[36] The issue becomes truly problematic in the case of the payment of *riba* or interest because the civil codes of various Arab countries do not allow for interest, whereas the commercial codes stipulate the imposition of a certain percentage of the cost of money. This has led to litigation as to the validity of all the laws of the country dependent on the status of sharia as set out in the constitution.

This issue became particularly problematic when the Egyptian government, to appease the growing Islamist tendency in the country, passed a Personal Status (Amendment) Law (Law no. 100/1985),[37] which led to litigation as to the status of the prevailing laws.[38] A similar case arose in Pakistan, where the issue in question was whether the laws of Pakistan conformed to the objectives of the country as a Muslim state, and the Federal Shariat Court decided in this matter that the laws were not in accordance with the founding principles.[39] The Pakistan government was given a year to realign its laws to make them conform with Islamic principles. The geopolitical situation changed post 9/11 and the issue has been sidelined for the present. Yet this is an issue not only in the Muslim countries themselves, but one that emerges when courts in England give judgements that are to be enforced in Muslim countries, where payment of interest forms part of the decision. The judgement could be stayed on the basis that it is contrary to the public mores of the Muslim country where the enforcement is supposed to take place. The same problems arise with international arbitration.[40]

Practices in the Islamic World that Conflict with Human Rights

Besides the cases discussed above, there are other practices current in Muslim countries or carried out by some Muslims who live in the diaspora that are deemed by many, including the Western media, to be a part of sharia but which are not actually sanctioned by sharia. These are honour killings, FGM and forced marriage.

Honour Killing

Honour killing occurs amongst many social and cultural groups in the world. We shall focus our attention on what happens within Muslim communities.

Human Rights Watch provides the following definition:

> Honor crimes are acts of violence, usually murder, committed by male family members against female family members who are perceived to have brought dishonour upon the family. The misconduct in question may be actual or alleged. A woman may be targeted because she has been raped, has been seen talking to a man outside of the family, has refused to enter an arranged marriage, or even left an abusive husband. Any acts by the victim that may have brought dishonor or shame to the family can trigger attacks on the woman in question. Honor killings are more prevalent in Muslim majority countries, even though the practice has been condemned by Muslim leaders who deny that religion condones the practice.[41]

A man may also be the victim of honour killing by members of the family of a woman with whom he is perceived to have had an inappropriate relationship. The notion of honour is a collective value attached to an ancient idea of the self as a part of the communal identity; it affects the reputation of the tribe or family or other collectivities. Honour involves a profound feeling of shame, which weaves itself into the ethical structures of such communities. To kill a member of one's family is not an easy thing done on a whim but requires to be addressed by the family as a whole, and it is perpetrated as almost a ritual cleansing of the family's 'name' within the community, the blood of the victim in effect cleansing the family reputation.

Estimates of the incidence vary widely because of the lack of systematic methods of collecting data about these actions, many of which are done covertly and are reported as suicides or accidents. However, this brutal practice is not universally deplored, and various governments and those in authority, while not overtly supporting it, collude with it on the basis that it preserves an important social value concerned with reputation and therefore with a particular perspective of order. A Turkish study carried out in 2008 on honour killings in the south-eastern Anatolia region – a predominantly Kurdish area – indicates that little, if any, social stigma is attached to the act, which is notionally regarded as a crime by the Turkish authorities. The study also comments that the practice is not related to the male-dominated feudal social structure. As Professor Mazhar Bağlı from Dicle University in Diyarbakir, Turkey, states:

> It is not appropriate to associate honor killings with only one section of society. Some people think that it is related to a feudal structure, but this has proven to be false. There are also perpetrators who are well-educated university graduates. Of all those surveyed, 60 per cent are either high school or university graduates or at the very least, literate. The victims of honor killing are not always women; males have also been targeted.[42]

The causes of honour killings are many and include the views of a given society on women, its culture of honour and shame. And, of course, the act of killing itself involves the laws of different countries. Women in societies where such killings occur are considered to be the property of their family, with no personal agency or indeed individuality. According to Tahira Shahid Khan, an academic specialising in women's issues at the Aga Khan University in Pakistan: 'Women are considered the property of the males in their family irrespective of their class, ethnic or religious group. The owner of the property has the right to decide its fate. The concept of ownership has turned women into a commodity which can be exchanged, bought and sold.'[43]

Family honour is a cardinal notion in many communities where the family is viewed as the central source of honour, which is valued by the community as a whole. According to Professor Bağlı, this sort of killing – which in the West is considered murder – is a form of necessity or inevitability when honour is at stake. Legal frameworks sometimes encourage honour killings: relevant laws show on the one hand leniency towards such killings and on the other they criminalise certain forms of behaviour such as extra-marital sex, wearing attire deemed immodest in public places and homosexual acts.[44] These laws effectively condone honour killings and those people who engage in such criminalised behaviour are viewed as deserving of punishment. The punishment is often carried out by individuals rather than the state apparatus, and the latter is often not effective in dealing appropriately with this as homicide.

Although some time has been spent examining this phenomenon, there is actually nothing in the Qur'an or larger system of sharia that permits or sanctions honour killings, even though they remain a scourge in many Muslim countries. Nor does sharia specifically forbid these practices. Tahira Shahid Khan blames this type of violence against women on attitudes across different class, ethnic and religious groups that view women as property without rights of their own. Women are thereby commodified and dealt with accordingly. Resolution 1327 (adopted on 4 April 2003) of the Council of Europe states: 'The Assembly notes that whilst so-called "honour crimes" emanate from cultural and not religious roots, and are perpetrated worldwide (mainly in patriarchal societies or communities), the majority of reported cases in Europe have been amongst Muslims or migrant Muslim communities (although Islam itself does not support the death penalty for honour-related misconduct).'[45] It must be noted that the law in countries where honour killings are prevalent tends to show leniency towards this crime for various reasons, including the patriarchal structures of those countries.

Female Genital Mutilation

We now examine the contentious issue of female genital mutilation (FGM). Although it is not strictly a sharia or, indeed, an Islamic issue, it is practised in several countries with a majority or a significant minority Muslim population. Defined in 1997 by the WHO, UNICEF and UNFPA as the 'partial or total removal of the external female genitalia or other injury to the female genital organs for non-medical reasons', it affects 133 million women, mostly in 27 African countries, Yemen, Iraqi Kurdistan and elsewhere in Asia, the Middle East and among diasporic communities around the world. The age at which FGM is inflicted varies from days after birth to puberty. While the practice of FGM is abhorrent to Western notions of individual rights and gender equality, it is founded in societies that carry it out based on notions of family honour, purity and modesty, and proper form with regard to respectability. It represents the expectations of a patriarchal culture in which women themselves participate, as FGM is inflicted by elder females intent on preserving cultural traditions and norms and thus protecting their families. It has been officially outlawed or restricted in most of the countries in which it is practised. However, the laws are often not enforced and the authorities turn a blind eye.

Since 1970, international efforts have been pursued to prevent this practice, and in 2012 the UN General Assembly, recognising FGM as a Human Rights violation, voted unanimously to intensify these initiatives. Yet such actions have given rise to criticism among some anthropologists. Eric Silverman writes that 'FGM has become one of anthropology's central moral topics raising difficult questions about cultural relativism, tolerance and the universality of human rights.'[46] Various surveys undertaken indicate that the practice is an ethnic issue which, at times, may differ along national lines. It is more common in rural areas and less common among girls from wealthy homes and where mothers have had access to education.[47] This is true except in the case of Somalia and Sudan, where the reverse applies. Common reasons for FGM cited by women in surveys include social acceptance, religion, hygiene, the preservation of virginity, marriageability and the enhancement of male sexual pleasure.

The practice requires further analysis. Its origin is pre-Islamic but it is reinforced by the Muslim concern, indeed obsession, with female chastity and the seclusion of women, which encourages the practice. Therefore, the Islamic university Al-Azhar's Supreme Council of Islamic Research ruled that FGM had 'No basis in core Islamic law or any of its partial provisions.'[48] However, it must be noted that some younger imams continue to maintain that FGM is Islamic and has its roots in religion. Perhaps this is because the practice is allegedly praised in a number of hadiths as being 'noble' but not required, along with the advice that the milder forms of FGM are 'kinder' to women. This makes the religious position regarding FGM ambiguous, although not openly supportive; as in other areas of Islamic legal discourse, hadith is used as a convenient tool to legitimise and co-opt a practice that is not clearly a part of Qur'anic injunctions but pertains to custom. Even so, certain Muslim countries, such as Egypt, have gone so far as to ban FGM and in 2008 made it a criminal offence under the penal code. The first charges in that country were brought against a doctor and a girl's father in 2014 when the girl died after a procedure. On appeal, the doctor was sentenced to over two years in prison for manslaughter and the father received a three-month suspended sentence.

In diasporic settings, FGM is attracting increasing attention today through the work of social activists, mainly women. Some of these activists have made documentaries based on their own experience.

One such activist is Jaha Dukureh, a Gambian woman who underwent FGM as a child and was married very young and then settled in New York. Encouraged by the movement in the United Kingdom, she championed the cause against FGM in the United States and managed to persuade the Obama administration to fund a study on the issue with particular reference to the Gambia. Dukureh then went to the Gambia, embarked on an educational programme, visited schools and also engaged with the chief imam, eliciting his concurrence that the procedure was voluntary and not compulsory in sharia. Taking a non-combative approach, she was able to neutralise the antagonism of the imam and the religious functionaries, to gain the support of government functionaries. She also succeeded in persuading her father to rethink his position and thus saved her younger sister from having to undergo FGM. With this non-combative advocacy, she eventually managed to convince the president of the country to outlaw this ancient custom and to declare that it had nothing to do with Islam.[49]

This example shows how meaningful social change can be introduced if it is championed through Muslims themselves in a context of transformative mediation that is non-adversarial, non-combative and also respectful of the other without compromising the principle which one is championing. Once again, cognisance needs to be taken of the fact that Dukureh's intervention in the Gambia was not projected as a Westernising crusade at the hands of Western NGOs as much as an attempt by a Gambian woman, respectful of local cultural mores, trying to understand the basis of the customary practice of the country in order to ameliorate the general well-being of women. It is noteworthy that in her advocacy there is no mention of women's Human Rights. Instead, she focuses on their health and well-being, including their right not to be subjected to domestic violence. As we noted earlier, in the case of adultery in northern Nigeria, where Huawa Ebrahim defended the rights of a Muslim woman against stoning by engaging respectfully with the cultural tradition of that country, Dukureh's experience is another example of how meaningful change can be made through both education and cultural engagement from within. We do not mean to undermine the role played by NGOs; however, greater sensitivity to local contexts and expectations on their part would contribute significantly towards this important work. With the increased migration of people from many countries where FGM is still practised, the issue has relevance today in countries of the Western world.

In 2011, there were around 137,000 females living as permanent residents in England and Wales who had been born in countries where FGM is practised, many of whom would perpetuate the practice. Although the practice is outlawed under a number of statutes, the UN Committee on the Elimination of Discrimination Against Women expressed concern in 2013 that there had been no convictions for FGM in the United Kingdom, and asked the British government to ensure the full implementation of its relevant legislation. The first charges were brought in 2014 with an acquittal of the defendant in February 2015 because of a failure to carry out an effective prosecution.[50]

Reflecting on the developments to date to eradicate this practice, women in diasporic Muslim contexts, through education, will have an opportunity to acquire greater economic independence which, in turn, will enable them to make effective changes in their societies as well as in their countries of origin, as has been the case for Jaha Dukureh who championed the cause with due sensitivity to the local culture and religious sentiments. This pragmatic solution reflects the existing unacceptable gender imbalance in national power structures. In an interconnected world where social media is becoming prevalent, sensitive approaches by Muslim advocacy groups, working closely with religious leaders and governmental institutions, appear to be one effective way forward in the present situation. Here NGOs can play and have played a positive role, but the extent to which Muslims themselves are empowered to bring about changes using convincing arguments from within the traditions of their respective societies, and eliciting support from religious leaders and state institutions, will determine both the nature and the pace necessary to bring about change.

Forced Marriage

Another contentious issue in the Muslim world that is perceived as being part of sharia is the question of forced marriage. This notion is often conflated with arranged marriage. Neither of these practices is sanctioned or condoned by sharia or *fiqh*. The border between the two practices, however, is thin and often it is not easy to distinguish between them, although they both entail an element of coercion and may amount to the crimes of abduction, assault or domestic violence. Arranged marriages are a customary practice prevalent amongst families from the Indian subcontinent settled in the United Kingdom and elsewhere in the Western world. While initially this practice had some degree of legitimacy amongst these communities as part of custom, which in turn formed an important element of self-understanding and identity, it is beginning to become less prevalent as new generations of Muslims, brought up in the West, attain adulthood and look to making their own life choices. Arranged marriage is therefore losing its appeal but remains a part of the culture of immigrant communities, especially those with a lower educational attainment.

On the other hand, forced marriages are an issue that has given rise to greater concern in Western societies. As stated above, this type of union is vulnerable to criminal activities such as coercion, kidnapping and domestic violence. Where they violate the laws of the country in which they occur, the police and legal authorities are obliged to take action. In the United Kingdom, Scotland has taken the lead by enacting legislation to combat forced marriage by passing the Forced Marriage etc. (Protection and Jurisdiction) (Scotland) Act 2011, which empowers the courts to protect people who are in danger of being forcibly married and to annul such unions. The Act makes the breach of a Protection Order a criminal offence punishable by a fine, a two-year prison sentence or both. Scottish law therefore goes beyond legislation in England, Wales and Northern Ireland, where the breaching of a Protection Order is not a criminal offence.[51] However, ignoring a Protection Order is regarded in these countries as contempt of court punishable by imprisonment.

Apropos arranged marriages, the unreported case in 1999 of *Akmal v Akmal* made legal history, when Nasreen Akmal became the first woman in Scotland to have her arranged marriage annulled by the courts. By using the subterfuge of a holiday when she was only 14 years old, her family forced her to marry a first cousin in Pakistan. She was not allowed to return to Scotland until she provided the family with a grandchild. As her marriage began to become problematic, she engaged a lawyer in Scotland and embarked on proceedings to have her marriage annulled on the grounds of being underage under Scottish law. Her courageous action led to over 100 women and men having their marriages annulled as a consequence. It has also deterred parents abducting their underage children to Pakistan with the aim of marrying them off.

Nasreen Akmal's case was followed by the case of *Sohrab v Khan* in April 2002, in which the wife sought annulment of her marriage on the grounds that her consent to it had been vitiated by family duress. The wife was aged 16 at the time and had been told of the marriage only a week before the actual ceremony. Her mother threatened to commit suicide if she refused to be married, with the further threat that she would be forcibly sent to Pakistan if she resisted. The court held that the wife had not given a genuine consent to the marriage but had been placed under such duress by her parents that whatever semblance of consent was exchanged at the ceremony was vitiated. The need to have a clear consent according to the law when the marriage is solemnised is a requirement that cannot be dispensed with, regardless of any registration that may follow. The Lord Ordinary,[52] Lord McEwan, in a reasoned judgement, set out the predicament of children born in

the United Kingdom who are subjected by their parents to different
cultural norms from those which prevail in the country where they
were born and continue to live. Lord McEwan observed that 'such
situations will continue to arise where ancient Eastern-established
cultural and religious ethics clash with the spirit of 21st-century
children of a new generation and Western ideas, language and
what these days passes for culture. There is inevitable tension,
and clashes will happen.'[53] In May 2018, two successful prosecutions took place in the United Kingdom, one in the Leeds crown
court of a couple of Bangladeshi origin,[54] and the other of a
Birmingham couple of Pakistani origin,[55] both of whom forced
their daughters into marriage. These two cases indicate a change
in attitude of the United Kingdom authorities towards these types
of coercive behaviour which are deemed to be criminal. It should
also be noted that this type of issue was litigated in a court in Pakistan where the Human Rights lawyer, Asma Jehangir, successfully
argued that a Muslim woman who was *sui juris* was entitled to
choose her own marriage partner.[56]

Extrajudicial Measures

Recognising that this is a cultural issue that will not be resolved
overnight, the British High Commission in Islamabad has
established a special unit to help victims of forced marriages.
Normally, by way of covert and confidential activity, the team at
the High Commission manages to enable the British victims of
such arrangements to obtain proper documents to leave Pakistan
and return to the United Kingdom. According to Dr Noreen
Khalid, an advisor to a Pakistani organisation called Struggle for
Change: 'Forced marriage is part of our custom, it has nothing
to do with law or religion. In fact, it is the very opposite.'[57] Such
rescue missions have been carried out in India, Bangladesh and
countries in Africa and the Middle East, but nowhere comes close
in scale to Pakistan, which has an estimated 80,000 dual nationals
and accounts for nearly 60 per cent of all cases handled by the
Foreign Office's Forced Marriage Unit. It should be noted that the
work of this unit, attached to the British Embassies, is worthwhile
insofar as it helps to extricate the victims from their immediate

situation. However, it does not address the issue of what happens to them when they return to the United Kingdom, where they are confronted with serious legal, social, cultural and economic problems that are not easily resolved.

It should be mentioned that there are human rights lawyers in Muslim countries who champion the rights of all under the principle of upholding the rule of law. Many of these practitioners are women, such as the late Asma Jehangir of Pakistan, Shirin Ebadi of Iran and Tawakkol Karman of Yemen. We should also remember the courageous stance taken by Malala Yousefzai who is the youngest ever Nobel Peace Prize recipient. The entire subject of Human Rights needs to be thought through carefully to avoid the error of being defensive instead of examining the condition of the law as applied in a positive but critical manner.

Incidents and Attitudes Conflated with Sharia

While there are cases that are adjudicated on the basis of what sharia states about such occurrences, and issues that arise which become conflated with sharia but are neither sanctioned by it directly or indirectly, there are a number of practices of Muslims living outside Muslim countries that are either projected as being part of sharia or are perceived as such although sharia does not clearly cover them. These attitudes and practices offend modern liberal sentiments and project the idea that Muslims are unable to engage with modernity. A few examples of such situations show that they are the idiosyncratic and interested inferences and interpretations of individuals who often claim religious and legal knowledge.

For example, a cashier at a retail outlet in the United Kingdom refused to process the purchase of a bottle of alcohol by a customer because her faith did not allow her to sell alcohol. The retail outlet, in line with political correctness, supported her position, to the chagrin of some Muslims living in the country, who claim that Islam does not forbid a Muslim from this in a non-Muslim country. Sharia is not clear about the practice. The Qur'an inveighs against becoming intoxicated, whether by the use of alcohol or other substances, but it is silent about the sale or other handling of such drink or substances by Muslims. While one can understand that the cashier may have acted out of genuine conviction, such action is demeaned by its over-exuberant construction of the prohibition against intoxication by extending it beyond its reasonable scope. It can be argued that if Muslims were forbidden to sell such substances, the Qur'an would have more clearly enunciated this in the first place. However, there may be jurisprudential arguments based on hadith that suggest that Muslims cannot deal in any way with intoxicating substances. This argument, if such exists, can be counterweighed by sharia on the basis of *darura,* or necessity, and *maslaha,* or public interest, which would surely dilute such an interpretation and allow a Muslim working in an enterprise in a non-Muslim country where alcohol is sold to carry out his or her duties as an employee with due respect to other cultures. Other prominent issues are those of *halal* meat and how Muslims relate to animals. In some Western countries in recent times there have been protests from non-Muslims about being served *halal* meat due to their perception of the method of slaughter. The media have also reported cases where a Muslim taxi driver, for example, refuses to carry a customer's guide dog.

The Quran has a number of verses that speak of animals as part of God's creation and a number of hadiths attest to the Prophet extolling the virtue of kindness to animals. However animal welfare practices in Muslim countries still leave much to be desired.[58]

These issues are the crux of the topical and deeply problematic question of how Muslims live in non-Muslim societies where they become integrated without losing their Islamic sense of identity – it raises the question of what makes an identity Islamic. Similar questions arise with regard to lifestyle issues such as homosexuality, stem-cell and biomedical research, organ transplants, same-sex marriages, end-of-life decisions and a host of others current in modern Western societies which are beginning to affect other societies as well through the influence of globalisation. We should remember that sharia concerns itself with the ethical purpose and vision of life, rather than with rules and specific prohibitions that came into existence by the practice of *fiqh* or jurisprudence, which introduced a necessary element of stability in Islamic law in its early history. However, *fiqh*, as we have seen, became crystallised over the centuries, thus often making the legal rules out of touch with the stresses and requirements of contemporary society. The arbitrary notion of Islamic law as being fixed once and for all has become impractical and unrealistic, and Muslim communities particularly in diasporic settings have had to reconsider some of these issues. For example, the Muslim College in the United Kingdom under the direction of the respected Islamic jurist and scholar Zaki Badawi, after consulting other legal scholars – Sunni and Shi'i – and medical practitioners, issued a fatwa on the issue of organ donation in the United Kingdom, which permitted crucial donations to be made by Muslims living in the country on the basis of *darura* and *maslaha*.[59]

Conclusion

We have described a number of situations in different Muslim countries and diasporic contexts that are subsumed under the general call of 'a return to sharia' with its draconian consequences. These situations are not clear-cut issues of 'sharia versus the rest'. For example, we have noticed that, in the case of Amina Lawal, it was a Sharia Court of Appeal in Nigeria that acquitted her on the basis of sharia principles that are similar to English Common Law. However, we also believe that the respectful behaviour of the lawyer defending Amina Lawal contributed significantly to her acquittal. In the case of Mukhtaran, it was the imam of the mosque in the area who took up her cause and persuaded the family to report the rape to the police, since he believed the act was contrary to sharia. In the matters of blasphemy we have discussed, it was individuals such as Salman Taseer, the Governor of the Punjab, who, at the cost of his life, took up the issue when a person from one of the minority groups was being unjustly accused. These so-called sharia cases show that the implementation of Islamic law is not a simple matter with predictably brutal outcomes. We also see a number of practices carried out by Muslims in Muslim countries and in diasporic settings that are neither sharia compliant nor endorsed by sharia, although in the popular imagination such practices are deemed to accord with, or enjoined by, sharia. However, we should also note that there are various harmful customary practices on which sharia is silent and thus they are practised without any constraint in the belief that they accord with Islamic law.

New thinking on many of the issues we have discussed in this chapter is taking place. The work of various NGOs has helped this development. This process of renewal affects civil society and enables Islamic law to adapt to new situations arising from the constant changes in the contemporary world that are fuelled by social demands, global interconnectedness and scientific research. In some cases Muslims themselves are responding to these challenges positively and are embarking on such new thinking in accordance with sharia, as enshrined in the principles of *darura* and *maslaha* through which they are moving towards a more *maqasid*-cum-*maslaha*-based theory of law that is better fit for purpose and responds to the needs of Muslims in the modern world.[60] The sharia councils in the United Kingdom are one example where new developments have taken place through the use of ADR processes. This has enabled the 'Islamisation' of divorces granted by a non-Muslim court, to the point where a Muslim woman can remarry in a manner deemed Islamic by the Muslim community. However, this change of attitude has been largely opportunistic and the councils do not appear to embrace the complete culture of ADR and all it implies with regard to the rights of the protagonists, proper power balancing and gender equity or the higher purposes of sharia, which ironically was one of the reasons for the establishment of such councils. Islamic finance is another area of modernisation and change. We shall discuss these two areas of new thinking or *ijtihad* that hold promise for a new mode of understanding Islamic law in Chapter 9.

9

Neo-*Ijtihad*

Necessity and Public Interest

Necessity has always been an important factor in Muslim juridical practice, giving rise to new modes of thinking and solutions to new problems within the Islamic framework of thought. Islamic finance, for example, is an area where novel and creative solutions are being developed within the Islamic paradigm. The oil crisis of the 1970s triggered by the OPEC countries following the Arab–Israeli war of 1973 led to an increase of revenue for most of oil-producing countries, particularly in the Middle East. This development, coupled with the movement of populations from the poorer parts of the Muslim world to the rich oil-producing countries, gave rise to the need for the utilisation of newly created wealth in ways that are in keeping with Islamic principles. Sharia finance, or Islamic finance, is one such area of the discourse of Islamic law where necessity plays a cardinal role.

Sharia Finance

Finance is a lively area of sharia, where change and necessity combine to make new law within the ethical boundaries of the faith that reflects and responds to new challenges in the world. This is a case where sharia meets the financial Leviathan and adapts to its demands, while endeavouring to retain an identity that remains faithful to the principles of Islamic law.

Islamic finance is largely based on the principle that money should not be commodified, being primarily a medium of exchange for goods or services. Therefore money must not make money in itself, namely through interest, which is a fundamental device for the flow of money in the international markets through the conventional financial system. Any unfair use of money is seen as unacceptable on account of creating an unjust enrichment of one party. Therefore it violates a basic ethic of the faith.

The actual practice and system of Islamic finance has developed during the last century in such a way that the structures that are sharia-compliant, or claim to be so, are complex and sometimes ambiguous but also pragmatic without endangering the quality of the vision of sharia. Yet the principles themselves are relatively simple and few and can be summarised as follows.

The first issue we need to be aware of is a point that bears repeating: money should not be a means of making money. It is to be used as an instrument of exchange, not a product in itself. Money itself does not actually create wealth but engenders an inflationary environment where the value of self-creating money loses its value by definition. This means that interest, or *riba*, which is at heart money making more money, is not allowed. There are arguments within the body of sharia scholarship that do not absolutely disallow interest. These arguments accept that the value of money may erode with time and the cost of money therefore becomes more expensive, so the interest that mirrors inflation in order to retain the value of the initial sum is deemed acceptable.

A second principle is that an investor should be investing in a product that is not forbidden, or *haram*. Investments in businesses that make, provide or sell alcohol or pork products are therefore not allowed by sharia. Nor is investment that does not actually create wealth; hence gambling (*maysir*) or any other investment where chance, rather than increase in productivity, is central is not allowed. Speculation (*gharar*) is not acceptable, nor are investments that are not clear or transparent. Since an investor should participate in the risk of the investment, fixed loans are not allowed. Investment in any licit business is open to the fluctuations in the fortune of that business. The ideal sharia position is one of an equity investor who participates in the business, in its fortunes and future, and is not protected from the vicissitudes of the enterprise. Clarity is ideally an important element of sharia-based finance. It is therefore arguable whether an investment based on the arcane art of algorithms is sharia compliant. Sharia rejects the type of investment where the outcome is dependent on the failure of another – in a win/lose equation, which is a form of gambling. This principle makes much of international finance out of bounds in sharia. Dealing in futures, for example, becomes problematic, even though there are legitimate reasons for investing in such financial products, as, for example, where an enterprise wants to ensure a predictable outcome with regard to income and price at any point in the future.

It can be argued that sharia finance is in reality a form of ethical finance where investing is limited to creating real wealth, sharing risks and avoiding opaque investments whereby the investor gains an unwarranted advantage against others and remains unaccountable. Islamic finance and its products are competing with the conventional financial system – a global behemoth of a continuously morphing web of interconnected and restless fictions, which are opaque and possibly unknowable as a whole – a system that dwarfs sharia finance. Furthermore, any new products that are developed to engage with the volatility of the market have to be acceptable to a small group of Islamic scholars who pass fatwas to legitimise or debar them within the orbit of Islamic finance. On top of this, certain conventional products and processes are, by their very definition, inimical to the principles of sharia, even though they play a necessary role in conventional finance. While certain products win acceptance from Islamic scholars, they may escape the prohibition of being *haram* but they may not be *tayyib* or wholesome, which makes them acceptable through a process of *hiyal* or fiction. The principles of sharia are therefore compromised at a deeper level. Some Muslim scholars of sharia finance today are starting to question the ethical validity of some of the more opaque formulations of approval through sharia-compliance advisory boards and scholars that, when examined more thoroughly, are of questionable morality and validity.[1]

Sharia scholars generally tend to view financial queries and issues presented to them in a narrow framework of legitimacy. When confronted with deeper purposes of the law, which is a part of sharia legal thinking, they choose to ignore these issues and defer to the pragmatic demands of the political power of their country or, indeed, the global economy. In theory, sharia finance is based upon ethical values derived from the Qur'an and Islamic legal thinking developed over time. In practice, we perceive an economical vision of what consists of proper Islamic principles, which reduces this vision to the demands of the market and investors who want to be comforted rather than guided in their Islamic obligations. This issue of authenticity and legitimacy has become a problem not only in sharia finance but affects the wider aspects of sharia. Many scholars are examining this problem in order to inject some wider ethical principles into the application of the law by reverting to earlier processes of judgement which took into account the social and economic purposes of law. The process, which has two aspects – *maqasid al-sharia*, the higher objectives of the law, and *maslaha* and *darura*, public interest and necessity – is being revisited by scholars today to make the law more relevant and flexible in its application.[2]

Issues Concerning Sharia Finance

There is a risk that Islamic finance may become simply another version of conventional finance, without any particular regulatory frameworks based upon established precedents and internationally recognised authority, and without the underpinning of an already flawed regulatory system – but one which claims to have God's fiat to support it.[3] Islamic finance thus will become corrupted by the failures of conventional finance but without being recognised as faulty, both in terms of processes and, more importantly, in terms of the ethical underpinning which is supposed to be at the heart of sharia finance. A fundamental rethink about the role and status of sharia finance, including the systems in place to legitimise specific financial products, needs to be undertaken. The purpose of the law and legal provisions – the *maqasid*, *maslaha* and *darura* aspects mentioned above – will therefore become an urgent question based upon the law's basic ethical principles that serve society as a whole, rather than enriching individuals and specific groups. While the global financial system demands continual reform and new thinking to enable at least a proportion of the multitude of transactions to subscribe to the principles of sharia, the way of monitoring this process is bringing into existence an awareness of the difference between a law or legal decision wearing the apparel of sharia compliance and those legal events that are infused with the deeper principles and wider purpose of sharia.

Maqasid al-Sharia

Sharia compliance can no longer be a rubber-stamping exercise but becomes a reality that enables investors to think in terms not only of profit but also of the effects of financial products on the community.[4]

This particular understanding of the law will have greater traction if the thinking is rooted in Islamic tradition rather than being perceived as an imposition of Western modernising zeal. It is here that the work of the 14th-century Maliki jurist al-Shatibi and others, who wrote about the *maqasid al-sharia*, will provide the necessary intellectual support and religious legitimacy to a process that will be of global relevance at a time when the global system itself is under critical scrutiny.

Laws, even those inspired by faith, have to conform to changing social and economic realities, and Islamic law is no exception. The issue of whether *riba* is allowed in Islam has been the subject of discussion and controversy for many generations, necessitating the Caliph Umar, one of the Rightly-Guided Caliphs, reputedly to have said that if only the Prophet had lived a little longer in order to clarify the situation we might not be facing some of the difficulties we do today.

The prohibition against *riba* is found mainly in six verses of the Qur'an.[5] The best-known is 2:275, which states:

> Those who devour usury will not stand except as stands one whom the Evil One by his touch hath driven to madness. That is because they say 'sale is like usury', but God hath permitted sale and forbidden usury. Those who after receiving Direction from their Lord, desist, shall be pardoned for the past; their case is for God [to judge]. but those who repeat [the offence] are companions of the fire: they will abide therein [forever].

The legal problem with this verse is that it does not deal with what should be done with the ill-gotten gains acquired by the perpetrator or what happens if he is a repeat offender. In both cases, the matter is left to the individual's conscience.

Sale and *Riba*

This Qur'anic revelation contrasts sale and *riba*, and in fact a sale contract (*bay'*) has always been considered as typical in Islamic law. According to Muslim scholars, this verse was revealed after the legitimacy of the prohibition of *riba* was questioned by some of the Prophet's contemporaries who chose not to see the difference between sale and loan. Hence the verse indicates the difference between these two transactions. Originally, the prohibition only applied to a loan agreement but later was extended to other transactions such as exchange of currencies and denominated articles such as wheat for wheat, barley for barley, dates for dates or salt for salt. The verse above is problematic from a law-creating perspective, for while it refers to the prohibition it does not in any way indicate a this-worldly sanction for its violation but focuses only on the hereafter, thus emphasising that whoever has accepted usury in the past will be pardoned, and those who refuse to desist from such practice will be consigned to hell forever. The verse is invoked in many modern cases on *riba* both in Muslim countries as well as in courts in non-Muslim countries where sharia has been stipulated as the proper law of a contract under review.[6]

Some Developments in the 20th Century

At the turn of the 20th century,[7] the Egyptian government set up the Egyptian Savings Fund (Sunduq al-Tawfir) which, like similar institutions in France and other Western countries, accepted cash deposits from individuals in return for which it gave them saving 'certificates' that yielded a return on their investment based on a fixed and pre-determined rate. Some 3,000 depositors expressed concern about the Islamic legality of the return arising from this transaction. The matter was referred to Muhammad

Abduh (1849–1905) a leading Muslim reformist, who a few years earlier (1899) had been appointed Grand Mufti of Egypt. According to Rashid Rida (1865–1935), who was his disciple, a respected reformist in his own right and the editor of the journal *al-Manar*, Abduh issued a verbal response in 1904 indicating that such operations should be carried out 'according to the rules of the *mudaraba* (partnership), for the use of monies deposited in the Fund'.[8]

Rida himself published a short fatwa on this issue in 1904 in which he referred to his mentor's opinion of that year as acquiescing in the operation of the Savings Fund on the basis that 'the postal administration is a rich governmental administration that uses the monies deposited in the Savings Fund in a manner that is beneficial both to the depositor and to those who work in that administration and in the government'.[9] In 1906, Rida published an essay in *al-Manar* commenting on the Qur'anic verses dealing with usury attributing to Abduh statements in which he, Abduh, criticised the prevailing banking practices in Egypt, though not the Savings Fund.

According to Chibli Mallat, the fatwas issued by Abduh and Rida on the subject of banking heralded the emergence of a new field where 'two great reformers of the early 20th century … became involved in a matter that marked the meeting point of certain Qur'anic statements regarding commercial transactions and the prohibition of *riba* (e.g. Q 2:275) on the one hand, and a complex web of Western economic models and commercial instruments on the other'.[10]

In the 1920s and 1930s fatwas on banking appeared regularly in journals published in Islamic circles in Egypt including that of al-Azhar. In subsequent years, a number of distinguished jurists contributed to the discussion, which included commentaries on the contract of loan included in the much-discussed Civil Code of Abd al-Razzak al-Sanhuri (1895–1971). Muhammad Abu Zahra (1898–1974) a reputed traditional scholar, issued a lengthy opinion on subjects related to lending and Western-style banking. Mahmud Shaltut (1893–1963), the Egyptian Shaykh al-Azhar, issued a fatwa in the 1950s conferring legitimacy on the Sunduq al-Tawfir operations, which is quoted at length by Muhammad

Sayyid Tantawi (1928–2010), a later Grand Mufti of Egypt, in a fatwa pronounced in 1989.

Relevance of the Sharia Today

This issue has assumed critical importance in the light of the resurgence of political Islam from the 1980s on and the call for the reinstatement of sharia that pervades Islamist discourse. In Nabil Saleh's words, the issue is that of 'an inevitable clash or mutual tolerance'.[11] An earnest plea has to be made for an attempt to co-ordinate the financial system based on sharia and the conventional international financial system. William Ballantyne, a leading academic-practitioner in this field, calls for an international Arab Code of Sharia in reference to the Arab world and also for a greater flexibility on the part of the conventional system with regard to the Islamic concept of creating and sharing wealth. Since the key element with regard to *riba* is the issue of money breeding money, there is, he argues, a need for a uniform code for Muslims to follow.[12]

According to Ballantyne, three issues arise. First, where sharia applies in a country, basic illegality is something to address. Secondly, some Muslims may justifiably view the Islamic system as being better than conventional finance. Thirdly, there should be recognition of the fact that an alternative to co-operation is confrontation, and that this would not be viable in the contemporary financial world. On the issue of basic illegality, even in a case where the proper law of contract is stipulated and there is a non-exclusive jurisdiction clause, there would still be a need for a 'clearing opinion' because the plaintiff may need to sue in the courts of a borrower's state or to enforce a judgement in such a state. In a case like this, it would be important to have an idea beforehand through such a 'clearing opinion' given by a lawyer of the jurisdiction that states how the courts of that jurisdiction would regard the contract in question. Under the principles of conflict of laws, an English court may also wish to review the laws of some Muslim countries for *ordre publique* (public policy based on moral order). With regard to whether Muslims would view Islamic finance as being a better alternative to conventional finance, the question arises as to what extent most

Muslims are committed to the system of Islamic banking. Ballantyne asks whether Muslims, looking at the world situation as it exists today, could not in fact say that the Islamic system is superior, both from religious and practical perspectives.

Since the Arab oil crisis of the early 1970s we have seen a steep increase in the income of oil-producing countries in the Middle East, a subsequent economic downturn, the collapse of some Western banks, the recurring international debt crisis and its attendant debt-rescheduling – all of which affects the global economy. This has led to the amassing of vast liquidity of funds in oil-producing countries generally. Ballantyne argues that Muslims could therefore legitimately question whether these drastic uncertainties and imbalances in the international financial system could have been avoided if the principles of sharia finance – which are in essence a form of ethical financing – had been more widely adopted.

For Ballantyne, it is sobering to reflect that in many Arab Islamic jurisdictions, should there be a difficulty in repaying a loan, an argument could be put forward both on a legal and constitutional basis with regard to sharia that would favour a renegotiation or rescheduling. Under sharia, if the loan is onerous for any reason the borrower has some right to have it rescheduled so that it can become more equitable. Even though generally it could be argued that loans (with interest) are not acceptable under sharia, there is also the argument from a pragmatic and practical perspective that since they do exist they should be administered in an equitable manner.

With regard to the complexities of conducting business with the Arab world and by extension with other Muslim countries, Ballantyne notes some of the issues on this theme. These range from what is stated in their respective constitutions regarding the status of sharia to a careful examination of the various statutes and regulations passed under these constitutions and to actual practice. Emphasising that there are some irreconcilable differences between the conventional Western and Islamic systems, he highlights three which are absolutely repugnant to the values of sharia. These are *gharar*, which roughly translates as risk or uncertainty; *riba*, which represents any unjustified one-sided accretion of wealth; and cases where there are a number of transactions within one contract.

The question as to whether Muslims would choose between a confrontation or an accommodation remains open. However, Ballantyne stated in his foreword to the Newsletter of the Arab Regional Forum of the International Bar Association in 1995 that there is a need to devise the necessary bridges with mutual respect to each other's values. However, he cautions that these bridges may only be built if there is an understanding based on 'knowledge on all sides of the basic elements and problems involved'.[13]

Whichever way one looks at the issue, it is a basic conflict between the laws of God and the laws of Mammon. The Egyptian government's change in the constitution of that country from sharia being *a* source to *the* source of law led in 1986 to a case being brought by the Rector of al-Azhar, who argued that the change in the Constitution meant, inter alia, that sharia must be applied in its entirety and thus henceforth those provisions of the Civil Code which provided for interest became ipso facto unconstitutional and therefore illegal. However, the country's Court of Cassation sent a circular to the judiciary informing it to the effect that this change made no difference to the laws until further notice. The court held that the change was not effective retroactively but would only be applicable to future laws. A similar issue arose in 1992 in the Kuwait Constitutional Court with regard to the provision of the Kuwaiti Commercial Code. The court stated that the fact that in the Kuwaiti Constitution sharia was *a* principal source but not *the* principal source of law and certainly not the sole source, helped to salvage the legislation. This issue also emerged in the UAE Civil Code which, for the first time, referred to the principle of conflict of laws and the principle of *autonomie de la volonté*.[14] However, the same provision has a sting in the tail which states that no choice of law is valid if it offends against the principles of sharia.

In the civil laws of most of these countries *riba* is prohibited but it is allowed in their commercial codes, which can be perceived as being tantamount to evasion, with many Muslim countries finding themselves in a global strait-jacket that precludes them from giving effect to sharia in their commercial laws. When the economy works successfully, Islamist rhetoric is largely ineffective;

however, when economic conditions deteriorate, an ideological vacuum develops, and this does not disappear unless governments genuinely embark on democratic reforms which, in themselves, present new problems of governance in countries where democratic values still need to be adopted.

According to Nabil Saleh, writing in 1988, financial transactions were up until then 'governed by statutory provisions, secular by and large. However, the challenge presented by the Sharia's champions is everywhere on the increase.'[15] In some cases, as in the banking sector, it had caused total disarray, compelling Saudi and UAE legislators to take immediate action with the aim of appeasing sharia's champions and reassuring international financial and banking communities. Saleh pointed out that another type of challenge had emerged during the previous decade: this was the revival of operations 'traditional to *fiqh* such as Islamic partnership (*musharaka*), the cost-plus-profit contact (*mudaraba*), as well as other operations of lesser importance. Altogether they represent a modus operandi promoted by banks which claim to function on the basis of Islamic ethics.'

Saleh warned that 'we are not any more presented with abstract principles and tenets which could well be uttered with no intent to see them implemented', and describes what was happening as a daring move as a financial system which described itself as Islamic was made to compete with an already existing and confirmed system. But the stakes are high. Saleh continued, saying that if such a newly introduced system 'fails or wanes, such a setback will bring a lack of credibility to the Islamic financial system as a whole'. He cautioned that in such a case it would lead to resentment, frustration and a further mistrust of Western standards and values. 'Only religious radicalism', he stated, 'will reap advantage from such a situation, and the divorce between East and West will be nearly complete in case the financial and economic systems collide and their legal systems segregate.' He completed the warning by stating that 'what is unreasonable is to take for granted that total rejection will be devoid of consequences which will be adverse to both West and East'.

Referring to the macro-economic scene as it was in 1988, Ballantyne emphasises the fact that, notwithstanding the shortcomings of Islamic finance, some in the West had begun to find the idea of equity-sharing as distinct from lending at interest attractive. 'It gives the provider of money a strong incentive to be sure he is doing something sensible with it.'[16] He argued that this element of sharing rendered the free market system more democratic and responsible. Ballantyne's thinking is even more applicable to the post-2008 financial world, when the system was near collapse because of doubtful investment policies, opaque products and practices carried out by major international banks. Quite independently of the academic discussions which were taking place in the United Kingdom and in some Muslim countries at that time, in September 1989 Muhammad Sayyed Atiyya Tantawi, the Grand Mufti of Egypt, and arguably the most prestigious *mufti* in the Sunni world, issued a fatwa entitled 'On Some Banking Operations'. Approximately 12 pages long and containing no reference to a specific question, the general form and style of this text according to Mallat 'place it squarely within the modern tradition of fatwa giving on the subject of banking, replete with citations from both classical and modern jurists'.[17] Mallat argued that Tantawi's fatwa represents a significant break with the earlier tradition of issuing fatwas in that

> at a critical juncture in his response, the mufti assumes the role of *mustafti* [the person who poses the question in order to develop the argument of the fatwa] by addressing a question to a lay expert, in this instance, a bank manager. Tantawi includes in his fatwa both his question to the bank manager and the latter's response. Although the authority of the response resides ultimately with the mufti himself, the act of seeking clarification from a lay person with no training in Islamic law is noteworthy and may signal a new and different type of *ifta* [fatwa issuance].[18]

Mallat's prediction has come true, as today's Islamic scholars are working closely with Islamic bankers and others involved in the field of finance and investment including insurance. What is noteworthy of Tantawi's fatwa, which Mallat describes as being in four sections, is that he establishes on the basis of his reading of the Qur'an and hadith the obligation of wise men (literally those who are rational – *al-'uqala*) to search for the truth, the principle of *ijtihad*, the virtue of avoiding fanaticism (*al-ta'assub*) and the importance of expertise in unravelling arcane subjects. What is further to be noted is that the fatwa, inter alia, highlights the complexity of banking, marshals the points of view of some 14 jurists belonging to the four schools of Sunni thought, distinguishes them, reiterates an earlier fatwa of Mahmud Shaltut on the issue, suggests certain changes in the language in which the products are described, and exhorts individuals to buy 'these certificates to help the state to develop worthwhile projects for all'.[19] The approach of reasoning is similar to the case law method in Common Law of arriving at a decision. It must be noted, though, that unlike a precedent in English law, a fatwa is not legally binding nor is the case law method endeavouring to establish the 'truth', as Tantawi suggests he aims to do. This difference occurs because modern jurisprudence is essentially rules based rather than a search for a 'truth'. Most important is Tantawi's awareness 'of his own intellectual limitations in the field, acknowledging that, irrespective of his competence in sharia, a *mufti* trained at al-Azhar has very little knowledge of the banking world and that the alien vocabulary associated with modern banking quickly transforms an imprudent *mufti* into a 'fish out of water'.[20] His candour about his weakness, coupled with the explanation included with his account of the methods by which he researched the subject, and the fact that he inserts lengthy quotations from secular specialists, makes his fatwa remarkable. Mallat continues: 'This example suggests that the mufti in late 20th-century Egypt recognises the limitation of religious knowledge (*ilm*) in the modern world and acknowledges the necessity of appealing to authorities trained in secular institutions.'[21] He states: 'The modest tone of a religious expert who himself seeks the advice of experts in other fields can only strengthen the moral authority of the mufti, both in Egypt and in the Sunni Muslim world at large.'[22]

We should note that Mallat's description of the *mufti*'s changed and enlightened approach may be a cause for hope, but it does not address the issue fundamentally and, being pragmatic, it is always vulnerable to contrary points of view. Muslim societies will still have to come to grips with the issue of whether *riba* is allowed in an Islamic dispensation. This problem of the role of sharia in Islamic finance reflects a wider problem in a modern, democratic society where secular values prevail. The contemporary scholar of Islamic law, Mohammad Rasekh, points out in his article 'Sharia and Law in the Age of Constitutionalism' that this interface between sharia and modernity presents a 'conundrum'.[23] He argues that 'there are several types of problems that may arise if sharia were to comply with modern law. In particular, the relationship of a sharia-compliant legal system with basic citizens' rights, on one hand, and with a democratic legislature, on the other.' While modern rights are embodied in the constitutions of Muslim countries, their ambit is always curtailed by the requirement of their conforming with sharia. This prevailing condition, argues Rasekh, 'can hardly accommodate modern rights which are amoral entities readily prone to be used in both moral and immoral ways'. Democratic legislatures, usually called Islamic national assemblies in most Muslim countries, are not normally elected by a nation in a free and fair election – a necessary precondition – thus they 'do not meet ... the characteristic of their rule making function which is limited by the compliance requirement'. Finally, according to Rasekh, the limits that sharia imposes are not in keeping with the pluralistic nature of modern societies where the assertion of rights has to be conceived within both a moral and amoral universe. On this basis, he maintains that the nation state has to be moral and immoral at the same time, which is not possible in terms of sharia. These types of issues also pertain to the role of sharia in modern finance, which is complex and rules based.

Meanwhile, the question remains as to whether Muslim countries will amend their commercial laws to conform to the values of sharia. This, in our view, may not happen in the short or medium term but it may take place gradually. It is also pertinent to ask to what extent sharia itself would have to adapt to the existing international financial system without jeopardising the principles upon which it is based and without developing face-saving devices to dress up a façade of sharia-compliant products which, in effect, evade the underlying ethical demands of sharia finance. Meanwhile, although sharia finance remains a small part of international finance, it is growing fast and significantly, and this has been recognised by various Western institutions and laws so that the United Kingdom, for example, has passed legislation to enable the sharia financial product of *sukuk* (Islamic bonds, more fully defined on the section on *Takaful* and *Sukuk* below) to be formed and traded on the stock exchange. Since the 2008 global financial crisis, interest has increased in ethical finance and socially responsible investment, and the World Bank Treasury has brought different investment streams together by helping the International Finance Facility for Immunisation (IFFIM) issue two *sukuk*s within a year. The IFFIM issued its first three-year USD 500 million transaction in 2014, the largest debut *sukuk* to be issued by a supra-national entity.[24]

Sharia finance principles create the ground on which this type of financial system can operate and upon which various financial products that are compliant with sharia principles are developed. Most of the products, some of which we outline below, have a long history, but they are not static in form or, indeed, in content. Sharia finance is an area of sharia which has not remained still or become ossified under the edicts of legal scholars intent on keeping to the minutiae of God's commands as they understand them.[25] Sharia finance has a pedigree and aims to be in line with the essential principles that underpin it, but it is also driven to be innovative and pragmatic to supply appropriate financial products in a fast-moving globalised financial world which is dominated by a vast, often opaque, complex financial system driven by the need to invest surplus funds, and the ambition of investors to make these funds work to increase their wealth even in cases where the actual process of investment is murky and tantamount to gambling, which is not allowed by sharia.

We shall now describe briefly some of the concepts and the products developed by Islamic finance.

Mudaraba and *Murabaha*

One of the earliest products to be developed in the modern financial market is *mudaraba*, in which one party provides the capital and the other uses his skill and knowhow to invest the capital in a profit-making venture. The parties agree beforehand on how consequent profits will be shared and how the losses will fall.

The investor of capital therefore bears any losses, while the other party also suffers by not getting any reward for his involvement in the transaction. Thus the risk is shared between the parties concerned.

Another product is the *murabaha*, whereby a financial institution, usually a bank, purchases an item at a particular price at the request of its client who wishes to own the item and then sells the item on to the client with an agreed mark up (which is regarded as its profit margin rather than interest). The client then pays the final price in instalments to the bank. This product is not dissimilar to that in conventional finance, where the bank makes a loan to its client who then pays it back with an interest-bearing cost. The main difference is that in *murabaha* ownership and risk first pass to the bank which, in turn, sells the item on to its client, who repays the final price in instalments. In this way the problem of *riba* is evaded by a construct relating to the ownership of the item.

Musharaka and *Ijara*

Another means of obtaining bank financing for a business venture is through *musharaka*, which in essence is a joint-venture partnership. In this case, the bank invests with others in a business and an agreement is made between all the participants (some of whom will be managing the business) whereby the profit is distributed in pre-determined ratios and the loss is borne in accordance to the size of each partner's financial contribution. We should note that there are differences of opinion between different legal schools on whether profits should be paid out on a pro rata basis or can be agreed otherwise.

A variant of this product is a diminishing *musharaka*, which entails an equity participation in a project, company or asset and the sharing of profit derived from the entity on a pro rata basis. The entity is theoretically divided into units which are transferred at a fixed price over an agreed period from the financial institution to the ultimate owner(s), who will finally own the entire equity of the entity. The ultimate owner agrees by contract to pay rent on the units yet to be transferred from the financial institution in accordance with the character of the asset. As an example, rent is due from a house which is jointly owned from the ultimate owner to the financial institution on that part which is not yet owned by the occupier, or in the case of a company the profit share. This type of sharia product is underpinned by a network of multiple contracts which in effect protect the financial institution by imposing binding promises on the ultimate purchaser to pay rent on the outstanding units, and also to purchase those units over time.

Ijara is another form of mortgage lending. This is a leasing contract whereby the borrower essentially rents the property, which is owned by the lender, on agreed terms over an agreed period, and during this period the borrower pays to the lender both rental and capital. At the end of the term, the borrower may purchase the asset or the lender may continue to retain it. A variation of this contract is *ijara wa iqtina* (commonly used for the purchase of a home or of machinery), whereby the borrower is obliged to finally purchase the asset at the end of the term.

Takaful and *Sukuk*

The above contracts often include insurance cover, which in sharia terms can be problematic. A form of sharia-compliant insurance is *takaful*, which is based on the Qur'anic principle of mutual assistance known as *ta'awun*. This contract entails joint risk sharing in the event of a loss by one of its members and provides for mutual protection of assets and property. A further development of this product is *re-takaful*, or reinsurance based on Islamic principles. This contract spreads the risk.

One of the most important products in sharia finance is *sukuk*, which has enjoyed significant growth over recent years. It is similar to a conventional bond but is always attached to an underlying asset which produces the income. The asset is leased to the client to yield the return on the *sukuk*. While this product is convenient, it does have its detractors who deem it not to be sharia-compliant, but a device to produce fixed returns which are akin to interest.

There are a number of other sharia-compliant products that have been developed and there are others in the pipeline. This reflects the active and dynamic nature of sharia finance today.

Future of Islamic Finance

Sharia finance is becoming more 'professionalised' as courses are established in universities both in the West and in Muslim countries on the subject; these are actively enrolling students, including imams. Consequently, a new cadre of sharia finance advisors is springing up, with young graduates fluent both in the principles of sharia and also in economics and banking who are advising banks and other institutions that apply sharia finance. Whether these professionals will also explore and develop new authentic sharia finance products has yet to be seen.[26] The pressures of the global international financial system are immense, and sharia finance is still a small part of the financial world. Funds traverse continents, trillions of dollars are used on a daily basis and the circulation of money grows faster and faster, helped by technological innovations that occur at a breathtaking rate and create new and often elaborate methods of investment; these require immense ingenuity for practitioners to use them successfully. Ethics is a victim of oversight in the pursuit of profit. Sharia advisors and scholars have to keep up as well as keep faith, and this is a tremendously difficult task that encourages participants to stretch and downplay the basic ethical principles of sharia in order to provide convenient solutions rather than real ones. This danger is encountered by sharia finance advisors on a daily basis.

According to Iqbal Asaria, an Islamic finance academic, the four-decade-old Islamic banking, finance and insurance industry is now ripe for evaluation. Islamic finance assets are said to have grown to over USD 1.5 trillion and the industry is featuring on the radar of all banking, finance and insurance regulators across the globe.[27]

As the replication of most conventional financial instruments or arrangements proceeds apace, two key questions are increasingly being asked: how true is the contemporary Islamic finance, banking and Insurance industry to the *maqasid al-sharia*, and is it delivering the distributional justice and equity which are supposed to be the core propositions in the *maqasid al-sharia*?

The debate has started by dissecting the reverse-engineered nature of most contemporary Islamic finance products. These sharia-compliant products appear to be delivering a similar outcome to conventional finance, so there has been a call for sharia-based products. But the question remains whether these terms have been adequately addressed. There is now a need to articulate more clearly the underlying issues. This can be done by exploring the concepts of *halal* (permissible), *haram* (not permissible) and *tayyib* (wholesome).[28] Scholars in this field are beginning to grapple with issues such as: if a product fulfils the conventional *halal/haram* test, is it wholesome or *tayyib* to invest in ventures which, though not specifically prohibited, are not in the best interests of the wider community? Examples are projects that may harm the environment or food and beverage companies whose products are deemed to cause childhood obesity. Scholarship is looking beyond the *halal/haram* dichotomy to the purpose of the law, whether it is wholesome and beneficial to society – which is the basis of sharia. Asaria asks: 'is the present arrangement of using Sharia Supervisory Boards capable of delving into the *tayyib* aspects of Islamic finance, banking and insurance? If not, what arrangements may be put into place to incorporate this aspect in the practice of Islamic finance?'[29] In today's world, which is driven by a neo-liberal capitalism intent on profit and the exploitation of resources, Islamic thought could play an important role in contributing to this seminal and vital discourse of global concern.

Alternative Dispute Resolution

Alternative Dispute Resolution (ADR) is another area where new thinking concerning sharia is taking place. ADR is a global movement that has taken root over the past four decades largely in the Western world, and diasporic Muslim communities have had to embrace it out of necessity by developing mechanisms to deal with their family disputes, ensuring that the dispositions of wealth, succession, custody of children and matrimonial rights and obligations are conducted in an Islamically sensitive manner.[30] In the United Kingdom, the emergence of sharia councils, while having contributed towards this process, has also given rise to a number of concerns with regard to women's rights, minority rights and Human Rights in general. It should be noted that Western

Human Rights discourse is largely geared to the notion of rights, whereas sharia, in the shadow of which Muslim negotiations generally take place, emphasises the notion of duty or obligation. This finds resonance in Qur'anic principles, but at times is at variance with Western liberal values and thought.

What is ADR?

First, we shall briefly discuss what ADR is and how the sharia councils mentioned above came into being in the United Kingdom. This will illustrate one way in which sharia works in a Western, non-Muslim society, and what Muslim communities can do to bring their ADR practice in line with contemporary ADR principles. As part of this process, we show how Muslims can uphold the higher purposes of the law – what the 14th-century Andalusian Maliki jurist al-Shatibi referred to as the *maqasid al-sharia*, mentioned above in this chapter.

ADR has arisen as a response to the challenges faced by the civil justice system worldwide which, over the past few years, has been unable to process the increasing number of cases brought before it. Therefore the courts are clogged in many countries and cases drag on for long periods through the adversarial process, often being eventually settled before they are heard.[31] According to the Law Dictionary, 'the most recently-available statistics [show] about 95 percent of pending lawsuits end in a pre-trial settlement. This means that just one in 20 personal injury cases is resolved in a *court of law* by a judge or jury. It also means that planning for a pre-trial settlement is a crucial component of any sound legal strategy.'[32]

In India alone, it is estimated that some 30 million cases will not be heard in the lifetime of the disputants. One notorious case has now been running for some 118 years and has gone through a series of courts both in India and England, having survived the partition of India during which some of the disputants emigrated to Pakistan and were given land there by the government. However, the disputants continue to fight the case, even though they received some compensation.[33] In many parts of the world today, disputants are more inclined to resolve their issues informally outside the adversarial process because of these challenges, which are not only time consuming and costly but are also destructive of human relationships.

We should recognise that ADR as a process fits in well with sharia. Muslims have been practising a form of ADR for centuries, because it is supported by verses in the Qur'an – namely 4:35, 4:58 and 4:65 – which encourage believers to enter into negotiated settlement known as *sulh*, rather than using a full-blown legal process.[34] Clearly, *sulh* was traditionally, and remains, deeply influenced and informed by patriarchal tendencies in Muslim culture and is now being adapted in some countries to modern contexts. This is an example of sharia being able to respond to modern conditions. However, we should note that in many Muslim communities, cultures and countries – where *sulh* is part of the public legislation and community practice – the traditional mode of resolving disputes amicably continues.

UK Sharia Councils

In the case of diasporic Muslims in the United Kingdom, the embracing of contemporary ADR principles came about almost by accident. In the 1970s a Muslim woman from Pakistan, having obtained a civil divorce in the English courts (the only jurisdiction where a divorce performed in England or in any other jurisdiction recognised by the laws of England can be dissolved), required a Muslim divorce necessitated by sharia principles. While this disputant was entitled to remarry under English law, she was not so entitled under sharia law, which required her to apply for an additional Islamic divorce that only her husband could grant – and he refused to do so.[35] Failing this, she was obliged to obtain a declaration from an Islamic panel of jurists. The woman sought help from the London Central Mosque. Initially, the imams of the mosque, largely trained in the subcontinent of India, were unable to grant her a divorce in accordance with the strictures of the *fiqh* to which she and her husband belonged, and also, as England was not a Muslim country, the imams felt hampered in helping the disputant to complete what was a non-Muslim legal decision.

At that point, an Egyptian scholar-jurist named Mohamed Zaki Badawi, trained at al-Azhar University and the leading imam of the London Central Mosque, recognised the injustice of the case, and examined the original texts of sharia of the Hanafi school of jurisprudence to which the parties belonged. He discovered that according to the eponymous founder of the school, Abu Hanifa, where Muslims were living outside a Muslim context or environment and were faced with a problem that required a sharia solution, then Muslims may constitute themselves as a body to mete out justice to anyone who was being unfairly treated, since Islamic law does not wish *darar*, or harm, to befall any person. Badawi opined that if two prerequisites, which are *darura* and *maslaha*, coincided, then the rigours of the law could be mitigated and subordinated to the higher principles that sharia aims to protect which, according to the Andalusian Maliki jurist al-Shatibi, drawing on the theories of al-Ghazali several centuries earlier, are defined as the protection of the person (*nafs*), the intellect (*'aql*), property (*mal*), offspring (*nasl*) and religion (*din*).[36] Using his intellect and reason to arrive at a just solution that would meet the exigencies of the time, the process known as *ijtihad*, Badawi was able to provide justice to this female disputant who, according to him, was suffering from the abuse of the principles of sharia by her intransigent husband, who was acting inequitably.[37]

It is unlikely that Badawi was conscious of the details of the ADR discourse then taking place largely in the United States, but his rationale and solution found immediate resonance with ADR. It also claimed indigenous legitimacy for ADR amongst the Muslim community in the United Kingdom. Since this decision, they saw the emergence of the phenomenon of sharia councils established on lines similar to the Beth Din rabbinical courts. Over the past four decades, while the sharia councils have succeeded in helping thousands of Muslim women obtain an Islamic divorce,[38] there remains today a concern about the patriarchal nature of some of their deliberations and, in some cases, their over-dependance on *fiqh*-based formulations of the law that potentially conflict with the norms of liberal values that essentially underpin secular laws in Western countries.[39]

In the context of the general ADR debate that continues throughout the Western world, the phenomenon of the sharia council is gradually being accepted, though its practice and its patriarchal nature continues to give rise to concerns particularly among groups who champion Human Rights women's rights and, indeed, children's rights.[40] Approaches to these issues have been influenced by the prevailing Islamophobia in the West which, in turn, has fuelled the debate further, particularly in Canada. The Boyd Commission Report,[41] in which former Attorney General Marion Boyd shows how the initiative to introduce sharia law into the Canadian legal system was projected, has been controversial and highlights the development of a polemical debate that polarised the Muslim community itself, in addition to dividing Muslims from the larger population of Canada.[42] This unfortunate occurrence, which has caused distrust and even hatred between communities, does great harm to the presence and identity of Muslims living in the West. However, recent scholarship on this phenomenon both in the United Kingdom and in Canada has helped to make the debate more rational and informed, rather than being driven by fear and ignorance.[43]

There are reputed to be about 85 sharia councils operating in the United Kingdom at the time of writing, and they are mostly unregulated and operate informally. Some of these councils apply sharia in a judicious manner using the notions of *maqasid* and *maslaha* to ensure that their decisions take account of contemporary issues and values, while others continue to apply sharia in a literal and rigid manner. In this regard, one must mention the issue of *halala* which comes into effect when a man has stated impetuously to his wife three times that he wishes to divorce her and then repents and wishes to annul the divorce. In this situation she must first consummate a marriage with another man who will then divorce her, allowing her to remarry her first husband. This practice, intended to protect women from arbitrary and capricious divorce, in effect subjects them to abuse.

These councils have always been regarded with a degree of suspicion by the authorities in the United Kingdom, and in 2016 the then Home Secretary, Theresa May, set up a commission to investigate the workings of the councils and more specifically to examine their treatment of female disputants and the rights of children. Some criticism has been expressed by various writers about the terms of reference of the commission. While we agree with some of the issues raised, there is a danger that the debate may become eclipsed by Islamophobic sentiment rather than being informed by genuine concerns about the role of ADR as a whole in society.[44] On 1 February 2018, the UK Home Office published the report of an independent review, chaired by Mona Siddiqui, into the application of Sharia law by sharia councils in England and Wales. The report makes three recommendations: for legislative change, awareness campaigns and regulation.[45]

Some Examples of Negotiated Settlement in Sharia

Negotiated settlement (*sulh*), as mentioned above, is deeply embedded in Muslim juridical thought and ADR is recognised as an Islamic ethical value.[46] Negotiated settlement is not only mentioned in the Qur'an but it is also referred to in the hadith of the Prophet. Two examples are prominent, the first being the Prophet's decision following the reconstruction of the Kaaba when he resolved the dispute between the Quraysh leaders about who would have the honour to replace the sacred stone by placing his own cloak on the ground and having all four disputants carry the stone on top of the cloak. In today's ADR parlance, this would be deemed a win–win solution. The other example is the forgiving of a woman who threw rubbish over the Prophet's head each day as he passed by her window. On one occasion, when this did not happen, he enquired about her, and on hearing that she was unwell sought permission to enter her room and gave her water, as she was too ill to help herself. This is an example of the principle of forgiveness which also lies at the heart of modern transformative mediation.

Elsewhere in Muslim juridical tradition there is the famous letter of Caliph Umar to Abu Musa al-Ash'ari on how he should conduct himself with his subjects by acting impartially in his dealing with the populace. Umar said: 'And in the court room so that the rich be not greedy for your partiality and the weak be not fearful of your injustice ... avoid impatience, vexation and annoyance with people and denying the rights of the litigants.'[47] Ali, the fourth Caliph and the first Imam, also spoke of those most in need of justice and who have no resources – the destitute, the disabled, the elderly, orphans – those who are most in need of justice from you who should be treated in a manner such that 'God may excuse you on the day you meet Him'.[48] All of these and others who are in need but refuse to beg should be helped by the governor who, according to Ali, should appoint an officer with the specific task of bringing to light the needs of the most destitute and providing for them. This is onerous for the governors and the fulfilment of all rights is difficult but, as Ali stated, 'God makes it light for those who aspire to the hereafter, who restrain their souls in patience and trust in the truth of that which is promised them by God'.[49]

According to Shah-Kazemi, a respected scholar on Ali, 'What needs to be highlighted here is that the spiritual element is what makes practicable an ideal that otherwise would be a heavy "burden": divine assistance is assured for those whose attention is not confined to this world alone, but whose aspirations extend beyond it to the hereafter. It is only when this world is seen through to the next, that a fully justified attitude towards this world emerges.'[50]

This notion of amicable dispute resolution is also highlighted in the works of Shi'i Imams such as Muhammad al-Baqir and Ja'far al-Sadiq as well as in the practice of the Ottoman Kayseri courts,[51] and in the family law statutes of most Muslim countries in the world.[52] According to Wael B. Hallaq, the notion of negotiated settlement was an essential part of the Islamic juridical landscape and often was the method of first resort for Muslims.[53]

Discourses among Muslim scholars today revolve around a model that would be more appropriate for Muslim communities – one that is not suffused with excessive individualism but focussed on the notion of relationality and communitarian ethics. Amr Abdalla, a leading exponent of this principle, emphasises the point that Muslim ADR personnel today have a positive obligation to ensure that it is used to bring about greater social justice, fairness and equity, which are meant to be the principles of law and sharia.[54] This idea finds resonance with the thinking of the leading Muslim modernist Fazlur Rahman who, in his book *Islam and Modernity*, argues for the higher principles of sharia – its *maqasid* – to serve as the basis for reform today. Rahman emphasises the argument that ethical sharia needs to be retrieved from the legalistic cloak in which it has come to be wrapped historically.[55] This idea finds sympathy with various Muslim thinkers and social activists as well as with many younger Muslims,[56] as such an approach locates reform within an Islamic tradition which is regarded as dynamic rather than a static body of rules. Obviously the legitimacy of this reform process will also depend on how well it is situated within public narratives that are both familiar and progressive. It can be argued that ADR could serve as a practical area of legal application through the creative use of ethical principles.[57]

As we have seen, the notion and practice of resolving disputes outside the rigour and limitation of the legal process has a home in Islamic thinking and has been used throughout the history of Islam. The basis of the procedure of all ADR processes is to seek justice by enabling the conflicting parties to find a solution that allows them both to obtain a level of satisfaction by compromise and by encouraging one party to recognise the claims of the other. Muslims who live in non-Muslim countries and who wish to observe sharia as far as possible in those countries, which means that sharia decisions or agreements must accord with the public law of those countries, have become more flexible or sophisticated in their understanding of sharia which, certainly where it plays a role in ADR decisions, has to take into account principles of justice and Human Rights as generally understood in non-Muslim countries. Patriarchal tendencies in sharia thus have to be modified to take into account the equal rights of women, even though in some cases this may be a difficult exercise. However, in the Muslim ADR process this can be achieved more equitably and without offending the Muslim sense of identity.[58]

One area where new thinking has taken place is in the field of international child abduction. A large number of Muslim countries have not signed up to the Hague Convention on the Civil Aspects of International Child Abduction promulgated in October 1980 (hereafter called the 1980 Hague Convention), and to date only a little over a third of the countries of the world have signed up or adhered to it. To respond to the practical problems arising from this situation, a German organisation called Mediation bei international Kindschaftskonflikten (MiKK), in collaboration with Child Focus of Belgium and the Catholic University of Leuven, put together a manual in which the need for a chapter dealing with the issue apropos Muslim countries, where mediation could be considered as a way forward, was mentioned. One of the authors of this book, Mohamed Keshavjee, contributed a chapter showing that mediation was not incompatible with sharia but was akin to the negotiated settlement (*sulh*) enjoined by the Qur'an.[59] The organisers of this project established a training programme in Brussels in 2009 attended by representatives of 27 EU countries and in which the Islamic segment was taught through a role-play of a bicultural, binational and biracial marriage by two Muslim mediators (male and female). Independently of this exercise, under the auspices of the Permanent Bureau of The Hague Conference on Private International Law, a working committee was set up to review the possibility of utilising mediation as a method of resolving this problem. The Canadian government promoted this endeavour and the working committee was jointly chaired by a former Canadian diplomat, William Crosbie, and a Pakistani Supreme Court Judge, Tassaduq Hussain Jillani, with members from 22 countries – 11 from the Western world and 11 from Muslim nations. This endeavour was set up in 2009 following the Malta 3 Conference. Over a seven-year period the committee had several meetings, including two regional seminars, in Qatar and Malaysia, during which it developed a framework of collaboration between judges in Muslim countries, scholars and other institutions. Reporting to the 4th Malta Conference in Valleta in May 2016, Judge Jillani reminded attendees of the genesis of the Malta process, quoting the former Deputy Secretary General of The Hague Conference, Professor William Duncan, stating that a common understanding should be developed on the basis of 'equal respect for different legal traditions and systems' and 'a willingness to explore and consider new solutions'.[60]

Since this process began, Morocco has become a party to the 1980 Hague Convention and representatives from various other Muslim countries who attended Malta 4 are taking steps to ensure that their countries sign up as well. In the final declaration of the conference, mediation was highlighted as an important method of resolving these problems regardless of whether a country had joined the Convention or not. A resolution to that extent was unanimously passed. States were encouraged to promote mediation training using the services of training organisations in their respective jurisdictions as well as online services provided by various EU civil society organisations whose representatives were present at the conference. Most importantly, this was an example where initial reluctance on the part of Muslim countries to engage in the process of resolving disputes between parents who experience the abduction of children was transformed into engagement. This was because the countries concerned realised the processes involved did not contradict the principles of sharia but were in fact in keeping with them and that the process was a collaborative effort based on mutual trust.

Conclusion

In this chapter, we have noted that a great deal of new thinking is taking place both as a result of migration and increased globalisation fuelled by the digital revolution and the vast flow of financial resources across borders. Given this reality, the principles of *darura* and *maslaha* become more urgent and understanding the purpose of the law took on greater importance. At the same time, there is a need for deeper thought on aspects of genuine purpose and greater social justice, so that any changes enacted are not merely cosmetic but correspond with the more genuine purposes of sharia and also ensure that they can be brought into better alignment with some of the most challenging ethico-legal issues of the day, such as those pertaining to Human Rights, minority rights and children's rights. There is, therefore, a growing recognition today that a *maqasid*-cum-*maslaha*-based theory of law is critical to the Muslim modern reformist project.

Sharia and Human Rights

Historical Background

Only a few centuries old, the history of Human Rights is problematic. The discourse that now plays a distinct role in international relations and is beginning to form a part of international law was mainly developed in the 20th century and especially after the Second World War. It is largely perceived as a Western development that is dominated by the West to serve its own geopolitical interests. Yet Human Rights the rights of each human being to be treated with dignity, respect and accorded a common humanity, can arguably be found in the traditions of all the major religions – Judaism, Christianity, Islam, Hinduism, Buddhism and so forth. These general ethical tenets underlying the great faiths have to be read and received in the context of other competing principles that concern the sanctioned duties and obligations of the faithful; they exist as a reminder of the central importance of each person who is also part of a greater whole, of the community of faith which forms an integral part of the God-created identity of the individual. However, before considering how Human Rights have developed in recent times, we should note that these rights in various degrees and forms were already being discussed in the West, independently of religion, by philosophers from the 17th to the 19th centuries such as Locke, Rousseau, Kant and, in a contrary manner, by Jeremy Bentham, who indicated an element of scepticism about them when he called them 'nonsense upon stilts'.[1] For Bentham, real rights were legal rights rather than natural rights, which were mainly the topic of philosophical speculation as he saw it.

He argued that even to suggest that governments were constrained by natural rights would be dangerous since it could be a prelude to anarchy.

Justiciability

This issue of the normative status of Human Rights and its justiciability is taken up by the contemporary Nobel Laureate Amartya Sen in his book *Development as Freedom*,[2] in which he recalls Bentham's attitude and points out that these rights suffer from a 'legitimacy critique', whereby their status as law is questioned by virtue of their unenforceability. Therefore it could be argued that they continue to be in the domain of philosophical discourse rather than enforceable 'legislated legal rights'. 'Human beings in nature are, in this view, no more born with human rights than they are born fully clothed; rights would have to be acquired through legislation just as clothes are acquired through tailoring.' Sen then speaks of the second line of attack, which he refers to as the 'coherence critique'. This concerns the form that the ethics and politics of Human Rights take. 'Rights are entitlements that require, in this view, co-related duties.' Sen cites an example: 'If person A has a right to some x, then there has to be some agency, say B, that has a duty to provide A with x. If no such duty is recognised, then the alleged rights, in this view, cannot but be hollow.' He argues that these rights are 'heart-warming sentiments' but at the same time they are, 'strictly speaking, incoherent'. Finally, Sen also points out that Human Rights do not have the universal credibility and acceptance that the rhetoric would claim for them. This is what he calls a 'cultural critique'. Here the critique does not take quite such a legal and institutional form, but 'views Human Rights as being in the domain of social ethics'. Human Rights are conditional on the nature of acceptable ethics, and Sen questions whether such ethics are truly universal. He asks what if some cultures do not regard such rights as particularly valuable compared with other rights. Perhaps scepticism arises mainly from Asian perceptions of Human Rights and, even here, Sen questions whether we can be certain of what constitutes Asia or the differences within East Asian cultures themselves, cautioning that attempts at generalisation about 'Asian values' could be extremely problematic and crude.[3]

Working from different perceptions, Human Rights have also been disowned by the intelligentsia and governments of former colonial countries as a gigantic and continuing Western imperialist imposition. They argue that this notion of rights, posited as a global phenomenon, does not fit into the indigenous values of their own countries and regions which, in many cases, place greater regard upon the idea of obligation, community and authority. In fact, this critique goes so far as to argue that the emphasis on 'rights' can lead to contradictions and a lack of accountability, to competing claims and superficial application in societies where late capitalism encourages consumerism by which rights have become abstract, obsessive and trivialised in place of deeper social values. This critique has gained some degree of recognition by contemporary writers and thinkers such as Michael Sandel, Alasdair MacIntyre and Charles Taylor. David Selbourne, a conservative thinker, writing in 1994, referred to a culture of 'dutiless rights' where civic society, which is based on rights but also on shared duties and the moral obligations that underpin it, is being eroded by mindless freewheeling and the self-interest and status-seeking pursuit of private wealth and power at the expense of the common good and wider society.[4]

Persistence of Discourse

The discourse of Human Rights continues to be a living issue, even though Sen, like others before him, has argued that Human Rights lack legal status, and since the Second World War they have moved towards becoming positive law, starting with the work of the laywers, Raphael Lemkin and Hersch Lauterpacht, who brought into legal consciousness the terms 'genocide' and 'crimes against humanity' respectively. Their work influenced the development of the UN's Universal Declaration of Human Rights (UDHR), adopted in 1948, followed by a series of Human Rights treaties and conventions. Since that time, subsidiary treaty obligations and jurisprudential developments, for example the International Criminal Courts, have taken on derivative life from the UDHR, whose fundamental principles most, if not all, members of the UN have agreed to accept. We do not wish to over-emphasise the effectiveness of a universal declaration of Human Rights which most states still acknowledge in a haphazard way depending on their particular national interests. The problem of instituting the UDHR is common to all states, which are now challenged by Human Rights as they become more than postulates and transit into enforceable legal rules – thus the United States has not signed up to the International Criminal Court for fear that its citizens may be indicted for Human Rights infractions, while at the same time it claims to champion Human Rights as part of its constitution and liberal democratic ethos.

Muslim States and Human Rights

This issue of the UDHR becomes crucial, however, when considering the position of Muslim countries who have signed up to the UDHR and subsequent treaties and have joined institutions aimed at promulgating and protecting Human Rights. Muslim states have difficulties in accepting the UDHR, not only because it is regarded as a Western colonial construct but also because, according to them, it does not accord with sharia in some aspects and therefore is not entirely acceptable. At the same time, as part of the comity of nations, these states remain accountable for Human Rights infractions within their borders as they are obliged to respect Human Rights, if not solely through their treaty obligations, then by virtue of the principle that Human Rights have now become accepted as part of customary international law. Yet the point remains that they view the Declaration from an Islamic perspective, which has its own world view. Therefore, we need to examine the rights as covered by sharia and how they differ from those expressed in the UDHR. Due cognisance needs to be taken of the fact that the constitutions of many Muslim states declare explicitly that the state is either a Muslim or an Islamic entity. In such cases, sharia acquires a degree of significance as a source of law and the question arises whether it is *a* source of law or *the* source of law, as mentioned in Chapter 9. If it is the former, other systems of law may be called into play in cases of internal conflict. However, if the latter pertains, then any law that conflicts with sharia is viewed, even by the country's law courts, as being contrary to the moral and religious fabric of that country and thus, ultra vires, the constitution. Such situations demand an understanding of sharia's conception of Human Rights which is not clearly enunciated within the Islamic legal system as a single body of doctrine but is deemed to arise from various readings of the holy texts and the subsequent legal interpretations of those texts which become positive law or *fiqh*.

The Human Rights discourse is mired in the binary context of Islam versus the rest of the world,[5] whereby the 'origins' of Human Rights become problematic, giving rise to questions such as why a discourse that arose in the West should attract Muslim support and whether it is an expansion of the colonial venture. Note needs to be taken of the fact that the UDHR was not accepted by Saudi Arabia and certain other Muslim states, ostensibly as being in contravention of sharia. Saudi Arabia argued, for example, that rights are God's gift to people and the treaty contravened the Qur'an by asserting the right to change one's religion.

The noted Islamic scholar Mumtaz Ahmad (d. 2016) acknowledged the abysmal Human Rights record of many Muslim states but did not blame Islam per se for this state of affairs. Human Rights abuses prevail, he argued, because of the political disorder that appears to be endemic in Muslim states.[6] The Sudanese-born professor of law, Abdullahi An-Na'im, is more direct when he says categorically that Muslims, if they implement historical sharia, 'cannot exercise their right to self-determination without violating the rights of others'.[7] An-Na'im's argument appears to be based upon the absolutist claims of sharia, which denies the legitimacy of other modes of ethical values. In fact, An-Na'im is also firm in his opinion that the validity of Human Rights discourse is one that is capable of being accepted widely, since it is 'appreciated by a wide variety of cultural traditions because they pertain to the inherent dignity and well being of every human being regardless of race, gender, language or religion'.[8] In effect, he argues that although the discourse may originate from a Western tradition it does not belong exclusively to the West.

However, another well-known scholar, Bassam Tibi, posits that, given post-modern affirmation of difference, one could see something that is condemned in one place being culturally appropriate in another. Tibi is aware of double standards and argues that it is 'significant that Western politicians never address Human Rights violations in Saudi Arabia'.[9] Consequently, Tibi sees the difficulty of persuading Muslims that a discourse that originated in the West does not somehow also favour the West. However, he criticises those fundamentalists who castigate Western cultural relativity yet exploit multicultural openness and tolerance to establish legitimacy for themselves, something that manifests a profound intellectual dishonesty and political chicanery in the name of authenticity and the good. Cultural relativity, Tibi warns, 'virtually prohibits a critique on non-Western culture'.[10]

Islamic Approach to Human Rights

To gain an insight into the Islamic approach to Human Rights we need to review the writings and polemics of the Islamist ideologues Abul A'la Maududi and Sayyid Qutb, of Hizb ut-Tahrir – an Islamic Liberation Party founded in Jerusalem during the 1950s by Taqi al-Din al-Nabhani (d. 1972) – and of the Universal Islamic Declaration of Human Rights which, according to Clinton Bennett,[11] represents the right of the political spectrum, as well as the writings of Tibi and An-Na'im, which represent the left. In the remainder of this chapter, we shall examine this range of thought and highlight some of the problems inherent in all these perspectives in order to establish a credible Muslim approach without indulging in apologetics. The fact is that the parties of the right reflect the thinking of a large segment of the Muslim world, which is profoundly influenced by a narrative of grievance, while those of the left can be regarded as a group who are beginning to provide a critique that would enable Muslims to live more readily in a globally interconnected world.

Muslim Writers on Human Rights

Maududi's 1977 tract *Human Rights in Islam*[12] is regarded as an influential text in the field of Human Rights for a large segment of Muslims who tend towards the salafist/radical spectrum of the

Islamic faith.[13] He compares and contrasts Western and Islamic notions of Human Rights and attacks the idea that the West invented Human Rights while the rest of the world was steeped in ignorance. Maududi's main criticism of the Western concept of Human Rights is that it is humanistic and posits only a secular understanding of man, in contrast to Islam's conception based on divine disclosure and mindfulness of God's rights (*haqq Allah*), which always supersede Human Rights (*haqq adami*). He refers to Human Rights as 'part and parcel of Islamic faith', implying that these rights existed from the beginning of Islam, whereas the West had no concept of Human Rights before the 17th century.

Maududi continues by arguing that the Western charter of Human Rights has no enforcement of sanctions to make it effective. Since Islam's 'charter of Human Rights' was conferred by God, Maududi argues that it is transcendent, inalienable, perfect and permanent, and inherently enforceable as God's commands over Muslims. This cannot be changed or rescinded by human action. Maududi supports his position by citing a number of verses in the Qur'an that bolster the notion of Human Rights. Thus, for example, he refers to Q 5:32 ('whoever kills a soul … it is as if he had slain mankind entirely. And whoever saves one, it is as if he had saved mankind entirely'), where murder is equated with the slaughter of all humanity. According to Maududi, all necessary rights are guaranteed by the Qur'an and Islamic law. Maududi's certainty about the independence and the all-encompassing expression and legitimacy of Human Rights as established in the Qur'an and generally underpinned by Islamic law prevents him from concerning himself with the substance of Human Rights as understood in the West, since he regards that as unnecessary. His accusation of the West's arrogance in its espousal of its version of Human Rights has an element of ironic and apparently unwitting overstatement on his part, since his position could also be perceived as the epitome of arrogant assertiveness. From this point of view, the argument of the two sides is locked in a disconcerting impasse.

Maududi's dichotomous and simplistic division between the Islamic notion of human rights and that of the West was adopted in the Arab world by Sayyid Qutb, another Islamist thinker who developed the arguments propounded by Maududi by asserting that Islam balances individual and social rights in the correct proportion since it is decreed by God. The commentator Heiner Bielefeldt, a German professor of Human Rights, suggests that Maududi's choice of rights reflects an a priori assumption that Islam needs no supplement or correction and that it is complete in its doctrine of Human Rights.[14] However, he also points out that Maududi remains silent on the rights of women which, under the international standards as espoused by the West and enshrined in the UDHR, demand the equality of women as a human right. He points out that Maududi 'fails to … address … the ban on conversion from Islam to another religion and the restriction on interreligious marriage',[15] which violate Article 16 and Article 18 of the UDHR respectively. Bielefeldt's comments highlight the lack of self-critical awareness by such Islamist writers as Maududi and Sayyid Qutb, which prevents any debate or discussion between their notion of Islamic Human Rights and that contained in the UDHR. Equally, a similar observation could be made towards Western positions from an Islamic point of view.

While Maududi and Qutb argue for the existence of Human Rights even though they give the concept an exclusive Islamic flavour, Hizb ut-Tahrir posit that the notion of Human Rights itself is an invention of the West used in its campaign against Islam. This version of Human Rights is covered in a tract developed by Hizb ut-Tahrir entitled 'The American Campaign to Suppress Islam'.[16] The aim of this document is to warn Muslims that the West is engaged in an ideological struggle against Islam with a view to dominate the faith and establish its power over the world. This group regards the world as a global battlefield for supremacy between Islam and the West: the West propagates the ungodly ideals of democracy, pluralism and Human Rights laced with free-market ideology, which, according to Hizb ut-Tahrir, are anathema to the core of Islamic beliefs. This bleak ideological battlefield has no place for compromise or indeed for the examination of nuance and subtlety that may indeed problematise the perceived power struggle between these two competing ideologies. According to Hizb ut-Tahrir, an Islamic state cannot accept the freedoms championed by the West, including the freedom to choose one's religion. Muslims have no choice but to remain Muslims. Indeed, they should be endeavouring to convert (which they refer to as 'revert') non-Muslims to the true and final faith, which is Islam.[17]

Universal Islamic Declaration of Human Rights

In 1981, the Islamic Council for Europe drew up and published its Universal Islamic Declaration of Human Rights (UIDHR),[18] which was followed by the Cairo Document of 1990 published by the Organisation of Islamic Cooperation (OIC). In its foreword, the Declaration states, that 'human rights are an integral part of the overall Islamic order'. The drafters of the UIDHR regarded Human Rights as part of Islam and saw no need for any reform or new thought on this issue in the light of later historical developments or external standards. As with Maududi and Qutb, the OIC declared that the rights enshrined in the UIDHR are 'of divine origin, no ruler, government, assembly or authority can curtail or violate them'. It elevates duties above rights, implying a criticism of the UDHR's exclusive focus on rights. The UIDHR charter sets out 23 rights regarded as inviolable and inalienable. Amongst these, Article 13 includes the right to religious freedom: 'Every person has a right to freedom of conscience and worship in accordance with his religious beliefs.' This right is, in effect, more limited than it appears, since no mention is made of a Muslim being able to change his faith. The same Article also states: 'All persons are equal before the law and are entitled to equal opportunities.' This right appears to contradict Q 2:282, a literal interpretation of which equates two female witnesses as the equivalent of one male, with implications that are inimical to women's rights for equality as female testimony may consequently not be deemed 'basic evidence' (*hujja asliyya*).

Therefore, the Professor of Islamic Studies Ron Shaham points out:

> The majority of jurists agree that female testimony is entirely excluded, not only from all Quranic punishments (*ḥudūd*) and penal ('*uqūbat*) cases, but also from claims of marriage and divorce, because these fields encompass issues dealing primarily with the human body

and its status (for example, a marriage contract entitles the husband to exclusive enjoyment of his wife's body). As for financial matters, according to a literal interpretation of Q 2:282, the standard testimony is of two males; if, however, there is only one male witness, it is permitted to replace the second male witness with two females. The traditional rationalisation for the two-to-one ratio is that females are forgetful and imprecise in relating details. The two female witnesses remind each other about the details of the transactions under consideration, thereby complementing each other and producing a full testimony, equal to that of one male.[19]

Generally, Muslim legal opinion deems female testimony as not being 'basic evidence'. Reformers, such as Muhammad Abduh, explain – apparently without irony – this discrepancy of regard towards women by arguing that 'women's testimony is disregarded because females [are] preoccupied with domestic responsibilities which prevent them … from developing memory skills, precision in details, and proficiency in such public matters as contracts'.[20]

Thus it would seem that the discourse on Human Rights in the Islamic world is today dominated by Islamist ideologues. However, another current of thinking developed by Muslim scholars and intellectuals is more critical of this type of polemical exchange dividing the Islamic world from the rest of the world in absolutist and dogmatic terms. Writers such as Abdullahi An-Na'im and Bassam Tibi, mentioned above, come to mind, while there are other important thinkers, such as the leading Algerian scholar Mohammed Arkoun, who was Professor of Islamic Thought at the Sorbonne, and Mohamed Charfi, a Tunisian professor of law and Human Rights activist. All these thinkers go beyond the closed corpus of the Islamists towards a more open discourse that encourages Muslims to think more widely about their faith, heritage and the limits of the legal framework provided by a conservative reading of Islamic law, especially as constructed through classical *fiqh* or jurisprudence. An-Na'im's starting assumption is that the normative understanding of Islamic law, which he calls 'traditional shariah', and Human Rights are incompatible. He emphasises the fact that if Muslims wish to assert their right to self-determination – the notion of personhood based upon their particular view of Muslim identity – they will not be able to do so under traditional sharia without violating the right of others. By this argument he touches upon issues where Islamic law fails to measure up to what is understood elsewhere as universal Human Rights. In his view, the inferior status of women and non-Muslims and even the continuing existence of the possibility of slavery, which has not been abolished by Islamic law, therefore derogate from the universal principles of Human Rights. An-Na'im is clear that this is an impediment in Islamic law and, therefore, it requires to be reformed, so that these issues are addressed and, in effect, done away with.[21]

An-Na'im sets himself an agenda to 'identify areas of conflict … and seek a reconciliation and positive relationship between the two systems'.[22] Conceding that there is a debate about the 'genuine universality' of the UDHR, An-Na'im states: 'this does not mean that there are no universal and binding standards' or that 'enforcement should be abandoned'. He argues that a normative principle that runs through all cultures, and which calls on others to treat us as we wish to be treated ourselves, opens up the possibility of discussing and developing a framework of a 'universal standard of human rights'. He further contends that the type of rights that qualify as universal are those which people are entitled to by virtue of being human, hence they do not belong exclusively to any specific culture or religion. Although this argument is attractive to Western ways of thinking, we would suggest that it does not conform to authentic notions of what it means to be human in Islamic discourse, particularly in relation to gender.

An-Na'im, however, does recognise the problem of Islamic law's intractability concerning the status of women, slavery and non-Muslims. He claims that this important point may be addressed by a new reading of the holy texts that takes into account the fact that they came into existence in a particular historical context. Therefore, for example, slavery was not forbidden when Islamic law took shape because slavery was generally accepted in the 7th century and continued to be so for centuries afterwards. What Islam did was to regulate and humanise the practice in a number of ways, including encouraging the freeing of slaves and limiting the opportunities for creating slavery to during warfare, when prisoners could be taken as slaves. An-Na'im draws on the notion

of an evolving Islamic law as postulated by the Sudanese scholar
Mahmood Mohamed Taha (1909–1985). This approach advocates
a new methodology that gives primacy to the more metaphysical
and ethically driven Qur'anic verses of the earlier Meccan period
over those of the later Medinan verses that were revealed when
the Prophet was ruler of his community. This approach effectively
reverses the legal principle of abrogation (*naskh*) whereby verses
of the Qur'an revealed later are given primacy over those revealed
on earlier occasions. An-Na'im further lists verses that are
'discriminatory' and calls for such verses to be 'repealed' in favour
of laws based on the earlier Meccan revelations that encourage
Muslims to value equality and justice between people.

An-Na'im argues that this radical rereading of the Qur'an
may be achieved by recognising that the relevant Qur'anic rules
developed in Medina have fulfilled their transitional purpose
and, therefore, can be set aside for earlier more general revelations. Hence Q 4:34, which establishes male guardianship over
women, would be displaced by an earlier verse such as Q 33:55,
which affirms the spiritual equality of the sexes. Spiritual equality
is therefore deemed to include legal and social equality in
conformity with what An-Na'im refers to as the original intent of
the Qur'anic message. This line of thinking is controversial and
has not been readily accepted by traditional Muslims never mind
by Islamic radicals. The idea of verses being 'transitional' or being
'repealed' is in itself highly problematic. It could be argued that
An-Na'im's position is optimistic at best, since there is nothing
to prevent the process of abrogation, as argued by him, being
reversed again by other Islamic scholars or groups. Underlying
this entire approach are other difficulties, including the fact
that, in Sunni Islam for example, there is no central authority to
legitimise changes and sharia itself has a piecemeal aspect since
it is made up of a series of juristic pronouncements without any
final consensus among the schools of law. This problem becomes
even more urgent in the light of current global pressures and
stresses, especially in the Muslim world. We confess this is a
pessimistic assessment of An-Na'im's proposed solution to the
difficult passages in the Qur'an and hadith. Such changes as he
would like to see require a new world view which has to arise

from the Muslim world itself as an organic and evolutionary process.

An-Na'im recalls the Rushdie affair.[23] He points out that the death sentence for apostasy pronounced by Ayatollah Khomeini was incorrect in Islamic law, given that it is not a lynch law but a developed legal system that demands due process. Therefore no Muslim leader has a right to call for anyone's death by issuing a fatwa in any circumstances, nor can a death sentence be passed upon a citizen of a non-Islamic state as this is beyond the ambit of sharia.

Bassam Tibi's Views

Bassam Tibi shares many of the views of An-Na'im, stating that an Islamic definition of international law that claims the right to impose the faith on the entire world contradicts the idea of a worldwide 'cultural pluralism'.[24] Tibi calls for 'an inter-civilisational morality covering human rights and democracy' – principles that he regards as standards of civilisation necessary for a peaceful and just international order. Without this philosophy, Tibi believes that conflict between Western globalisation, which fuels modernity, and the new Islamic absolutism, which drives contemporary Islamism, is inevitable. Both sides, he argues, wish to dominate the present world order. However, he claims that neither side will achieve its aim to be the sole paradigm of the world order.

Tibi argues that the Western world has to set aside its aim to be the dominant global ethos and to recognise that the North–South economic gap has to be addressed. Furthermore, the present Eurocentric legal discourse has to adapt to a new world view. Equally, he points out that the claim for 'the dominance of an Islamic notion of law' is also impractical and indeed, invidious. He calls for a dialogue because replacing one ideology with the other is not feasible. Tibi desires to establish a genuinely pluralist 'international morality' and regards the UDHR as a working basis for such a project.[25]

There is a profound problem in this argument when one considers the claims of political Islam, which are dogmatic, absolutist and totally exclusive and which reject the right of the 'other' to any claim for acceptance. Only an Islam that embraces pluralism in its broadest sense would be able to contribute to this essential discourse. Such a generous world view, Tibi argues, was part of an earlier enlightened Islam as practised, for example, in Umayyad Spain and among the Muʻtazilis or rationalists in the medieval period. Islam therefore has resources in its historical experience on which Muslims have been able to draw and assimilate into the Muslim world through conversation, examination and cultural borrowing from other traditions. Tibi's discourse does not support multiculturalism, as such – as opposed to pluralism which entails an active engagement with the 'other' which can be deemed an Islamic value. He believes that multiculturalism leads to a ghetto mentality, ostensibly encouraging a sort of passive tolerance that is based on cultural relativism where everything goes and is tolerated in an opportunistic manner.

Tibi champions, on the contrary, a mode of thinking that engages with other cultures in a positive manner, so that both or all parties may learn from one another in a desire to create a more habitable world for all. He criticises such ideologues as Maududi for denying that Muslims are 'human' by excluding them from the UDHR and stating that there were Islamic Human Rights separate from, and prior to, the modern philosophy of Human Rights that belong exclusively to Muslims. The problem with this ahistorical position is that it appears to deny any substance to Islamic discourse on Human Rights – according to Tibi, Human Rights are a modern invention rising from the cultural and political history and experience of the West which is evolving through the auspices of the UN and its agencies into positive law applicable to the community of nations that make up the UN and, consequently, the world at large.

In fact, Tibi is attempting to rethink the basis of Islamic thought by inviting contemporary Muslim discourse to rediscover the rationalist and ethical underpinnings of early Islamic thought and indeed the overriding ethos of the Qur'an, which seeks to establish a just and balanced society. Tibi's argument claims to be based on Islamic ideas and ethics, which are not foreign to modern notions of Human Rights based upon the dignity of the person. These ideas and ethics would not only subsist in such a worldwide conversation but would also take an active part in deepening it into an ethical convergence between cultures and peoples to create a more habitable human world providing the basis for peaceful co-existence. However, Tibi's position can be regarded as essentially secular and humanistic, no matter how much he dresses it up in an Islamic garb, and so may be unaccept-able per se by Islamist thinkers and ideologues whose positions are subscribed to by many Muslims worldwide, which grants it a normative legitimacy in keeping with the Foucauldian notion of power that creates knowledge. The identity and world view of most Muslims are thus inextricably tied to a belief in the One God and His commands as set out in the Qur'an, the sacred texts derived from it, and the life and sayings of the Prophet as they understand them.

Tibi's position could be regarded as heretical and, as it stands, may not be heard but would be simply rejected. A more practical approach is provided by the Iranian scholar Abdolkarim Soroush, who argues that 'contemporary advocates on Human Rights can claim no monopoly on truth and justice: nonetheless, religious societies, precisely because of their religious nature, need to seri-ously engage in discussion of the issues they pose ... extra-religious debates of our day, which happen to concern Human Rights must be viewed as worthy and useful exchanges of opinion in Islamic society'.[26] Soroush's position, less didactic than that held by Tibi, may open the door for a reasonable exchange of views between conservative Muslim scholars and those who call for new thinking with regard to Human Rights and indeed on the status of sharia.

This debate about the role of Islam and Human Rights is a continuing one, with many Muslim voices taking part. For example, Mohamed Charfi, who was at one time Minister of Education in Tunisia, writes in his book *Islam and Liberty* that: 'a large number of rules in classical Muslim or sharia law are contrary to human rights as these are today understood by the international community: each such rule is an affront to the principles of individual liberty, human equality in general and gender equality in particular, and to respect for the physical integrity of human beings'.[27] Charfi argues that these elements of Muslim law were not sent down by God but shaped by human beings and are capable of being revised and reshaped by them.

To ask for a new attitude from Muslims is to request a change not only of heart but of identity. For Charfi, 'Muslim law is based on three fundamental inequalities: the superiority of men over women, of Muslims over non-Muslims and of free persons over slaves'.[28] Therefore, he advocates a profound revision of Islamic thought that requires a new reading of Islamic history and law and a society that enables dissent, secularism and freedom of belief. This condition presumes a re-evaluation of the role of education, even a critique of faith, a revolution in governance in Muslim countries, and a new conception of the role of Islamic scholarship and modes of thought.

Another North African, Mohammed Arkoun, in a paper entitled 'The Foundationalists and the Problems of Foundationalism',[29] puts forward the argument that, by locating the law in texts where it did not really exist, Muslims sacralised it and in turn gave it the authority to authenticate oppressive regimes. This gave rise to a certain symbiosis between the state and the religious law that has operated in a toxic interdependency and has continued to this day. He calls for the development of new modes of thinking utilising modern methods of intellectual and textual analysis that recognise the fact that Islamic law has been sacralised and ossified in this way, by sourcing the Islamic legal system from sacred texts where they are only partly located.

Muslim female writers in modern times, such as Fatema Mernissi, Amina Wadud and Leila Ahmed, have started writing from a new female perspective, asserting feminist ideas and women's rights, not only about the law but also about the values and ethos underpinning traditional Islamic mores and societies. This is in striking contrast to the orthodox male conservative juristic writing and it has destabilised the conforming and hardened modes of thinking about the role and meaning of Islamic law, opening the way to new thinking on the original sources of the law in the Islamic world. Their work, which is based within the Muslim tradition, is just a beginning – but it is a momentous one that is already having an important influence in the Islamic world, where feminist currents of thought, which are inevitably connected to Human Rights are disseminated by the new media (including social media) and are taking root. We discuss this more fully in Chapter 13, the critique at the end of this book.

Notwithstanding the superficial reflection of Islamist discourse and its depredations of Human Rights in the Western media, and its influence in existing power structures in the Muslim world, if we look more closely at the intellectual developments in the Muslim world and among the Muslim intelligentsia, some of whom are working and writing in the comparative safety of academic institutions in the Western world, we notice the birth of new thinking not only about Muslim culture in general, but also about Human Rights and indeed about the role of law. Fawaz Gerges of the London School of Economics discusses these tumultuous changes in the Middle East, which he describes as creating a '[p]sychological and epistemological rupture [in the region] that has shaken the authoritarian order to its very foundation and introduced a new language and a new era of contentious politics and revolutions'.[30] As the failure of the Arab Spring – a series of protests and demonstrations which took place across the Middle East and North Africa from 2010 – has shown, change is still an ideal rather than a process in place.

Discourse on Human Rights as a whole is a continuous process and new thinking is being developed constantly. As Human Rights lawyer Professor Ann Elizabeth Mayer states: 'international human rights have been reconfigured and expanded, as the comparison of the skeletal 1948 Universal Declaration of Human Rights with the vast panoply of subsequently developed instruments reveals'.[31] Mayer cites, among others, changes made by the 1999 International Labour Organisation's Worst Forms of Child Labour Convention, the International Criminal Court, established in 2002, and the Right to Water, enunciated in 2002 by the Committee on Economic, Social and Cultural Rights in General Comment 15. These particular instances of the enactment of Human Rights provisions cover problems that affect the entire world, including Muslim societies. In her article 'The Islam and Human Rights Nexus: Shifting Dimensions',[32] Mayer makes the point, based on her years of experience in this field in the Muslim world, that neither Islam nor Human Rights are static entities and their relationship is not conflictual or essentially so, but rather they are the products of politics, which creates a changing and malleable relationship both hostile and promising. She terms this relationship hostile, as it is driven to an extent by the foreign policies of countries, especially that of the United States towards the Islamic world, which is negatively perceived by millions of Muslims; but as she points out that can also be seen as promising, in that Muslim intellectuals and even some politicians see Human Rights not as the sole product of Western thought any longer, but the evolving realisation of other societies including Muslim societies. She states that they are moving towards a more global understanding of Human Rights. Mayer's analysis thus suggests a new accommodation between Human Rights and Muslim societies that is not driven by the old and misguided contradiction between Western notions of Human Rights and the countervailing idea of an essentially Islamic conception of the issue, exclusive to Muslims.

Conclusion

We tend to agree with Mayer's cautious but optimistic assessment as global developments in today's electronically connected world are helping shape debates and discourses in new ways. Many younger Muslim men and women in their own countries as well as in the diaspora are beginning to realise how the term Islam is often used instrumentally through programmes of Islamisation that violate the basic rights of their citizens, who, when they speak out against such conduct, are often branded as apostates (in the case of Muslims) or accused of blasphemy (in the case of non-Muslims). Depending on their particular geopolitical interests of the moment, Western countries that arrogate to themselves a proprietary relationship to Human Rights often help to bolster or discredit such regimes. This factor is a constant threat to the implementation not only of Human Rights but of international law as a whole. Both are liable to be used for ulterior purposes. As more people, both in the Muslim and Western worlds, begin to realise that this body of international law is a foundational principle today, accepted as a universal set of values regardless of their origin, Human Rights will have a greater chance of becoming a standard by which human action will be judged. No longer will either camp have the opportunity of obfuscating issues affecting humanity on the basis of narrow ethno-centric, religiously obsessed, gender-oppressive political aspirations that hold their societies in bondage. Notwithstanding the important misgivings expressed by Amartya Sen and others about the efficacy of Human Rights and, indeed, international law, we would argue that in a globalised world, where the knowledge society embellished by social media is beginning to become more prominent, this seems to be a positive trend.

Regarding the larger epistemological problem faced by Muslims confronting modernity, there is a need for using new disciplines of knowledge, including those of social anthropology, semiotics, linguistics and critical thinking, amongst others. Whether this new thinking will take place in the Muslim world, where the intellectual environment is not yet conducive to this type of discourse, is doubtful. Muslim scholars working in the West will also have to break down barriers regarding the generally negative way Islam is perceived in the Western world, and the paucity of resources for genuine scholarship. However, there is more hope for such new thinking in the Muslim diaspora. There is still an element of independence and intellectual daring among the intelligentsia working in Western academic institutions of higher learning, where they are in the privileged position of being able to critique Western notions and at the same time, while not being apologetic about Islam, to develop an authentic Human Rights discourse from an Islamic viewpoint that could be useful to the wider debate on the issue.

Criminal Justice in Islam

Criminal justice in Islam, or a perceived lack thereof, has unfortunately become the standard by which the entire notion of sharia is regarded. Punishments for certain acts, which in the Western world have been de-criminalised or viewed as being outside the purview of the state, are seen by many as sharia's inability to come to grips with the modern social realities. Calls to 'bring back the sharia' are at times accompanied by draconian punishments for offences such as theft, adultery and apostasy, some of which have either been abolished in many countries of the West and are no longer deemed criminal offences. They are relegated to the sphere of private actions which may be deemed 'immoral' by some but not justiciable.

In those Muslim countries where harsh punishments are meted out, they are projected as being mandated by the Qur'an, and so carry the maximum (*hadd*) penalties. However, there is an authentic and respected tradition and interpretation of these offences that argues that these penalties were established as deterrents but are not easily implemented owing to the exacting evidentiary requirements. In an imperfect world, such offences were open to a discretionary approach (*ta'zir*) that takes into consideration the type of mitigating circumstances that populate the real world. As the sharia system historically was incapable of enacting the penalties on account of the onerous and sometime irrational evidentiary requirements, more realistic and pragmatic discretionary punishments were developed by the political authorities instead.

Given this complex background, this chapter aims to explore whether or not Islamic law has a comprehensive criminal justice system and, if it does, how it is to be implemented. If punishments were prescribed in the Qur'an, which entity should be responsible for implementing them? Was it the *qadi* courts, with their idealist notions of evidentiary requirements, or was it the political authority, which took upon itself the right to uphold public order under its *siyasa* jurisdiction? This chapter will also highlight Islamic criminal law under the classical system, outlining its main characteristics; the interface of such a system with the requirements of the Muslim political authority to maintain an orderly society; the reform of the criminal justice system, leading to penal codes that created more certainty; and the abolition of the penal codes in some Muslim countries in the last quarter of the 20th century when a call arose for 'the return of sharia' without the safeguards that originally protected the individual, either under classical sharia, or the *siyasa* developments that were underpinned by it.

Criminal Law in the Classical Period

Classical Islamic law developed within a particular political, legal and epistemological context. Its structure and content can only make sense when viewed within this context. Criminal law as we now understand the term is the product of a different outlook and time and connected to the theory of the modern state that developed in the West during the 17th century. The punishment of crime in the modern world is the signal application of state power over its citizens. According to the sociologist Anthony Giddens, 'in the pre-modern world, the state asserted authority over a fairly narrow range of matters. States lacked the means to regulate social life generally.'[1] The modern conceptualisation of crime and penal law, as pointed out by the legal historian Wael Hallaq, was not shared in any marked way by the Muslim jurists of the pre-modern era, for, as he points out, their notions served 'epistemic imperatives that fundamentally differed from those enshrined in the modern state and its systems.'[2]

What is today called Islamic criminal law is actually drawn from three categories of rules within classical legal literature. The first of these incorporates the rules on *hadd* (pl. *hudud*), which signify the limits prescribed by God. These *hadd* offences (between five and seven in number) refer to a group of punishments given in the Qur'an for crimes considered to be against the rights of God. These can also include punishments stipulated in the *hadith* – notably the punishment for illicit sexual relations, as Esposito defines it, fixed by the second caliph Umar. The rules covering *hadd* protect four central interests and values of society, namely public order, private property, sexual behaviour and personal honour. Those who violate these interests are threatened with severe punishment. *Fiqh* offers a diversity of interpretations of offences attracting *hadd* penalties. Five are recognised by all four Sunni schools of law. These offences include illicit sexual relations (*zina*), false accusation of illicit relations (*qadhf*), imbibing alcohol (*shurb al-khamr*), theft (*sariqa*) and highway robbery (*qat' al-tariq*). The Shafi'i school also considers murder and bodily harm as a *hadd*, while the Maliki school considers insurrection and apostasy (*ridda*) as a *hadd*.[3] Traditionally in Shi'i Islam some scholars argued that in the absence of the Imam the *hudud* could not be applied. Twelver Shi'is hold that their twelfth and last Imam, who is descended from the Prophet's cousin the first Imam, Ali b. Abi Talib, is in *ghayba*, 'hidden in the world'. At the end of time he will return as the Mahdi and restore justice to mankind.

By today's standards, the punishments for *hadd* are considered extreme, for example stoning or lashes for illicit sexual relations and amputation of the hand for theft. At the same time, *hadd* offences are subject to stringent and highly technical proof requirements. Circumstantial evidence, for instance, is not permitted and the law provides various means by which the accused may escape punishment. One of the significant limitations is the doctrine of uncertainty based on a Prophetic report that states: 'Ward off the fixed punishment from the Muslims on the strength of *shubha* as much as you can.' *Shubha* here means the element of doubt.

The second category commonly included in Islamic criminal law is *qisas*, or retaliation, and deals with murder and the infliction of bodily harm short of death. The principle of *lex talionis* governs *qisas* offences and the punishment for murder or inflicting bodily harm is either retaliation or compensation. Here, equivalence limits the law of retaliation and the guilty party suffers the same harm as he/she inflicted on the victim. Compensation is sometimes an alternative to retaliation and is at the election of the victim or his/her relatives and is measured against the full blood price for the killing of a free Muslim male. Unlike *hadd* offences, which are enforced by the political authority, homicide and bodily injury are private actions prosecuted by the victim or his/her family. This operates by way of a tort, and the court's role in these cases is essentially civil rather than criminal.

The third category under the heading of Islamic criminal law is *ta'zir*, a residual category in the sense that it serves as the basis for punishing actions that are considered sinful or destructive of public order but are not punishable as *hadd* or *qisas*. The type of actions punishable under *ta'zir* are not clearly categorised and *ta'zir* applies when *hadd* or *qisas* penalties cannot be imposed on account of their strict procedural requirements, which are subject to detailed regulations in the *fiqh* literature. By contrast, *ta'zir* is essentially a discretionary power of the ruler and governed by standards rather than strict rules. It is a means of achieving a level of public order and morals in a pragmatic manner where the strict rules of *hadd* do not apply. The political authority enjoys considerable flexibility and *ta'zir* can be used to avoid the stringent and impractical evidentiary requirements of *hadd*. However, in applying penalties the ruler had to be guided by the culpability of the offender, the heinousness of the act and the needs of public welfare.[4]

The panoply of rules that we group together today as Islamic criminal law did not constitute a unitary body of law in the classical period. They appear arbitrary from the modern perspective. The categorisation is based on the nature of legal rights in Islamic law as the rights of God and the rights of man. The claims of man (which includes those of women) are conceptualised as property, and disputants are viewed as proprietors who control its disposition. The political authority merely adjudicates such claims when individuals turn to it for help. The claims of God, on the other hand, are rights and obligations belonging to God, and here the political authority (initially the caliphate and later the sultanate acting on behalf of the caliphate) represents God against individuals. These claims include largely acts of worship, prayer, fasting, pilgrimage and so on. *Hadd* punishments are also claims of God, while *qisas* is viewed purely as a claim between individuals.

Interface between the Classical Formulation and the Political Authority

Understandably, a system of classification that was largely arbitrary, idealistic and impractical would not have been able to meet the growing needs of a Muslim polity that was expanding geographically over many cultures. Consequently, the political authorities did not regard sharia as the only law and the *qadi* courts as the only arena for disputes to be resolved. In fact, in the field of criminal law the *siyasa* ('government in accordance with the revealed law'), which was largely implemented through administrative regulations underpinned by the different judicial functionaries and institutions such as the *shurta* (police) and the *muhtasib* (market inspector), began to take over many of these types of activity, included criminal jurisdiction.

The classical position continued alongside the expanding *siyasa* dispensation. It was only in the time of the Ottomans, whose sultanate extended from North Africa to Iraq and into Eastern Europe, that a clear delineation and relationship between these two streams of law were worked out. The Ottoman Empire drew on the earlier influence of the Hanafi law in Anatolia and developed a system not dissimilar to the *siyasa* precedent whereby Hanafi doctrine was transformed by the state into an unambiguous body of legal rules and of state-enacted laws known as the *qanun-name*s. The earliest Ottoman criminal legislation dates back to the reign of Mehmed II (r. 1444–1446 and 1451–1481).[5] This was revised and extended by his successor, Bayezid II (r. 1481–1512). Around 1534, during the reign of Suleyman the Magnificent (r. 1520–1566), a new *qanun-name* was promulgated.

All these Ottoman rules gave rise to what Rudolph Peters, a leading specialist in this field, refers to as the Ottoman Criminal

Code, which contains detailed procedures on crimes, their definitions, their fiscalisation, the relationships between *qadi*s and the political authorities, and the protection of the liberty of the individual as understood in the context of that time. While the Ottoman dispensation may not be representative of the entire Muslim world, it involved most of the Middle East for some four to five centuries and therefore is highlighted as a case study by Peters because it offers elaborate reports of what happened in *qadi* courts and in the institutions set up by the political authority.

Reform of the Criminal Justice System

The late 18th century onwards witnessed the eclipse of Islamic criminal law through the modernisation and Westernisation of the Muslim world as Western powers and Russia extended their influence resulting in colonial conquests in places such as Indonesia, India, North Africa and Central Asia.[6] This historical development called for reform of criminal law in areas where Western countries colonised Muslim countries as well as Muslim lands that were not colonised by but interacted with different cosmopolitan demographics, such as those of the Ottoman Empire, including Egypt. This development also had an impact on countries where Islamic justice was being conducted along tribal lines, such as Arabia, Yemen and Afghanistan. Here, classical Islamic law remained in place, but implementation was defined through penal codes.

Reform took place in three basic modes, namely the complete abolition of Islamic criminal law, a reform of Islamic criminal law and reform of the *siyasa* justice system. In traditional areas such as Arabia and Yemen, a tribal form of justice continued. In India and northern Nigeria, British colonialists used different methods. In India, for example, between 1790 and 1807 the British totally transformed Islamic criminal law. Private prosecution was replaced with prosecution by the state. Anyone who had committed an act of wilful murder could be sentenced to death and the heirs of the victim, in murder cases, could no longer rely on talion for compensation. *Hadd* offences remained in form but lost their significance in substance, in that the penalties of stoning and amputation were abolished and the numerous defences for *hadd* cases were repealed. Islamic law, which had existed only in name, was effectively abolished in 1861 when a new Indian Penal Code was established.

In the Ottoman Empire, including Egypt, Islamic law was reformed through the introduction of Criminal Codes from Western countries as part of the *Tanzimat* reforms and more particularly with the promulgation of a penal code in 1840. Various penal codes and Codes of Criminal Procedure were introduced in the Ottoman Empire, which had an important bearing on a large part of the Arab Muslim world, which was under the suzerainty of the Ottomans. In Egypt, legal reform commenced during the rule of Muhammad Ali Pasha (r. 1805–1848), when a short penal code was introduced. Reforms continued well into the 19th and 20th centuries.

In 1899, Sudan, still under British influence, established a penal code based on the Indian Penal Code of 1860. In 1925, it was thoroughly revised. The Sudanese Code differed from those of its Arab neighbours in that it was based on Anglo-Saxon law. Saudi Arabia and North Yemen continued to use traditional Islamic law in penal matters, but other Arab and Islamic countries introduced modern criminal codes based on Western laws. Iran adopted the French system in 1939, and in 1943 Lebanon introduced a system based on French, Italian and Swiss codes. Pakistan inherited the Indian code in 1947, when it became independent. Libya, using Italian and Egyptian precedents, established its penal code in 1953. Morocco took on the French code in 1962, as did Algeria and Egypt in 1966. Iraq also adopted a new code in 1969, based on the Egyptian code.

In Nigeria, the British, who continued to have influence in that country, followed a similar course and allowed Islamic criminal law to continue, not influencing its application except for those parts that were repugnant to the values of natural justice as understood by them at the time. Islamic law was thus domesticated and the implementation of Islamic criminal law ended as late as 1960, with the introduction of the 1959 Penal Code for northern Nigeria.

Certain principles, well known in the West, characterised the penal codes in these countries, such as the legality principle – there can be no crime or punishment except by law (*nullum crimen nulla poena sine lege*). Another principle is the non-retroactivity of laws, a third the concept of territoriality of jurisdiction, with some exceptions, and a fourth the tenet that certain crimes committed abroad by citizens or non-citizens that affect the vital interests of the state may be tried by the state. The last principle enabled a state to try a citizen for an offence or misdemeanour committed abroad if the act is also a crime in the mother country. The past few decades, however, have seen the resurgence of a strong movement to reapply the Islamic laws of *hadd* and *qisas* in certain Muslim countries as part of their commitment to the establishment of what they consider an authentic Islamic order. In the next section, we shall examine the impact of this development on the rights of the individual and on sharia as a whole.

Abolition of the Penal Codes and the Reintroduction of Islamic Criminal Law

Since 1972, Islamic criminal law has been reintroduced in some countries of the Muslim world which have either repealed the penal codes they inherited from the Western countries as part of the modernisation process mentioned above or made additions to them, as in the case of Pakistan, which inherited the Indian Penal Code of 1860 when it became independent in 1947. Traditional Islamic criminal law, as mentioned, also continued to be applied in countries that were not affected by the modernisation process, such as Yemen, Qatar and Saudi Arabia. In the latter country, traditional Islamic law is applied in full, based on the Hanbali school of law. As a concession to modernisation, both Qatar and Yemen promulgated penal codes that did not affect the substantive content of the law but only the method of implementation.

With regard to the rallying call to 'bring back the sharia', the reasons are many and the role of ideology cannot be ignored. For any of the political elite that repeat the call, it is a mark of their Islamicity and a validating factor for their form of rule. It makes a statement in defiance of Western laws that were premised on a philosophical principle that attributes little or no significance to religion. Moreover, Western law is viewed as hegemonic. For large segments of the populations of Muslim countries, Islamic law is seen as the best way of providing for a just and fair society as predicated by the faith, and many people view its observance as a religious duty. It is also seen as a hedge against corruption on earth, a check on venal functionaries and, above all, a method of swift justice, which, in the case of homicide, gives the victim's heirs the right to prosecute for the offence, giving the individual, rather than the state, full control. One often hears of people in countries of the Middle East extolling the virtues of the draconian punishments for their very powerful deterrent effect on crime. For the political elites, a demonstration of Islamic criminal justice has a strong deterrent impact on would-be detractors, and often criminal justice has been used instrumentally to silence dissent – as was evidenced in Sudan with the 1985 execution of Mahmoud Mohammed Taha, the religious thinker, for apostasy when he challenged the regime of the Sudanese president Gaafar Nimeiry.

The implementation of Islamic criminal law in its reintroduced form has not been uniform and has been effected through accretions to existing penal codes, their repeal in some cases, the repeal of some of their sections in others and the introduction of new edicts. Equally, standards of evidence differ across countries and institutions of implementation are also very varied. All of them refer to *hadd*, *qisas* and *ta'zir* in one way or another, but the evidentiary requirements do not conform to the classical Islamic position. While punishments range from amputation, lashings, stoning to decapitation and crucifixion, not all those with authority have resorted to these punishments, though flogging seems to be generally prevalent. In some cases, the judiciary, many of whose members have been trained in methods of Western jurisprudence, have shown a marked reticence to implement strict sharia punishments, and where they do, interference with their decisions by the ruling authority is not unheard of. In some cases, inherited penal codes were tested and impugned for not conforming with the principles of Islam and were consequently repealed, whereas in other cases, in Nigeria for example, the power assigned by the federal constitution to the individual states brought into question the very nature of the state and its commitment to any one religion, particularly given its multi-confessional population.

Other serious issues that have arisen are the question of equality in cases of homicide where a Muslim kills a non-Muslim, the value of a woman victim of homicide being half that of a man, and questions of evidence and the value of a woman's testimony. On many of these issues the new codes are silent.

What we are beginning to notice is that in many cases classical Islamic law, which historically had an inbuilt balance in that *hadd* offences called for a very high degree of evidentiary exactitude before a penalty was imposed, are now implemented not by religious functionaries operating under a sharia system but largely by military or other autocratic regimes operating outside it. So-called sharia is meted out in the name of sharia without any sharia safeguards or due process.

There is no doubt that the new penal codes violate the fundamental principles of many Human Rights conventions such as the International Covenant on Civil and Political Rights, the Convention on the Elimination of all Forms of Discrimination Against Women, the UN Convention Against Torture (CAT) and the Convention of the Rights of the Child. In fact, countries such as Libya, Saudi Arabia and Sudan have acceded to the CAT without reservation, even though their criminal codes may be viewed as openly violating many of its principles. This therefore takes us back to the issue of Human Rights and how these are viewed, which we discussed in Chapter 10.

To reiterate, many Muslim countries view Human Rights as a Western invention aimed at undermining Islam and subordinating Muslims at worst or buttressing Western geopolitical interests at best. Selective adherence to Human Rights tenets in many Western countries, coupled with support given to autocratic Muslim and non-Muslim countries by Western states on a selective basis, has undermined the value of Human Rights as a universal principle. Unfortunately, the debate between the Muslim countries and the Western world is locked in an impasse.[7] The way forward does not appear easy, given the conflictual times in which we are living. Rudolph Peters argues that stances taken by Muslim countries have placed them into intractable positions whereby any detraction on their part would appear to their constituents as a capitulation to foreign interests at the cost of Islam – something akin to apostasy. He posits that coercion in the form of strong-arm tactics by Western countries may not work. Instead, he calls for indigenous groups to take a greater lead.[8] From a practical point of view this does not seem a viable proposition, as the moment a foreign Human Rights institution is seen as backing a local NGO, that support itself will discredit the local organisation.

Peters' second proposition is that support for Human Rights could be garnered from within the articles of the Islamic Human Rights Charter itself. However, he recognises its limitations when he says that it upholds certain principles but only to the extent that they do not conflict with sharia.[9] The issue arises as to what should happen if sharia principles, particularly its criminal punishments, conflict with Human Rights principles. One option that could work is a new epistemology and a reading of the text in the context of the modern world, and here approaches posited by Abdullahi an-Naʿim and others have some merit. The question is, who has the authority to pioneer such a process in today's world? Meanwhile, Islamic criminal justice will prevail in those countries where new penal codes are promulgated, and cases that hit the headlines will need to be resolved in a manner that is acceptable, given the needs of the state, the opinions of the various Islamists, the influence of various Western countries, the growing power of social media and the ability of the Muslim nation state to balance the various interests with which it has to work.

Islam and Ethics

While morality springs to mind when considering Islam, ethics does not readily lend itself to our present-day notions about Islam or indeed about Muslims. However, this attitude is misleading to say the least. We attempt to explore the essential and enduring relationship between faith and ethics and survey some of the practical effects of ethical thought on Islamic life and Muslim discourse. First, we shall distinguish between ethics and morality.

Morality is a subset of ethics which, from an Islamic perspective, deals with rules, obligations and duties set out in seminal texts that constitute the Islamic world view, namely the Qur'an, hadith and the subsequent positive law or *fiqh* drawn from these foundational texts. Islamic morality draws on the sayings and life of the Prophet along with the reports of the lives and sayings of the Prophet's immediate followers who make up the *sahaba*, and the Rightly-Guided Caliphs who presided over the young Muslim community in the years following the Prophet's death. For the Shi'a, morality is founded on the guidance of their Imams as well as the Sunna of the Prophet as transmitted through their Imams. Morality, in this case, is underpinned by the sovereign fiat of God as presented in the holy texts and the exemplary lives of the Prophet and his immediate followers, which provide its legitimacy and efficacy. Where the obligations are not clearly set out, the texts are open to interpretation according to agreed hermeneutical readings that developed amongst learned legal scholars over time.

Ethics, on the other hand, does not have ready answers to guide the faithful. It is more a mode of reasoning that seeks to ascertain the good life, something that hypothesises values organically connected to societies that engage in ethical debate and the search for the good. Ethics seeks to establish the good from bad, recognising the qualities of these concepts which are continuously interpreted, discussed and argued about, since definitions in this type of discourse fail to provide final answers. While ethics deliberates appropriate responses to particular problems that confront societies and individuals, it points the way rather than ordains. On the other hand, morality commands and establishes duties that members of a faith group – in our case Muslims – are compelled to fulfil if they are not to suffer punishment of one sort or another. The Islamic spectrum of right conduct and the measure of the good covers what is clearly right and what is clearly wrong – these are the pillars of Muslim morality. However, there are shades of actions and thoughts in between, of varying acceptability, that are open to choice by individuals and societies where morality's presence is not so emphatic. It should be noted from the outset that, for Muslims, both morality and ethics consist of actions and intention. Ethics is in constant search of foundations but it does not look to God to provide them through divine impress. Thus ethics, as we suggest above, is a form of moral reasoning open to contradiction and constant reappraisal, as opposed to the imposition of duties and obligations. On the face of it, it is intellectually or conceptually evasive, always slipping out of focus, and the concepts that make up its discourse are never quite possessed or defined, yet ethics is necessary for all societies and individuals if they are to function meaningfully and with a degree of common accord and cohesiveness. We never escape ethics, although it always escapes us.

Muslims therefore have to engage with their lives and live in their society on the – albeit nebulous – basis of ethics. However, as a cohesive discipline, Islamic ethics does not exist per se and its principles are dispersed in various Islamic sciences such as *fiqh*, *tafsir* (Qur'anic exegesis) and *kalam* (scholastic theology).[1] We should be aware that these ethical principles and values are supported by various texts including philosophical, allegorical and indeed fictional writings, as narrative has always been a potent form of articulating meaning, purpose and the forms of the good life to enliven and engage with an individual's own dilemmas, as we see in the parables in the Qur'an, the life of the Prophet, the Bible and the great Hindu texts of the Upanishads and the *Bhagavad Gita*, as well as in Buddhist teachings.

We should note that there is no specific term for ethics, as understood in Western discourse, in Arabic. Two Arabic words that come close to signifying ethics are *akhlaq* and *adab*. *Akhlaq* signifies a number of qualities, including that of virtue and moral disposition as exemplified by Islamic theology (*kalam*) and in the philosophy (*falsafa*) discovered from Greek antecedents and developed in Islamic civilisation and cultures. It is aligned to the character, nature, temper, culture, morals or manners of an individual. Character is regarded as the site of the good and is driven by an intuitive sense of right and wrong. This essentially subjective awareness of ethical conduct is clearly not evidence in itself that a right choice is being made – it does not 'prove' rightness or good, which are probably not propositions open to 'objective' verification – but it is a real and powerful motivating factor in the choices that people make in their interaction with each other and with the society in which they live.

Adab,[2] on the other hand, is concerned with the Islamic notions of etiquette or refinement of manners, decorum, decency and human engagement, based upon the Prophet's saying '[t]he best amongst you are those who have the best manners and character'.[3] While the bases upon which ethical values are predicated may not be dissimilar to those in the West, their development in the Islamic world differs in that in Muslim culture the distinction between ethics and morality, as articulated in Western culture, is not so apparent. Thus *ilm al-akhlaq*, literally understood as knowledge of morality, is also regarded as the science of ethics. *Adab* encompasses a wide range of meanings and also represents a specific genre in Arabic literature. As the scholar Azim Nanji states, *adab* represents 'the linking of learning and knowledge to right and appropriate human conduct... That is the foundation of the human personality.'[4]

The distinction, as perceived by Muslims, between their notion of ethical conduct and that of other cultures affects the way Muslims approach moral issues. Secularisation in the modern world is largely an instrumental function, part of the economic, political and technological drives of globalisation, which atomises the individual at the expense of a sense of community and communality. This gives rise to a feeling of anomie and alienation in an impersonal world order. The Muslim world is not immune to this disarray of thought, feeling and identity. The relational ethos that Islam (and indeed the other great faiths) engenders is under threat, and Muslims are being challenged to review their own values and perhaps to restore them in new ways. These entail ethical premises that will recreate a teleological sense of direction, containing their humanity as well as their interconnection not only with each other but with the world at large. This is the theoretical position, entailing a desperate search for an authentic but responsive sense of identity, which has to contend compulsively and comprehensively with the pragmatic, apparently enticing attachments of modern societies. This notion of betrayed relationality is extant in all cultures and traditions today. We see it in the notion of *ubuntu* in South Africa, the *agape* as described and lived by Martin Luther King Jr and the notion of *satyagraha* as developed and practised by Mahatma Gandhi.

For Muslims, authenticity is rediscovered in their foundational scriptures. However, this raises questions about the extent of these scriptures. Clearly we have the fundamental scripture of the Qur'an and hadith, or actions and sayings of the Prophet, and the development of jurisprudence or *fiqh*, but there is also an important attachment to this quest, which has to encompass the rediscovery of *kalam*, *falsafa*, *adab* and *akhlaq* in the vast corpus of Islamic literature. These additional forms of discourse present modern Muslims with challenges from within their own tradition, which counteract the present fixation in the Islamic world with sharia and *fiqh*. This has become an urgent need for Muslims, since ideas such as freedom, Human Rights, the rule of law, civil society and good governance, education and ecological responsibilities, including the distribution of wealth, are global concerns that affect the entire world population, and these ideas are endangered in today's political turmoil. For Muslims, especially for those living in non-Muslim countries, while all the above are important, medical ethics, by virtue of major scientific breakthroughs, is creating moral problems on issues ranging from abortion and stem-cell therapies to organ transplants, surrogacy, euthanasia and the prolongation of life. We shall therefore focus on medical ethics and Islam below, and also provide an example of how the issue of ethics generally is being dealt with internationally by a Muslim institution, the Aga Khan Development Network.

Medical Ethics

Islamic medical ethics has a long history dating from the beginnings of Islam. During the classical era, literature on this topic was based on the notions of *adab* and *akhlaq*, which were used to set out the ethical basis of medical practice. The earliest scholar in this field was Ishaq b. Ali al-Ruhawi, a 9th-century physician who lived in Iraq whose works continue to influence the thinking on the topic today. While *adab* writing is concerned with what is considered as universal values, other texts draw on Islamic legal tradition. Today, this discourse on medical ethics is not academic or overly philosophical; it takes many of the values it espouses for granted, looking particularly at their implementation in practical situations whereby, for example, professions are encouraged to ground their practice on ethical precepts. Judges and lawyers, doctors and students and other people holding public positions are therefore invited to act in accordance with ethical values as understood from the holy texts but also from the Hellenic, Abrahamic and Persian medical traditions that established an ecumenical basis for the discipline. Thus al-Razi (d. 925), a great physician and theorist, argues for the necessity of both doctors and patients to have a good moral character including the traits of honesty, sincerity, truthfulness, compassion, patience, tolerance and humility – values that are universal but which are also reinforced by the Qur'an and hadith and which were, and are, regarded as integral to a Muslim's identity. Al-Razi's work has taken on a modern form in the Islamic Code of Medical Ethics, which was established at the First International Conference on Islamic Medicine in Kuwait in January 1981 and is used in various medical schools across the Islamic world.

However, Islamic medical ethics is also governed by sharia and its tributaries – hadith and consequent *fiqh* – whereby an ethical stance is constructed and developed over time, including the pervasive use of fatwas or legal opinions, which have always played an essential role in providing guidance to the good life lived in accordance with the will of God, as interpreted by legal scholars and individuals claiming special distinction in giving knowledge concerning the role of sharia in these cases. As we have shown in this book, sharia and *fiqh* are not, contrary to the ideology of Salafist thinking, a fixed set of divinely inspired rules to be implemented at all times and places. We argue, therefore, that sharia contains a degree of flexibility supported by such doctrines as *maslaha, maqasid, darura* – public interest, purpose and general necessity – but this capacity to change in accordance with contemporary circumstances is countermanded by the firm belief in the integrity of the law as reflecting the commands of God, in providing predictability and uniformity, a common problem of all systems of law, and by the real fear of tampering with a sacred body of law. This structure of comprehending the law gives rise to the problem of how to approach new medical and ethical issues with a sufficient degree of flexibility, while retaining the needful propriety of not ignoring the strictures and rules that underpin sharia, which, we argue, constitutes a central element in the identity of Muslims.

While sharia and its ethical underpinning provide the necessary stability within which new medico-ethical issues can be viewed, some of the presuppositions on which sharia is predicated require re-examination in the light of new scientific breakthroughs in medical science that occur with increasing rapidity, for example as the scholar Fazlur Rahman mentions in respect of test-tube babies.[5] In vitro fertilisation would be a laudable solution if the process was carried out between a married couple. However, the process is compromised when the egg is provided by a stranger to the marriage. In effect, this could be regarded as adultery under sharia, which is concerned not only with the physical act of sexual intercourse but, more importantly, with the genetic descent of the child, which is of fundamental importance to Islamic society on account of protecting the integrity of the family unit and laws of inheritance. For this reason, the Qur'an prescribes a waiting period (*'idda*) after divorce or the death of the husband before the woman may enter into another marriage. Interestingly, this issue is also covered in various national legal systems and private international law – a system where national laws interact – where international surrogacy, for example, is giving rise to complex problems around the nationality of the foetus, the rights and responsibilities of the various parties, and jurisdiction generally.

Another area where an ethical issue could arise concerns anatomical research. Historically, this was sometimes hampered on account of the paucity of bodies available for dissection, but also because of the religious opinion that the cadaver is inviolate and cannot be dissected: post-mortems can present a problem for devout Muslims. An argument can be made that post-mortems in countries that require them may be carried out on the basis of *darura*, because this is called for by the national law which Muslims must respect. Another argument supporting post-mortems and anatomical research is based on the notion of *maslaha* or public interest, and postulates that anatomical research can lead to the furtherance of medical knowledge, which in turn aims to protect life. There is also the question of human transplants of organs. Religious opinion remains divided on this issue. While the *'ulama* remain strongly resistant, general attitudes in many Muslim countries are more amenable to the procedure, holding that it is based upon necessity and the need for sharia to ensure that no harm befalls an individual. Often the debate is complicated by the desire of Muslims not to interfere with God's creation, as humans are cautioned that they should not tamper with this.

The prolongation of life also presents a problem in that the Qur'an enjoins believers to protect life but also describes the afflictions of old age, including the loss of cognitive faculties.[6] This presents a case for not prolonging life where it is a source of suffering or where the individual is in a vegetative state, and also a possible case for euthanasia, although this could be regarded as interfering with God's will – He is deemed to give us life and take it away as He wills. These issues have divided opinions and courts in the Western world as well.[7] There are no clear-cut answers, even in secular jurisprudence.

In these issues and many more – touching upon lifestyle, sexuality, environmental matters, methods of food production using new scientific knowledge, such as genetic modification to enhance harvests, the more equitable distribution of resources in an over-populated world, and the globalised knowledge society where new approaches arise – Muslims will need to engage with sharia. While sharia is a major point of reference in providing Muslims with a moral compass to navigate these new developments, they will be compelled to resort to understanding the basis and the purpose of the law at a greater depth rather than simply following the established rules. Muslims must therefore be prepared to resolve problems and engage with the issues arising from the rapid scientific changes that are occurring in the world today in a constructive and positive manner, rather than being mired in the minutiae of the 'authentic' responses common in today's Islamist discourse. The larger values inscribed in the Qur'an, such as the sanctity of life, the idea of privacy, the principle of fair distribution of wealth and caring for the less fortunate, can be the basis of the new thinking that will be required in the future to develop appropriate responses from the Islamic world. We see one of these modern responses in the decision made by the *'ulama* in the United Kingdom in the 1980s under the presiding influence of Zaki Badawi, where they decided that organ transplants were acceptable under sharia as understood through the prism of *maslaha* and *darura*, namely public interest and necessity. This opened the door to British Muslims being able both to donate and receive organs in the interest of the preservation of human life, and at the same time demonstrated that Muslims were not only beneficiaries but also contributors to society at large.

Serious thinking on ethical issues is taking place amongst some Muslim scholars, such as Abdallah S. Daar, Amyn Sajoo, Abdulaziz Sachedina, Azim Nanji, Zulfikar Butta and Muhammad Rasekh – working in the Muslim world and beyond. We notice, however, a paucity of Muslim engagement with debates on medical ethical issues in contrast to those bodies dealing with such issues in the Western world – for example, the National Health Service in the United Kingdom and various hospital boards in Canada, Europe and the United States. A Muslim chaplain may be invited to respond to specific issues involving Muslim families, but this requires only a normative response rather than a more philosophical contribution based upon the general principles underpinning Islamic thought and law. Islamic legal discourse today is reaching out beyond legalistic formulae. Various elements of Muslim culture, including those of literature and speculative reasoning, are used to find new ways of dealing with new issues while remaining true to an Islamic world view. We should also note that in many religious centres of Iran and Iraq, such as Qum and Najaf, *mujtahids*, or scholars, deal with modern issues such as gender reassignment and the prolongation of life. In the Arab Middle East, doctors, including female doctors, in hospital wards have the final responsibility concerning ethical issues, which they carry out on the basis of *darura* and *maslaha* as outlined in Islamic legal thought.

Ethics in the Institutional Context

Ethics and its essential role in Islamic culture is expressed in practical terms by various Muslim organisations such as the Edhi Foundation in Pakistan, Building Resources Across Communities (BRAC) in Bangladesh and the Hariri Foundation in Lebanon. One of the major Muslim development initiatives active across both Muslim and non-Muslim countries in the world is the Aga Khan Development Network (AKDN), a contemporary endeavour of the Ismaili Imamat to put into practice the social conscience of Islam through institutional action. The AKDN links the values that derive from faith with the requirements of society (*din* and *dunya* – the spiritual and worldly), whereby Muslims are enjoined to act with right purpose and intention. Therefore it has as its underlying ethos principles such as inclusiveness, the search for knowledge, compassion and sharing, self-reliance, respect (for health care, sound mind and sustainable physical, cultural and social environment) and good governance. These principles, which are rooted in Islamic thought, are also universal, and they give rise to practical consequences that the AKDN is able to put into programmatic action.[8]

We have seen that ethics is based upon moral reasoning rather than prescriptions or obligations. They are to be found not only in the holy texts of Islam and its law but in its literature, in its humanistic thought and philosophy. And they arise from the daily engagement of individuals, including people practising their professions, but also the general populace, who are confronted with everyday moral issues. Islam looks to the notions of *akhlaq* (moral traits), *adab* (courteous behaviour), *ihsan* (spiritual virtue), *iman* (faith), *fitra* (intuitive discernment) and *taqwa* (piety), which are the formative norms that infuse the identity of a Muslim as God's servant (*'abd*) and trustee invested with obligations to promote the good and prevent evil; these are, indeed, the universal tropes for leading a good life within society. As professor of Religious Studies Charles Mathewes states with a degree of idealism:

> The outer person is brought into alignment with the inner person, the individual is reconciled to the community, the believer's experience is given determinate sanctifying shape. In all these ways, and more, the pillars of Islamic practice are meant to transform the self from a bundle of loosely aligned drivers and streams of thought into a coherent self, serving God by working for God's cause here on earth.[9]

These ethical values spring from an Islamic world view, but they also provide the ways or intellectual instruments to bring about creative thinking. This can engage with the problems of the modern world within the ethos of Islamic culture, thus giving them legitimacy amongst Muslims.

Ethics plays an integral part in Muslim society and indeed in sharia, yet as one would expect when dealing with humanity there is a gap between the ideal and reality. When we consider ethics, we also consider our human fallibilities. Therefore, in the field of ethics where values are expressed as abstractions to be treated with due scruple, utopian idealism can trump reality. One is reminded of the German philosopher Kant's memorable remark about human beings: 'Out of timber so crooked as that from which man is made nothing entirely straight can be built.'[10] Muslims are in good company when it comes to turning ethics – which could be labelled as the mind, that intimate site of sanity and delusion, talking optimistically to itself – into real acts and intentions where deception and duty make good bedfellows. Kant, who attempted to create a notion of ethics apart from what the Enlightenment regarded as the cul-de-sac of divine command, also believed that ethics as a rational discourse had its limits, especially in the devil's playground of politics with its seductive betrayals and necessary compromises, when external rules have to play the overriding role if we are not to descend into cruel anarchy. The rules, of course, have to reflect the surrounding and supporting values of the society in which they are to be observed. They have to have a purchase on the daily lives and the experience of everyman or they simply float into the ether.

There are many instances where ethics, which we argue is closely connected to sharia and the world view of Muslims, fail to assert the values they proclaim. Hence there is silence or passive acquiescence with regard to the 'crimes' of apostasy, blasphemy, honour killing (again, not licensed by sharia) and so on. However, we argue that Muslims are enjoined to live their lives with virtue or God-awareness (*taqwa*), intelligence and forbearance, to prevent the worst attributes of fanaticism which tend to ignore the attribute of God's mercy and compassion and make duty cousin to crime laced with perverted ideas of right and wrong, which turn crime into a deviant notion of duty personified. This lack of compassion and common endeavour makes space for bigotry and extremism. Such iron-clad dogma, we argue, is regarded by Muslim ethical standards as the antithesis of the faith.

No doubt new thinking is taking place in today's world, for circumstances are compelling Muslims to think in new ways to accommodate the reality of a fast-changing and globalised environment, which, as we write, has become a darker place of incipient and open hostilities between various groups, nations and, indeed, faiths. The Muslim world is also presented with these challenges and is called on to face them and renew the deeper values of its culture, presenting them to the world at large so that it is not demeaned and distracted by vilification and demonisation. Muslims, after all, are a part of the human family, warts and all.

13

Critique

In the preceding chapters we have tried to show that sharia developed in real time, subject to the same vagaries that any law has to face. In reviewing the role sharia can play in helping some 1.6 billion people to engage with a world that is undergoing unprecedented transformation, certain critical questions need to be posed. We do not believe there are clear-cut answers, but we feel that this process of interrogation remains critical if Muslims wish to embrace modernity on terms that are compatible with the ethics their faith teaches, and here we feel that certain questions are imperative. The law developed for Muslim communities as a result of actual situations that they were exposed to and had to grapple with as Islam expanded into new territories covering many cultures and many people. This empire conquered peoples but also had to find a modus vivendi of engaging and accommodating the subject population and their existing practices. Early Islam did not have a fully developed legal or, indeed, political system but had to adapt to and adopt existing systems. Islam's creative genius was in accepting pre-Islamic norms and adapting them to the vision of a new paradigm that Islam was bringing forth.

Sharia and *fiqh* also accommodated the cultural norms of the new, non-Arab Muslim subjects of the empire. Thus, in time, many of the legal devices and norms, such as *waqf* and *fides* (the Roman Law notion of trust and reliability between parties in transactions) for example, became a part of the growing body of legal practices that formed sharia, and continue to be used today. This accretion and selective adaptation was the norm in the Islamic world – the notion of pure origins was not an issue. Muslim thinkers contributed to a discourse that distinguished between essence and form, with such thinkers as the Persian polymath Ibn Sina (ca. 980–1037), the Persian Ismaili thinker Nasir Khusraw (1004–1088), the Persian theologian al-Ghazali (ca. 1058–1111), the Persian Shi'i scholar al-Tusi (1201–1274) and the Andalusian scholar al-Shatibi (1320–1388), looking to the broad purposes of society and life that the law should support in principle. However, the ideas of some of these thinkers were accepted with reservations by the legal scholars who developed *usul al-fiqh*, a narrow prism of legal interpretation through which law was understood and implemented.[1] Some legal scholars, such as Abu Hanifa, though they were eponymous founders of their respective schools of law, did not expect their ideas to become reified or frozen in time. Abu Hanifa wanted there to be a continuous response to the new claims of society by the law, which in his view had to retain a degree of purposive dynamism and contemporary relevance. We should note that there was no pristine legal system that could be imposed on Muslims, but a developing account of the law influenced by other legal systems and by evolving circumstances in order to provide the structure of law and order of the developing society that was the early Muslim empire. Therefore, to ossify or anchor the faith and law of Islam to one particular and imagined point in time is contrary to its ethos, which enjoins the faithful to seek knowledge widely, even 'as far as China', and to read and interpret the text according to time and contemporary circumstances. In fact, the first command to the Prophet is to be found in the first two verses of Chapter 96 of the Qur'an: 'Read. Read in the name of your Lord who created – created man[kind] from a blood clot.'

Reading is not simply mindless learning by rote but an attempt to understand and, therefore, to be mindful of the various levels of meaning that underlie even a seemingly simple text.[2] While texts are not moribund, without readers they project signs without meaning. There is inevitably a poetics of reading whereby readers create meaning out of the language by which the texts are produced. As the philosopher Wittgenstein argued, there is no such thing as private meaning, an autistic universe that accommodates only one being. Meanings are always a communal construct, but they are received and adapted, they are embellished and developed by individuals and groups with varying degrees of knowledge and sensibilities, and this takes place in different contexts. Texts are seldom monolithic or monotonous, unless they are read by minds or persons so inclined or brainwashed to explicate them as such. This inherently ambiguous condition of language compels us to learn to receive different interpretations and dissonances that we may not find congenial. By its very nature, the practice of interpretation should blot out bigotry, encourage debate and accommodate the ethos of uncertainty.

We wish to note an additional paradox here that attaches not only to us, as the writers of this book, but to most of the 1.6 billion Muslims across the world. We neither read nor speak Arabic; for us it is a foreign language. Therefore, the sacred texts that are deemed to form an essential part of our identities as Muslims escape us in great part because, as Q 12:2 states: 'Indeed, We have sent it down as an Arabic Qur'an that you might understand.' We are second-hand readers at best and translations, as we know, are approximations. Meanings, in our case, are not purely communal constructs but are mediated through a different language from that of the original. This paradox affects not only most Muslims, who recite the primordial text of the Qur'an, but we would suggest that it also affects the status of the faith of Islam itself, which claims to be a universal religion.

This attitude of engagement applies not only to reading texts but also to human relationships where each party's narrative, explicit and tacit, can easily dominate their world view and thus prevent an understanding of the other or indeed themselves. This is a perennial problem of the human condition which applies not only to sharia but to all aspects of social endeavour and engagement. There is no simple solution, although the notion of mediated settlement is an optimistic and promising process of human exchange in a troubled world. Mediation may not be the panacea but, in spite of its shortcomings, it constitutes an effective form of engagement between contesting parties, provided the process transcends technicalities, excavates the archaeology of discord and attempts to understand the universe of meaning within which each disputant lives, believes and acts. In this way we may be better able to address the roots of our disagreements and misconceptions. Both narrative and transformative mediation hold great promise because they give primacy to the principles of empowerment and recognition that enable disputants to see the world from the perspective of the other. Clearly, this process can only be effective where the parties are willing to hear each other's narrative in a non-combative manner. The transformation consists of a psychological and ideological reorientation. Interpretation of texts, including holy texts and those dealing with sharia, are also subject to this dynamic form of reading, engagement and understanding.

Each reader, each authoritative teacher or law giver, is finite with a finite comprehension, while language, even though it may not be infinite, is a varied and even mysterious construct of our minds and our differing levels of (self-)consciousness. There are, of course, texts that appear to set out clear commandments, but generally the sacred texts are open to discussion, disagreement and continuous interpretation. This applies especially to the Qur'an, an ancient Arabic text with lexical gaps and occlusions that are barely understood by scholars, never mind the mass of Muslims today. The Qur'anic text, like all sacred texts, should be read with a degree of humility rather than the dogmatic proclamations common in today's Islamist discourse, infected with an ostensibly triumphalist exceptionalism that seems to be an integral part of a particular mindset with its proclaimed final and perfect message. This creates a tedious and dangerous refrain, promulgating a supposed orthodoxy which effectively defames a great and varied civilisation with simplistic statements supporting division and discord in the name of authenticity.

Reading a text is a challenge, an excitement, a pleasure, and it can present us with a number of possibilities of self-understanding and understanding of the world about us, which implies a degree of awareness and openness from the reader, who is encouraged to take a principled and balanced approach towards comprehending an issue rather than holding on to a positional one. This often calls for a paradigm shift in understanding which affects both the sociology and the psychology of reading or receiving the

Qur'an that may not be readily visible to the searching eye and ear. Muslims in general need to remind themselves of this fact so as to ground their attitude of submission and awe towards the sacred text. To read the Qur'an with hermeneutic resolve is not to denigrate it but to read with self-awareness rather than with defaulting ignorance. Thus we enter into heartfelt and intelligent conversation with God's word by engaging with it and debating with it, which implies knowing about our own vulnerabilities and limits. The prodigal excessiveness of dogma has no role in this form of reading – but humility and intelligence do. The questing mind searches rather than asserts. We recognise that the position we adopt here can be regarded as a form of assertion, and thus we set out our case with a degree of ironic self-curtailment.

We present our argument in this chapter from a perspective or world view to which we belong because of where we were born, where we live and the education we have received. We are both Western-trained lawyers, born into a British imperial society which itself was traumatised by racism and colonialism. We now live in the United Kingdom, as part of its diasporic Muslim population. Education is a function of family, class and personal inclination, and it instils certain cultural norms. Our own education is part of a Western European Judeo-Christian and Classical heritage which developed over millennia into what we regard as the contemporary Western world with its secular, empirical, scientific and technological values and practices, including notions concerning the rights of individuals that infuse most of Western legal theory and practice. We do not espouse these values as the epitome of perfection, far from it – latter-day capitalism, with its obsession on markets, the exploitation of people and the planet, is no panacea for the perennial ills that befall humanity. There is no universal answer to the existential problems we encounter as individuals or, indeed, as a species. However, we are not advocating a debilitating form of relativism where anything goes because it is the custom or sincerely held belief of a group of people – we would not advocate honour killing or homophobia or the depletion of Human Rights, for example – yet it is incumbent on us to examine different values, to recognise they exist, as they do in much of Islamic discourse, and also to examine their nature, which often is not as pure as their advocates might proclaim. At the same time we have to be clear about where we stand.

In short, we see ourselves as Muslims living in the West, in essentially secular societies which are driven by an empirically based epistemology in the search for knowledge. Revelation is important, but reason and the benign streams of thought it entails (not necessarily, we admit) are also important. We believe that this principle is part of the Qur'anic ethos which calls for debate, discussion, disagreement, humility and a continuous search for knowledge; and, perhaps, even an attainment of wisdom in an imperfect world. These factors influence and indeed form our critique of sharia and *fiqh* that we share in this book, and which we hope both Muslims and non-Muslims may find congenial and thought-provoking.

To serve the needs of society, law has to emerge from the needs and requirements of that society. This entails a degree of flexibility and accountability, as well as acceptance by the wider community. However, it is important that the dimension of flexibility retains a degree of predictability so that a sense of orderly governance is maintained. When we study the evolution of a legal system, we see that change is constant, and this also applies in the case of sharia. Underlying the rules and regulations, the development of all positive law must be based upon an ethos of justice and fairness. These are highly abstract notions open to wide and sometimes contradictory interpretations, but nevertheless they are necessary to give law a degree of legitimacy.

In the case of religious law, this balance of flexibility and predictability is even more important, so that the law is understood not only as divine fiat but as a mode of ensuring a balanced and just society as generally understood at any particular time. This condition suggests that law cannot be set in stone; it cannot be immutable and draconian. In short, law is both temporal and contextual.

This brings us to the vexed issue of a modern Muslim nation state. The extent of the rights of a sultan or secular leader of such a state were initially fashioned in Abbasid times but are not clearly defined in Islamic history and continue to complicate the relationship between politics and faith to the present day. This lack of clarity raises questions about the notion of a nation state in conjunction with the idea of an *umma* or community of believers which has no borders. A number of implications arise. For example, who makes the laws? Is there one law for believers and another for non-believers? What are a modern Muslim nation state's obligations to its citizens and do they differ between Muslims and non-Muslims? Does the plurality of laws create an internal conflict, and what happens when religious laws are at variance with principles of individual rights and freedoms enshrined in the constitutions of modern states? Do some of these laws discriminate against Muslims themselves? How can such questions be resolved when they are presented in real-life situations and where international treaty obligations have to be adhered to by Muslim countries that also have to respect the principles of the Islamic school of law to which they belong?

This becomes even more problematic when some of the principles covered in the *fiqh* of a particular school of law that prevails in a country have not evolved adequately with changing values in the contemporary world.[3] Therefore, the laws against apostasy and blasphemy, for instance, become problematic, contrary to the general understanding of what Islam decrees about there being no compulsion in religion and what is said about Human Rights in international law and customary practice today. Often the crimes of apostasy and blasphemy are perceived to be the instruments of oppression in some Muslim countries.[4]

The question of identity also has a bearing on these issues, not least in the constitutions of Muslim states – are such countries Islamic entities? If they are, the logical conclusion is that sharia is the basis of the legal system. But then a further question arises, about how secular laws that contravene sharia – for example, the payment of interest on loans – are reconciled with the laws of that country. This issue has implications globally since it affects foreign legal judgements where interest is mentioned, and it also concerns foreign arbitral awards that have to be enforced in Muslim countries where the payment of interest is called for.

Most Muslim countries find stratagems to address this conundrum by stating that it only applies to new and prospective laws and does not have any antecedent effect. Our understanding is that a more fundamental approach has to be taken in comprehending this issue at the level of Qur'anic hermeneutics, rather than merely applying symptomatic solutions that do not go to the root of the matter. This important point of whether a Muslim country's laws are exclusively sourced in sharia also has significant implications for individual rights such as gender reassignment, same-sex relationships, citizenship, freedom of speech, apostasy, blasphemy and the rights of Muslim women to marry non-Muslims without their prospective spouses having to convert. This is because some of these issues have not been covered by sharia or because the *fiqh*-oriented formulations are of such a nature that they come into direct conflict with modern Human Rights principles as understood globally today. However, we often find that *fiqh* formulations are closer to Common Law principles, but also what sometimes passes in the name of sharia is pre-Islamic customary law which sharia itself does not countenance, such as forced marriages and crimes of honour. However, it should also be noted that sharia does not explicitly forbid these practices. Fatwas often seem to be the deciding factor, although in theory they are only opinions and not legally binding. There are no easy solutions to the problems.[5]

For sharia to play a role in a modern Muslim state, its classical formulation needs to be rethought and a more *maqasid-cum-maslaha*-based legal theory may have to supplant the original scripture-based notion of the law. Muslim modernists have been working towards making changes, but between the pre-modernist exponents of the principle of the purpose of the law and the handful of recent modern thinkers, sharia, in the form of medieval formulations (i.e. *fiqh*) seems to have taken centre stage in the debate. Although the original sharia, as was known to Muslim societies in pre-colonial times, has made way for newer interpretations of the law, there is a rupture in the memory of Muslims as to its original working and the ecosystems in which it operated. Consequently, there is little understanding of how what is projected as sharia today can function effectively in a modern Muslim state. What we see now is a shadow of the original sharia. While many Muslim countries profess to be sharia-compliant, in reality they are applying sharia unequally and, moreover, not in the same form as sharia was understood in the past by many scholars, but rather how it is interpreted by the state apparatus and by some traditional legal scholars. We do not intend to dismiss the varying applications of sharia as deleterious to Islamic law, but we highlight them as unavoidable challenges facing Muslim societies in their understanding of sharia's historical development, and thus its role in the contemporary world.

We have shown that sharia is not only a passive recipient of the challenges of modernity, with Muslim scholars being compelled to look again at its precepts. Rather, sharia's norms and principles could be used actively as a standard to challenge the deep-seated issues and problems of a modern, globalised world where change is constant and fast, where the environment is at risk, where ethics are being dangerously stretched. The situation in Malaysia is a case in point, where economic necessity and public interest are playing an integral part in the development of sharia finance, which is making important changes to the traditional medieval formulations of the law.[6]

We have used the term sharia throughout this book to mean not only sharia as an ethical path to the good as adumbrated in the Qur'an but as a concept conjoined with *fiqh*. We noted on page 3 that the legal verses in the Qur'an make up only a small part of the holy book, which means there are many gaps in legal matters that have to be filled in from elsewhere. Some Islamic laws have been drawn from customary laws of various parts of the Islamic domains, but, as we have seen, in time the legal scholars developed a 'science' of the law called *usul al-fiqh*, whereby the body of the law was developed by reference to the Qur'an, which was then supported by the notional sayings and actions of the Prophet Muhammad as well as by certain traditions that were reified and which were conflated with the idea of Sunna. The corpus of law in the course of time was perceived to be closed, and became fixed over the centuries. Furthermore, we have noted that this sharia/*fiqh* modality is an essential part of the sense of identity of a substantial number of Muslims today. This fact might appear strange to a secular notion of identity in which the law plays a necessary but external role, and is not warranted by God's command and made effective by the threat of divine punishment. Sharia thus plays a problematic role in the lives of modern Muslims and the contemporary

Muslim nation state where, in many cases, it is mentioned in its constitution as part of the state's identity. Sharia is necessary, theoretically definitive, and for most Muslims it defines their identity. The question arises about how one draws an identity from one dimension of Islamic textual sources that are perceived as a closed corpus, when lived Islam, consisting of diverse, changing and complex traditions, cultures, institutions and social relationships, constitutes such an immense part of Islam.[7] In addition, we should consider the fact that identity covers entire areas of feeling and wavering (self-)awareness, which means the psyche is more complex and more nebulous than the idealised notion of a Muslim person, solidly embedded in his/her community, enslaved to the demands of the law as adumbrated by clerics and those claiming exclusive knowledge, which inscribes his/her sense of self and his/her loyalty to an authority. Subjectivity therefore becomes static and emptied of agency.

We believe that the Islamic world is confronted with a profound existential question of meaning and purpose. This is because the core marker of Islamic identity has been deemed closed over a period of time by various factors, having been regarded as an icon of divine will. This has given it a sacralising authority, untouched and untouchable, unassailable to change, since such a move would be deemed by some pious Muslims as incongruous, if not actually blasphemous. We are left with the question of who has the authority to initiate a change in attitude whereby the closed corpus of self-understanding amongst Muslims may be reopened, reviewed, re-examined, and indeed made responsive to the powerful and disturbing changes in the modern world which call out for us to adapt if we are to survive. Where are the intellectual resources – analytical, cognitive, tools of comprehension which dare to think the unthinkable – to begin this process of change?[8]

As we have endeavoured to show in this book, we continue to hear, in different forms and places, a clarion call for a 'return to sharia', either in situations of political stress where sharia is regarded as the sole road to authentic renewal, or from Muslims in diasporic contexts who demand sharia's incorporation into the laws of the country in which they are settled, as a marker and protector of identity. In both these situations, we need to excavate the reasons behind the demands, to discover what motivates Muslims to regard sharia as a cushion for the stresses of modernity. In Muslim countries, sharia is regarded not only as a return to authenticity but as a catalyst for social justice where citizens want to hold their governments accountable for their impoverished lives, especially so when these governments claim to be Islamic. Social governance, social accountability, equity and fairness in the allocation of resources, enabling people to acquire dignity and become productive, and the eradication of corruption, are all concepts and ideals to be found in the Qur'an and Muslim juridical history. For the rank and file of people in the Muslim world, Islam then becomes the signifier of their grievances and yearning for a just society. Unfortunately, the call for the return of sharia is often a formulation that is antithetical to the very principles that motivate people to call for it – women, children, minorities and non-Muslims become the victims of repressive readings of holy texts which, in effect, make sharia, as thus understood, repressive and abusive.

In diasporic settings, the issue is complicated by different factors. Here, Muslims tend to have an exilic memory of sharia which is made up of medieval texts as expounded by their imams, as discovered on the internet, or as a memory of its presumed presence in their countries of origin, or an ideal of what it can do for them to protect their identity against erosion in a globalised world, where ethics appear to be depleted by a secular ideology. The idea of sharia in this context gives rise to concern on the part of Western governments and civil society because for them it is also a confused and minatory concept marked by some of the excesses of violence and repressive actions taken both historically and in our day in some parts of the Muslim world. Sharia therefore remains in the dock; the jury is out. This phenomenon, so closely associated with a Muslim understanding of their past, is not exclusive to Muslims, but in recent times we see its emergence in many non-Muslim countries, which dream of an imagined and idealised past inscribed with communal and personal authenticity – for example, in Serbia during the Balkan crisis, and most recently India with its Hindutva movement, or with Brexit in the United Kingdom. As the US political scientist Mark Lilla states, it is 'a World [where] we have lost narrative', something he refers to as 'an apocalyptic view of modernity as a kind of post-lapsarian state', a mind-cast in which 'the present, not the past, is a foreign country'.[9]

The role of history is critical to understanding the status of sharia not as an entity that is given once and for all, but a result of social processes that have taken place over centuries. History entails change, struggle and adaptation to new circumstances. The Charter of Medina,[10] for example, which was established by the Prophet, was itself a contingent, historical fact. We believe that it should not be regarded as a fixed icon, but as a guide to future accommodations especially in the fluid and pluralistic ethos of the present era. Caliph Umar's decisions on fiscal and administrative matters were moulded by historical necessities and demands. When he decided against the payment of booty to soldiers, or the paying of largesse to those who needed to be persuaded to join the faith, as adverted to in the Qur'an, he was acting with a degree of pragmatism rather than following a literal reading of the holy text. Recognising this act by the second Rightly-Guided Caliph should encourage Muslims to regard the holy texts which make up sharia and *fiqh* as not being immutable but open to interpretations that accord with the needs of the time. This necessary understanding of the importance of context (which is always a problematic notion in itself) should encourage modern-day Muslim exegetes and legal scholars to recognise the fact that law is an evolving institution, and Islamic law, in particular, was and should remain flexible in this way.

Finally, a better understanding of how sharia developed through its engagement with different customary processes and accommodated different foreign laws, administrative regulations and cultural mores while maintaining its fundamental ethos, will help to establish a new theory of legal knowledge. The fact is that all of us operate in society and with language, both of which are open to change and constant interpretation, as pointed out earlier in this chapter. This even applies to those values we regard as the inherent and essential ethical underpinnings of the law. For example, there is not a single, monolithic and fixed notion of justice; rather, justice is something that changes as societies develop across time. This idea, of course, is fraught with problems in itself, because it would appear to encourage a subversive, relativistic formulation that can be abused. However, we cannot ignore the fact that meanings change over time and place.

We discuss the importance of understanding the perennial role of history with a degree of caution. Clearly, history is the study of the past and a record thereof. But the past is always constructed by scholars and societies. We need to be aware of how it is constructed, by whom and for what purpose. History, like law, is not immutable but a discipline that is formulated through conventions of research, debate and exposition, and by the exercise of the imagination. This latter visualises the past as a creative re-presentation that is necessarily contingent and partial. History often verges on myth, and it is important for historians and the public to be constantly aware of this. It could be argued that historians pretend to enter the past, when all they really do is invent it. This allows them to retail an image of it to the present, in a continuous search for congenial meaning through narrative. This means that we should read the past, interpret it and, therefore, argue about it, to give play to competing ideas and speculate, while at the same time eschewing dogma and apparent certainty, which have a deadening effect.

Closed minds inevitably live in closed societies and are comfortable in them, but they do not serve honest disclosure or knowledge. We should understand the notion of historicity, the practice of historiography and the necessity to think historically with a degree of ironic reserve, thus keeping present events and processes in perspective. History can then speak to us continually and we may learn from it, both in terms of substance and form, in that we learn to realise that nothing is fixed but all is open to constant change and interpretation. Muslim scholars and the intelligentsia of today can ill afford to be oblivious to Islamic legal history and make ahistorical assertions in the name of a putative claim to authenticity. Even if the past has not been documented systematically, modern historical disciplines provide the tools of analysis that will enable Muslims to ask cogent questions about the past, with a view to developing a new understanding of our historical condition. This can inform our present thinking without us becoming trapped in a closed corpus of dogmatic assertions and naive readings of history, which are dressed as the pure and righteous exposition of the faith and its laws.

We recognise that law is a changing entity in any society, but it is not a freewheeling, unmoored institution. Law is concerned with orderly governance, with justice, with equity and fairness. These are high-level abstract terms but they are not empty of practical meaning: they have a vital role in the small print of our communal and social lives. We have to constantly concern ourselves about the purpose of law, and this idea of purpose is embedded in Islamic legal thought; it is known as *maqasid al-sharia*. In Jasser Auda's definition, it is 'a system of values that contribute to a desired and sound application of the Sharia.'[11] It has been employed as a legal hermeneutical tool since the 3rd century after the Revelation, and is based on the principle that Islamic law has a purpose to promote welfare and avoid harm. Its use is referenced in Islamic legal history, and modern-day Muslim thinkers and writers such as Rashid Rida, Muhammad al-Tahir ibn Ashur, Yusuf al-Qaradawi and Taha Jabir Al-Alwani have also written about this wide-ranging concept. In the pre-modern period, Muslim scholars had recognised that a definitive list of the *maqasid* or *masalih* did not exist in the Qur'an and the Sunna, that they were potentially limitless and that they evolve according to time and context, taking into consideration the demands of communal values.[12]

The majority of Muslim scholars, however, for reasons broadly mentioned in this book, restricted the scope of *maqasid* to those falling outside the realm of *'ibadat* (worship) and some explicit and unambiguous injunctions from the sacred texts. Over time, some scholars chose to move away from this rigid notion of law, notably al-Ghazali (d. 1111) and Najm al-Din al-Tufi (d. 1316), an important Hanbali scholar who considered *maslaha* as having a regulatory function over all established sources of law. This factor enabled scholars to provide a universal and humanistic status to positive law. Al-Tufi was followed by the 14th-century Maliki jurist of al-Andalus, al-Shatibi who developed a more systematic basis for this concept, which he considered to be 'the fundamentals of religion, basic rules of the law and the universals of belief'.[13]

Contemporary Muslim thinkers, such as the Egyptian philosopher Hassan Hanafi, the Moroccan scholar Mohammed Abed al-Jabri and the prominent Indonesian intellectual Nurcholis Madjid, view the *maqasid* and *maslaha* dimensions of sharia as the essence of the Qur'an, and hold that interpretations founded on these hermeneutical mechanisms can take precedence over clear Qur'anic texts.[14] According to Mohammad Hashim Kamali, a leading scholar of sharia and chairman of the Hadhari Institute for Advanced Islamic Studies in Kuala Lumpur, the early formulations of *usul* did not significantly address this dimension of the law until al-Shatibi's work. Kamali makes the further point that al-Shatibi's contribution came too late to make a visible impact on the basic schema and methodology of *usul* as developed by earlier Muslim scholars. Modern scholars have expanded the scope of the five traditional *maqasid* – life, intellect, property, offspring and religion – to include women's rights (Rashid Rida), justice and freedom (Muhammad al-Ghazali), human dignity (Yusuf al-Qaradawi) and equality, orderliness and freedom (Muhammad al-Tahir b. Ashur). Taher al-Alwani added the concept of developing civilisation on earth, and Gamal Eddin Attia, an Egyptian scholar of Islamic Law whose book enjoys great prominence in the Islamic world,[15] included 25 essential *maqasid* principles set out over four levels – the individual, the family, the *umma* and all humanity. This burgeoning scholarship not only helps to fill a gap but also builds on earlier formulations to expand the scope of *maqasid*-cum-*maslaha* approaches to the application of the law.[16]

However, we have to be cautious about how these tools are used. It is clear that the concepts covered by these two notions of the law are at a high level of abstraction and can be abused. Therefore it is important to ground them in a new communal understanding based on contemporary needs as reflected in modern societies, as Muslims endeavour to make sense of the contemporary world within the ethos of their faith. In this context, the role of the 'ulama has become diffused, and now we witness many other sources of influence which claim to speak for Islam and sharia. Sunni Islam has no central authority that can legitimately speak for all Sunni Muslims. This potentially fissiparous state, it can be argued, borders on a form of anarchy which can serve sectarian interests. For Shi'is, as we have noted earlier in this book, the law and legal mandatory pronouncements flow from the authority of the Imams. This process has its own problems as the Imam of the Shi'is is in occultation. It might be noted, however, that the Ismaili branch of Shi'ism has an Imam who is 'present' in the world and can provide authoritative opinions.

Historically, although Islam was embedded within, and expressed by, the Muslim community as a whole, the *'ulama* class held great authority through the institutions and functions that lay within its influence. With the bureaucratisation of the Islamic administrations in the 15th and 16th centuries, the status of this class changed. Firstly, they were incorporated into the power structures of the Ottoman, Safavid and Mughal states. In the late 19th and the beginning of the 20th centuries, massive modern-ising programmes in Muslim states, coupled with the impact of European imperialism, began to limit the influence of the *'ulama*. It was further diluted by the introduction of modern Westernised education in Muslim states, in some cases being at the behest of the Muslim rulers themselves. A new class of professionals came into being to whom the *'ulama*-based traditional system became increasingly irrelevant. Therefore, modern court systems, based on foreign legal procedures, coupled with the legislation process taken over by the centralised state, undermined the foundation of their relationship with sharia. *Waqf* (endowment), which had been a major source of the *'ulama's* income was appropriated by the state.

These developments have led to disparate and discordant voices speaking for Islam, many of whom are not formally trained in sharia and do not belong to the *'ulama* class. Their rhetoric uses novel idioms and arguments, adopting or mimicking the ideas of the modern Western world, while reflecting, if not creating, critical ruptures in the Islamic world today which is undergoing political, economic and intellectual ferment. Unless all these contradictory and countervailing voices and positions are able to engage in active and positive discourse with each other, the turmoil in the Muslim world will continue, and will be made more toxic in a digital era where information moves faster than the speed of thought.[17]

In discourses about Islam's views on certain issues, there is a tendency to regard the Prophet's actions and alleged sayings acontextually. We argue that retroprojecting to earlier periods when different norms prevailed is misleading, and generates a biased and polemical approach. We also believe that reifying the behaviour and values of that time for all times when, in fact, temporality necessitates the need for a more flexible view of any particular issue or course of behaviour, is also critical. This point affects not only those who castigate the faith for being inimical, for instance, to Human Rights but also those who wish rigidly to maintain the 'purity' of the faith by binding it to a past and its imagined perfection. Our position aims not to delegitimate the past but requires it to be read and dealt with historically and contextually. Respect is not the same as idolatry: it calls for a degree of realism that entertains change through evolution with wisdom in order to enable the present to be more adequately encompassed.

This brings us to the vexed issue of modernity to which we referred in citing Joseph Schacht in the Introduction to this book. The entire issue of how a faith is able to adapt to contemporary needs is a difficult one and is subsumed under the notion of modernity. Modernity, and the ensuing secularisation of society, itself is a complex notion and is subject to much controversy in the West as well as the East, although it is regarded by many Muslims as an idea created by the Western world to enshrine its own values and ambitions. In the Maghreb particularly the model of a secular society is fashioned on the basis of French culture and social practices. The Tunisian cleric Rachid al-Ghannouchi therefore argues that 'the "modernity-modernisation package" brought by the colonialists to the Arab region and then adopted by the national governments that succeeded them, was carefully designed to impose foreign hegemony on Arab and Islamic societies, especially in the Maghreb, denying the beneficial aspects of modernity that brought about political and economic successes in the West'.[18] For al-Ghannouchi, the secular elites in these Muslim societies, who claim to be the missionaries of modernity, inherited the role of the colonialists and their modus operandi of dealing with the masses, whom they viewed as primitive and backward.

This elite is losing any claim to an authentic relationship with the governed, who have begun to look for a licit, if instrumental, identity in their understanding of Islam, and the elite hold on to power with an increasing sense of collusion with their Western mentors. Al-Ghannouchi compares the Western and the Arab experience of secularism and argues that the ruling political mode in his home country of Tunisia, and some other countries in the Arab world since independence, does not resemble the Western liberal form of government 'except in its rebellion against religion and its inclination towards libertinism', which he feels is more akin to fascism and communism.[19]

Al-Ghannouchi draws a distinction between Western modernity, which slowly liberated the social mind from religious dogma and favoured science, empirical knowledge and critical thought, and the modernism played out in Arab societies, where governments took over religion as an instrument to control society and attempt to gain a modicum of legitimacy. This 'pseudo-modernity', which has infiltrated all the institutions of civil society, according to al-Ghannouchi, has been promoted by Western governments for their own interests. He posits a counter-narrative through an Islamic state and society which enacts the Islamic virtue of *taqwa* (piety). Al-Ghannouchi argues that Islam can restore the necessary relationship of the state and its citizens with the essential piety contained in *taqwa*, and that this relationship is the solution for the pervasive corruption of Muslim states today. We believe that this panacea is just that: it is facile and idealistic and does not take into account the complexity of the modern condition in which we are all mired. Nevertheless, we have to take al-Ghannouchi's position into account, as it represents a strand of thinking in the Muslim world which, is, in itself, complex and multifaceted.

We would argue that modern disciplines of cognition need to be taken on board by the Muslim intelligentsia even though such disciplines have developed in Western societies. This fact does not make them alien to Islamic societies, which in their early histories introduced the bases of this type of thinking into the Western world – for instance through the philosopher al-Farabi in around 951, who wrote a thesis on the merits of democracy. Islam was not immune to the influences of philosophy and science that originated in the Classical world. We should note that Plato and Aristotle have been presiding figures in Muslim cultures. From its inception in the 9th century, medieval Islamic philosophy was strongly influenced by their thinking, beginning with al-Kindi (801–873). The influence of Neoplatonism becomes apparent in the 10th and 11th centuries in the work of the renowned philosophers and jurists al-Farabi and Ibn Sina (d. 1037). Al-Farabi expanded on Plato's concept of an ideal city to develop his own political philosophy. Both al-Ghazali and Ibn Rushd reacted against this movement, and after the latter's death in 1198 the debate around Neoplatonism in Islam largely came to an end, surviving only in Ismailism.

Al-Ghannouchi is not unique in applying modern conceptual analysis to an Islamic situation using Islamic terminology. In the Shi'i world, a thinker such as Abdolkarim Soroush, an Iranian now working in academia in the United States, provides a new and challenging perspective. He argues, inter alia, that the Qur'an and texts relating to faith should be read with a hermeneutic discernment which historicises both texts and their interpretations, thus removing the tendency to idolise them in an ahistorical 'perfection', thereby making them more relevant to contemporary issues. In this way, Soroush and others like him are endeavouring to encourage alternative readings of hadith and the Qur'an which are in line with modern values, including those of democracy and Human Rights. Soroush develops a scheme of pluralism from three sources, namely mystical and literary theories as propounded by the Persian poets Rumi (1207–1273) and Hafez (1315–1390); second, the epistemological hermeneutics of the inevitable plurality of readings of any texts; and, finally, the intrinsic open-endedness of the Prophet's experience, which inevitably calls for new interpretations.

This call for new thinking has also been propounded by Mohammed Arkoun in his 2002 book *The Unthought in Contemporary Islamic Thought*. Arkoun writes that Muslims need to develop a new set of questions, new ways of approaching knowledge that take risks and enable them to find creative ways of resolving issues, while remaining grounded in Muslim cultures, thereby giving them a degree of resonance and relevance in today's world. This is an exciting, daring and ongoing process of social, communal and, indeed, individual renewal that arises from the historical context of each Muslim community. We argue, therefore, that sharia is not the sole but an essential element of identity amongst Muslims, and will require re-examination and rethinking that enables it to be applied to the galaxy of problems that beset the world today, and require a legal framework so that they may be dealt with in an orderly and ethical manner.

The first step is to think about the nature of law – jurisprudence – not only from a secular viewpoint, which considers appropriate rules and processes, but also from the albeit ambiguous underpinnings of ethical values that may not be sufficient but are necessary for a legal system to have traction in a state that respects law and civil society. Issues that may be relevant to consider in this context include whether or not there is an overriding Islamic law, and, if so, what makes such law 'Islamic'; which motivations that guided past Muslim communities to develop new approaches to problems faced by their societies can be used today with new intellectual vigour; what principles influenced Muslims in their interactions with non-Muslims, and how a legal system, based on a faith, can be applied generally across a nation state without being prejudicial to outsiders; and what the underlying principles are which have shaped the form and content of Muslim law, and how they can be applied today to develop appropriate responses to contemporary issues. All these will require a creative response to the present body of law, which, as we have pointed out, is not fixed but evolves, enabling it to become a vibrant, innovative and presiding presence in the modern world, while retaining legitimacy by respecting legal sources without reifying them. Here a sense of inclusivity and engagement would provide the best opportunity of drawing from the richness of the Muslim past through some of its own academic and cultural traditions and by combining them with the best in Western culture with a degree of intellectual equality, honesty and respect between Muslims and non-Muslims. In turn, this would enable the Muslim and Western worlds to share their experiences in order to enhance each other's cultural and intellectual capital. This process of intermingling discourse should draw upon a range of disciplines such as anthropology, sociology, psychology, literary criticism, linguistics, philosophy and the various specialities of law that exist in both Muslim and non-Muslim legal systems. Practising lawyers and scholars, governmental institutions, leading members of the judiciary and civil society, and religious experts, both Muslim and non-Muslim, should participate in this venture in order to develop a consensus or a jointly constructed discourse that is recognised by all parties.

This need for a profound review of the role of sharia as it affects the world in general, and its significance in Muslim societies in particular, grows more urgent in the contemporary world. However, our recommendations for change should not only be carried out in the abstract fields of the professions and intellectual discourse, which are essentially elitist; they have to gain traction with the wider populace, with Muslims in their daily lives, thereby providing them with a new but grounded vision of a future that entertains hope rather than the despair and loss of personal direction that pervade the Muslim world today. This entails a politics that is not self-serving but one that serves the wider needs of the general populace, including providing education, health care and employment. This is a major undertaking not only for the Islamic world but for contemporary society at large.

We should note that at a global level these issues affect not only the Muslim world but the wider world, which is now undergoing deep existential crises affecting, amongst other things, politics, economics, law, culture and the environment. Thus we find in Western societies an increasing loss of trust in government, where democratic politics is failing to provide honest governance, political discourse, accountability and the just allocation of resources. The public is being manipulated not only by governments but by social media, which can create a pervasive sense of disorientation, bewilderment, underlying fear and anger, and distraction. In the words of documentary film maker Adam Curtis, 'politics has become a pantomime and vaudeville in that it creates waves of anger rather than argument'.[20] The writer Jonathan Wolff argues that social media 'has become a world of bilious reaction to undigested information. It needs an antidote. Any university education – and not just PPE – when it goes well, combats lazy and destructive patterns of thought.'[21] Wolff calls for critical education which teaches people to understand the logical connections between different ideas in a rational manner, rather than simply consuming information which fails to distinguish assertion from fact. We are witnessing in the early 21st century the decline of Western hegemony not only in terms of hard power but also in its intellectual and cultural standing in the world at large. New social values are coming into existence which challenge the assumption of Western superiority.

With regard to specific legal disciplines, understanding constitutional law and how constitutions reflect changing societal needs, as well as how international treaty obligations operate, could be a good starting point to help Muslim countries to better ascertain what types of constitutional change are required to relate to the pluralistic realities of their changing demographics. In this process, in addition to sound constitutional thinking, we need to explore the type of *fiqh* which can engage with the changes needed to ensure that these countries provide a viable form of governance in a rapidly changing world in a more enlightened manner, while retaining sharia's integrity and ethical purpose which form its basis. We do not have easy or ready-made answers. However, we are asking for an honest enquiry which may be painful at times and daring, and which will provide a new way of living responsibly in our overcrowded planet. Innovative thinking on these issues will help to mitigate the practical internal conflict of law situations where the rights of the individual – Muslims and non-Muslims – are at stake.

Another area of legal enquiry could be family law and how different configurations of families are recognised in different legal systems. This would provide Muslim legal thinkers with an approach to the complexities of modernity and the requirement for calibrating a religious law to the needs of the time. Matters such as international surrogacy and its implications for national laws and indeed the relationship of national, secular laws with religious laws would be part of this search for new and relevant meanings based upon the ethical principles of the faith.

A better understanding of comparative law which studies the differences between legal systems, for example, would provide an insight into how different laws relate to each other in an increasingly interconnected and complex world. A good knowledge of business law, environmental law, criminal law, Human Rights, international arbitration law, global mediation processes and the complex workings of conflict of laws becomes important to see how a religious law, which, while not being applied uniformly in the Islamic world, finds its place in different legal systems. We believe that studying Islamic law as a linear process will not allow it to be understood and applied effectively in the light of its various interfaces in today's world. It has to be understood in the context of its interrelationships with other legal systems in existence today.

In recent decades, what we have been seeing is a clarion call for sharia's return, a call that has resonance in many Muslim countries as they have failed to provide healthy environments for good governance. In a sense, the call for sharia is simply explained as a legitimate demand for justice and for most orthodox Muslims is the core of their faith. However, in practice, this yearning for the retrieval of an authentic mode of individual and communal being is complex and contradictory. Therefore, while the masses in Islamic societies may think that they have a clear idea of sharia, in fact their notions are often vague, simplistic and, in many cases, misleading. Some Muslim governments, in turn, use the rhetoric of sharia to legitimise their power and the oppressive ways in which they use it. Sharia, in these cases, is not a basis for justice but a tool for wielding power. In diasporic settings, where Muslims are minorities – and especially where they are newly arrived migrants in states where they find work and a degree of safety but feel uncomfortable because of the values of a mainly secular society – sharia becomes a quasi-nostalgic yearning for the safety of an identity that is communally ratified within their groups.

In discussions on Islamic law and its development in the contemporary world, the work of Muslim women scholars and social activists is often overlooked, giving the impression that sharia's modern developments are an exclusively male-dominated discourse where women are barred or are objects to whom the law is meted out. In reality this is not the case, as Muslim women, educated at universities in Muslim countries as well as in the

Western world, have written on many issues impacting on the
rights of women and children under the dispensation of sharia.
These scholars, who are also social activists, are found today
in a number of countries, both Muslim and non-Muslim, and
embody a range of expertise that is contributing to new thinking
on law and social justice. They include individuals such as Azizah
al-Hibri (b. 1943), a lawyer and founder of Karamah – Muslim
Women Lawyers for Human Rights, an organisation based in the
United States and committed to the empowerment of Muslim
women through a focus on the Qur'anic principle of *adala* and
its egalitarian message of gender equity; Amina Wudud Muhsin
(b. 1952), a visiting scholar at Starr King School for the Ministry
at Berkeley, California, whose field of expertise covers theological
scholarship which critiques not only patriarchal and heterosexist
readings of the Qur'an but also gender, and ethnic and religious
dynamics among African American Muslim communities in the
United States; and Asma Barlas (b. 1950), formerly a journalist
and government official in Pakistan, who moved to the United
States and became the Director of the Centre for the Study of
Culture, Race and Ethnicity at Ithaca College, New York. Barlas's
2002 publication *'Believing Women' in Islam: Unreading Patriarchal Interpretations of the Qur'an* distinguishes between Muslim
'feminism' that dismisses Islamic tradition and believing Muslim
women who uphold gender equality as Islamic.[22] Barlas refers to
the Qur'an as an anti-patriarchal text.

While the above scholars operate mainly in the United States,
there are also in the Muslim world today a number of influential
women who are playing an active role in promoting women's
rights, such as Zainah Anwar (b. 1954), a Malaysian journalist,
author and former Commissioner of the Malaysian Human Rights
Commission; Siti Musdah Mulia (b. 1958), Research Professor
at the Indonesian Institution of Science (LIPI) and a veteran of
Fatayat Nahdlatul Ulama (NU), the women's wing of Indonesia's
largest grassroots Muslim organisation; Isatou Touray (b. 1955),
Executive of the Gambia Committee on Traditional Practices
Affecting the Health of Women and Children – advocating the
abolition of harmful traditional practices such as FGM and child
marriages; Fatema Mernissi (b. 1940), Professor of Sociology at

the Mohammed V University in Rabat, Morocco, and author of a number of books including *Beyond the Veil* and the *Veil and the Male Elite: a Feminist Interpretation of Islam* (1991);[23] and Shamina Shaikh (1960–1998), an anti-apartheid activist who opposed discrimination in all its dimensions from an Islamic feminist perspective.

In this new understanding of how the theory of knowledge of Islamic law is constructed, the contribution of Muslim male scholars is also to be noted. These scholars range from Abdullahi an-Na'im of Sudan, now working in the United States, whose expertise is in the field of Human Rights law;[24] Muhammad Khalid Masud (b. 1939), formerly Chairman of the Council of Islamic Ideology, in Pakistan, and one-time Academic Director of the International Institute for the Study of Islam in the Modern World (ISIM) in Leiden, the Netherlands; and Abdullah Saeed (b. 1964), Fellow of the Australian Academy of Humanities, whose field of expertise is the negotiation of texts and contexts, and *ijtihad* and interpretation. His publications cover Qur'anic hermeneutics, Islam and Human Rights, Islamic law reform, Muslim communities in Australia, and Islam and Freedom of Religion.

These scholars have lent their support to the establishment of an organisation in the 1990s in Kuala Lumpur, Malaysia, called the Sisters in Islam, a civil society entity which believes that Islam upholds equality, justice, freedom and dignity and whose work through social activism, training, publication and advocacy has given Muslim women a new voice globally through an organisation called the Musawah Global Movement for Equality and Justice in the Muslim Family. Musawah's principal remit is to strengthen women's voices at the regional and international levels through engaging with the Convention on the Elimination of All Forms of Discrimination Against Women (CEDAW) and its treaty body the CEDAW Committee, as well as with NGOs involved in the CEDAW reporting process.

We should also mention that the Sisters in Islam movement emerged as a consequence of the implementation of the new Islamic family laws in Malaysia in 1987. Enacted in 1984, these laws proved to be problematic for Muslim women seeking marital redress. A small group of women made up of lawyers, journalists, analysts and activists formed themselves into a sharia subcommittee of the Association of Women Lawyers (AWL) to discuss the ramification of the laws. Two members – Zainah Anwar, mentioned above, and Nor Faridah Ariffin, then President of AWL – took the lead. The group's discussions revealed that the origin of such anti-women laws stem from contentious readings of the Qur'an and that there was a need for reinterpretation. This movement coincided with a campaign by women's groups against domestic violence in Malaysia.

By 1989, this group, made up of eight women, started the Sisters in Islam and met each week to study the Qur'an closely and to examine verses that were used to justify domestic violence. The founding members discovered at these meetings that the texts showing that women should lead lives of equality with men were located within Qur'anic Islamic teachings, with the result that they came to understand that it was not Islam as such that oppressed women but male-centric interpretations influenced by cultural practices and values of a patriarchal society.

Around this time, a judge in the Malaysian court forbade a husband from taking a second wife on the basis that he had failed the four conditions stipulated in the Islamic laws with regard to polygamy. A media debate ensued, and this newly founded group lent its voice to the debate. In 1991, the Sisters in Islam published two booklets: 'Are Women and Men Equal Before Allah?' and 'Are Muslim Men Allowed to Beat Their Wives?' A public forum attended by more than 200 women and men from civil society groups, academia and government showed how important a role advocacy plays for law reform in a country. The Sisters in Islam began to submit memoranda to the Malaysian government and to initiate collaboration with international scholars of Islam. In 1992, the group held its first workshop, entitled 'The Modern Nation State and Islam', and in 1993 submitted a memorandum to the then Prime Minister of Malaysia, Mahathir Mohamad, contesting the proposed Kelantan Sharia Criminal Code (*hudud* law). To enhance their own scholarly capacities and understanding, Sisters in Islam members began to take lessons in the Qur'an, Islamic law, and social change and modernity from the renowned Egyptian reformist scholar Dr Fathi Osman, a Visiting

Professor of the Law Faculty of the International Islamic University. By 1998, Sisters in Islam became an established institution, able to discuss the necessary legal and procedural reforms with the government of Malaysia. It held workshops, ran education programmes and branched out into advisory services, setting up a legal clinic offering advice and counselling to some 1,700 clients in its first three years of operation. Through experience gained over a 20-year period, Sisters in Islam embarked on a project of Islamic family law research and advocacy – Musawah – which it launched in 2009.

In an informative article in *Critical Inquiry* in 2006, Ziba Mir-Hosseini, the current convener of its Knowledge Building area of work, traces the recent evolution of thinking in Iran with regard to feminist rights and emphasises that at the core of Muslim belief lie the cardinal values of justice and equality – principles that are not reflected in a state that claims to be guided by sharia.[25] For her, as for many other Iranian women, the Iranian Revolution of 1979 held great promise, only to be diverted by a pre-modernist interpretation of sharia based on a patriarchal culture. Following developments in the country over a 30-year period, during which time Mir-Hosseini visited various courts and interviewed a number of religious scholars, she makes the point that the relationship between the traditional approach to sharia and coming to grips with the reality of contemporary life as lived in Iran assumes a greater urgency today, because the rhetoric of Human Rights and women's rights as justifications advanced for the invasion of Muslim countries such as Afghanistan and Iraq by a Western superpower did not lead to an improvement in women's rights.

On the contrary, such acts caused a backlash and the repeal of hitherto progressive family laws in the place of which we witness the reinstatement of laws inimical to women's rights. In the process, ironically, what we see is the emergence of two important phenomena: first, the rise of a populist reformist movement spearheaded by a number of Iranian intellectuals such as Abdolkarim Soroush, Mojtahid Shabestari and Mohsen Kadivar; and second, a new gender discourse that argues for equality of women within an Islamic framework. Highlighting the fact that in the struggle between conservative elements in the country represented by the traditional segment and proponents of the New Religious Thinking, which is what Soroush's 'interpretative epistemological theory' is known as,[26] the so-called reformists may not have gained a victory because they failed to enable the necessary changes in the structure of power. However, according to Mir-Hosseini, 'they had one major and lasting success: they de-mystified both the power games conducted in a religious language and the instrumental use of religion to justify autocratic rule and patriarchal culture'.[27]

Drawing on the new wave of reformist thought and feminist scholarship in Islam, Musawah devised and published a framework for action in which it grounded its claim to equality and arguments for reform simultaneously in Islamic and Human Rights frameworks. Referring to the potential of these new movements to transform the patriarchal and non-egalitarian ethics in the Muslim legal tradition, Mir-Hosseini makes three important points. First, the key obstacle that Muslim women have had to contend with is the linkage between the religious and political dimensions of identity in Muslim contexts, which had its roots in the colonial era but assumed a distinct and more visible expression in the 1970s with the resurgence of Islam as a political force. The end of colonialism, the rise of secular and despotic regimes in Muslim countries and the suppression of progressive forces created a vacuum that was filled by Islamist movements that gained added strength from the Iranian Revolution of 1979 and the subsequent defeat of communism. However, with the US response to the events of 9/11, and more particularly with the invasion of Afghanistan in 2001 and Iraq in 2003, Muslim women found themselves in the crossfire.

Second, the rise of political Islam had certain unintended yet positive consequences – notably the 'demystification of power games conducted in religious language'.[28] This, in turn, led to the emergence by the 1990s of new reformist and feminist voices and scholarship in Islam that began to offer an internal critique of pre-modern interpretations of sharia.[29] For Mir-Hosseini, this has led to the change of the terms of debate amongst Muslims, paving the way for the democratisation of religious knowledge and for an egalitarian interpretation of sharia.[30]

Third, it is difficult at the present time to be optimistic when extremist and literal interpretations of Islam's sacred texts such as those espoused by various Islamist organisations 'are drowning out other voices'.[31] Speculating about the future of a process that is still emerging and contingent, Mir-Hosseini cautions, is risky, but viewing the connections that she sees and the trends that are emerging give her a sense of hope that 'we will look back at this time as one of a profound shift in Muslim identity politics and the understanding of Sharia from a body of immutable laws to a source of ethical and moral guidance'.[32]

Furthermore, and most importantly, these movements for the democratisation of knowledge, which displayed such vitality in the latter part of the 20th century, are today declining. The plight of Muslim intellectuals remains a perennial issue and the ability of Muslim feminist activists to operate from within the Muslim world has been severely curtailed by political and social turmoil in Muslim countries, which are also affected by global trends.

With regard to the notion of jihad, which dominates the global headlines today, there is a branch of sharia called *fiqh al-jihad* which regulates the lawful waging of war or jihad. The term 'jihad' has two meanings. The first, the greater jihad, denotes a personal inner struggle to do God's will, to attain a deeper level of spiritual understanding by an individual who overcomes the temptation of disbelief. The second meaning, which makes the headlines today, is the lesser jihad, which signifies the struggle against those who are deemed enemies of Islam and Muslims; this struggle, which also entails war, is a perceived means of ensuring the good and suppressing the bad. The term remains a complex and ambiguous one, originating in early Islam as the duty of individual Muslims to carry out the Qur'anic injunction to 'command the right and forbid the wrong'.[33] This undertaking does not entail a communal obligation; not every Muslim is called to carry it out actively. However, defensive jihad, where the Muslim community is considered to be under attack, places a duty on all Muslims – the *umma* – to participate in the struggle or war.

There are limits in warfare that were stipulated very early in the history of Islam which set out the criteria for those who cannot be attacked. Hence, old people, children, women, workers, slaves and hermits are not considered to be legitimate targets. Islamic *jus in bello* operates in this case. The maze of texts which make up sharia and *fiqh*, which are susceptible to competing and conflicting interpretations, become the pretexts of claimed authority by different groups of Muslims who seek legitimacy from them for their world view, thus creating a fierce politics of global division between the good and godly and the bad and ungodly. Suicide attacks have a particular toxicity in this narrative of seeking to purify and exact vengeance that surpasses the general sense of repugnance one feels about acts of violence against others. It enters the realm of unreason that contradicts our common humanity. No law, most would argue, and certainly not a law that claims to be God's law and is thus based on universal moral values, can support such evil actions. On the face of it, sharia does not condone such acts, and many clerics have so argued, citing the Qur'an and hadith. Indeed, suicide, according to sharia, is forbidden: it is a sin called *intihar*, which consigns the person committing such an act to hell. However, suicide bombings are justified by Islamists or jihadists, who argue that such acts are not suicide per se but a part of a war against the enemy, and thus allowed. Such persons are not committing suicide but are acting as martyrs or *shahids* for the greater cause of protecting Islam and Muslims. *Shahids* sacrifice their lives for a bigger purpose; their action is called *istishhad* and, according to the jihadists and their religious mentors, such action is to be commended. Rather than being consigned to hell, martyrs enter heaven directly upon their death where they enjoy a special status replete with eternal, and especially sensual, gratification. This link between martyrdom and paradise existed from the beginning of Islam. The Qur'an states: 'And never think of those who have been killed in the cause of Allah as dead. Rather, they are alive with their Lord, receiving provision.'[34] This verse appears to support the zeal of jihadists for death in martyrdom to fulfil what they see as doing God's bidding. Ironically, a similar situation existed in the early 9th century in al-Andalus in Muslim Spain where a monk called Perfectus provoked the authorities by insulting the Prophet. This was considered a capital offence and, despite the authorities' entreaties to him to recant, Perfectus persisted in vilifying the Prophet, and so he was consequently put to death. Perfectus was, therefore, regarded as a martyr for the Christian faith. His action gave rise to a cult of martyrdom in Spain, where many other monks who were searching for a distinct Western Christian identity, which they felt was being submerged by the dominant Muslim culture of the time, were put to death for insulting the Prophet, an action they used instrumentally to assert their distinct Christian identity.

However, the connection between sharia and suicide bombings or martyrdom actions is not clear and sharia scholars argue the case for and against such a link. This is an example of how sharia is manipulated or interpreted to suit a particular case, where the panoply of texts – the Qur'an, the hadiths and the processes of reasoning and group agreements – become the prey of scholars reaching out to legitimise the conclusion they wish to champion. Shi'i scholars and leaders such as Khomeini and Syed Hussain Fadlallah have therefore argued that sharia supports self-annihilation in war as part of jihad by pointing to the death of Husayn, the son of Ali and grandson of the Prophet, at Karbala where he resisted the army of the usurper Caliph Yezid against all odds and was killed. In itself, this opinion by analogy is insufficient, especially since Husayn was killed by the enemy rather than taking his own life. Therefore, other scholars have passed fatwas against the opinions of Khomeini and Fadlallah as being contrary to sharia and those Islamic rules concerning the conduct of war that forbid the deliberate killing of civilians, women (unless they are combatants themselves), children, the elderly and the wanton destruction of life and property.

While the verse in the Qur'an generally called upon to show that suicide is not permitted in Islam does not clearly prohibit suicide,[35] there is a hadith where the Prophet is deemed to have said: 'None amongst you should make a request for death, and do not call for it before it comes, for when any of you dies, he ceases [to do good] deeds and the life of the believer is not prolonged but for goodness.'[36] Another hadith from the Prophet, ascribed to God Himself, states: 'My servant anticipated my action by taking his soul in his own hand; therefore, he will not be admitted to paradise.'[37] Thus, prima facie, a suicide attack is acting against these commands of the Prophet and, indeed, of God. However, suicide attacks as part of jihad are deemed by many Muslim scholars not to be suicides but acts of martyrdom for the cause of Allah.[38] The jurist Muhammad ibn al-Hasan al-Shaybani (d. 805), who is regarded as a foremost exponent of Islamic international law, argues: 'It is permissible for a person to plunge into a group of enemy forces, or to attack them in cases where he hopes that he will be saved in the end, or – if there is no such hope – in cases where he will inflict damage on the enemy, and demoralise them, or will encourage his own combatants'.[39] However, this opinion does not openly support suicide attacks since it leaves the possibility of the attacker not being killed, and, if he is killed, responsibility lies with the enemy. It also makes clear that such attacks should be conducted as part of a war. Shaybani does not provide legitimacy for attacks carried out by civilians or those posing as civilians upon civilians and non-combatants, which is in contravention of Qur'anic commandments against acting treacherously.[40] There must be an initial breach of trust by the enemy before Muslims can openly proclaim that they will not be bound by any treaty made with them. To initiate hostilities with another group is unacceptable.[41]

The principle of reciprocity is a Qur'anic injunction that all Muslims are obliged to honour.[42] But reciprocity does not give licence to Muslims to carry out prohibited acts of retaliation. Suicide attacks are therefore condemned by Muslim legal scholars for many reasons, which they support by reference to the Qur'an and hadith; there is thus a consensus of legal and moral disapproval against such heinous crimes. Muhammad Munir, a Pakistani law professor, puts this clearly when he writes: 'When a suicide bomber targets civilians, he might be committing at least five crimes according to Islamic Law, namely killing civilians, mutilating them by blowing them up, violating the trust of the enemy's soldiers and civilians, committing suicide and, finally, destroying civilian objects or property'.[43] He argues that, for these reasons, this type of attack is not an act of martyrdom and ignores the strictures and values of sharia. However, this position is not as clear cut as he suggests: sharia is, as we have seen in this study, made up of texts, and texts are open to conflicting interpretations.

Those Qur'anic verses exhorting the protection of the innocent are interpreted by jihadist Islamists with extreme narrowness;

hence even those Muslims who do not agree with their ideology are deemed apostates (this practice is called *takfir*),[44] and therefore considered deserving of death by extremist groups such as Al-Qaeda, Daesh or IS, and others,[45] who thus find legitimacy in their own understanding of the holy texts and sharia for what they deem martyrdom operations. This conviction is buttressed by a Qur'anic verse that states: 'And do not kill anyone which Allah has forbidden, except for a just cause.'[46] The proviso in the verse enables jihadists to justify suicide killing and the death of bystanders even though they may be innocent, indeed believers themselves, since the 'just cause' overrides any other consideration – the end justifies the means and the collateral damage it creates.

This entire question of the legitimacy of suicide bombing should be viewed in the context of the new world (dis)order we are presently entering and which some commentators call the 'post-truth' era, where truth and lies are interwoven, where facts are denied or excoriated by populist rhetoric, where 'reality' is no longer clearly affirmed and accepted by the majority. We are indeed living both as individuals and societies in separate conflicting realities which are manipulated, polarised and constructed by the media, both formal and social, via the internet – creating what some deem 'echo-chambers' of what we wish to hear, of our differing anxieties and prejudices. Trust in society is becoming depleted, institutional and governmental credibility is waning, and a culture of public dishonesty has become the common exchange undermining social cohesiveness. It is in this churning environment that Islam is projected as a new enemy, with sharia as its Trojan horse which has to be rebuffed at all costs. Sharia itself, and Muslims generally, are also embroiled in this ongoing battle for legitimacy because some continue to champion an outmoded, pre-modern version of sharia that fails to command legitimacy in the discourse on the role of law in contemporary society.

The law has become even more important in securing an orderly society – especially in these uncertain times when the rule of law as understood in democratic societies as the pillar of a fair social contract and guardian of the rights of individuals against the inherent autocracy of government which it calls to account constantly. Yet the law is being severely threatened, with the complicit support of the media and acquiescence of governments who claim to champion freedom and democratic Human Rights. Muslims, we believe, can play a role in this global drama of power and responsibility if they understand that sharia is not simply a set of primitive, sometimes savage, legal rules but a system of ethical conduct – what we refer to in this book as *maqasid, darura* and *maslaha* – and instead look to the foundation of sharia to emphasise the wider social purpose of the law in protecting rights and ensuring moral values which continue to inform the lives of societies and citizens. We have argued in this book that this approach, in spite of the actions of various Muslim states and of radical groups, is regaining traction in Islamic discourse. We do not suggest that the greater purposes of sharia are in themselves the solution to the perennial problem of good government – they are too easily reduced to rhetorical signatures for oppressive rule – but they are an initial and necessary step for the Muslim world to engage in these problems and also to enter into a dialogue with other cultures in order to find a mode of living adequately, at least, together on this planet.

As we show in this book, the understanding of sharia is not solely attached to a framework of rules that were developed in earlier times and have failed to evolve adequately in order to be relevant to modern concerns no matter that many millions of Muslims claim they do. To appreciate and value sharia's wider remit raises the question of whether Muslims need to initiate a new world view based on a reformed theory of knowledge that challenges traditional modes of authority, thinking and sense of identity – an extremely difficult, if not perilous task for any society. Other, related, issues also come into play here. Do the new technologies that are developing exponentially today give any hope for this change of understanding to take place in the Muslim world? Do young Muslim men and women who live in the West have the opportunity to enter different disciplines of knowledge and do they have a role in this process of rebirth? What type of training and education is required to make this possible without destroying the valuable aspects of traditions to which they and their forebears belong? Would their education and new visions be able to influence change in Muslim societies themselves? These are critical questions (and there are many others) for which we do not claim to have answers, but an awareness of them is a good starting point for new thinking on sharia and allows it to have a realistic role in the formation of the identity of Muslims without it being fetishised as its fulcrum. This is not a revolutionary notion, as it has existed in the Muslim world over the centuries, where Islam was never regarded as a monolithic entity but seen as consisting of many cultures serving different dimensions of existence.

In his book *What is Islam?* the scholar Shahab Ahmed states: 'Unlike many Muslims of today, the Muslims of the Balkans-to-Bengal complex did not feel the need to articulate or legitimate their Muslim-ness … by mimesis of a pristine time of the earliest generations of the community.'[47] Ahmed describes the Muslim world as capable of being multifarious where the role of art, music, poetry, intellectual thought and other life pursuits were equally important as sharia and the explicit tenets of the faith – this world, as with all living social groups, was alive with apparent contradictions and paradoxes with which Muslims were comfortable, realising that the Revelation of Islam went beyond the Qur'an, hadith and the legal constructs of scholars. Islam was life, and the mystery of life extended beyond Islam in a healthy balance.

Fortunately, as we have noted, we are beginning to see a cadre of Muslim scholars who are challenging some of these perspectives and giving some hope. They are using new disciplines of knowledge that provide new modes of thinking that enable them to make sharia more relevant in the contemporary world. We consider that changes will only occur when new Islamic scholarship takes hold in the wider Muslim community, where scholars take on modern thinking that they can combine with the traditional streams of Islamic thought and religious discourse. Uprisings, such as the Arab Spring of 2010, will not bring about the reform of Islamic thinking in themselves. Instead, we believe that a steady evolutionary development of critical thought is imperative, but it has to be a sustained catalyst for change amongst the wider population.

In our study we have come to realise that law plays an important role in Muslim consciousness. However, we are not convinced that it holds the same position that Joseph Schacht assigns to it when he argues that sharia is the core of Islamic identity. We believe that Muslims, like Islam, are a diverse entity who share characteristics that may be deemed Islamic, but they do not all define themselves solely by sharia (although normatively all Muslims affirm the *shahada* or the belief in the One God and that Muhammad is His Prophet, and they share in certain common values that they ascribe to the faith). Even though sharia is not an exclusive marker of identity for all Muslims, it does embody practices and principles on how they pray, how they relate to each other, how their mundane actions affect their afterlife, and how they relate to the world at large, which is becoming increasingly interconnected. Muslims, therefore, need to reflect on how the ethical principles of the faith, which are beyond time and space, are able to inform the predicaments of the modern world to which we all belong. An understanding of this idea of sharia would enable Islamic values to play a role in helping human beings to negotiate some of the issues confronting us all.

Failure to take this route of reflection risks encouraging the preponderance of extremist thinking. Extremism, or the violent mask of alienation and the perennial quest for the comfort of certitude, is a toxic form of nostalgia for definite responses as opposed to the discomfort of asking awkward questions for which there may not be certain answers. As we can see at present in the Middle East, this is a dangerous frame of mind, one that creates enmity and brutal reprisals in the name of the good. We would argue that Islam as a faith and culture in which sharia is an essential part has a much greater and more generous vision, which attempts to realise the mercy and compassion of the divine, notions with which each Islamic prayer begins and which, we believe and hope, will provide the necessary impetus for change to take place organically from within Muslim societies rather than being imposed, or perceived to be imposed, from without.

Glossary

ahl al-bayt Members and direct descendants of the 'house of the Prophet' including the immediate progeny of the Prophet.

aya A verse of the Qur'an. Also the term used to refer to signs of God's creative power and the meaning of the universe.

Caliph Used in the Qur'an for Adam in his capacity of custodian of the earth. As a deputy or successor to the Prophet, the term was first applied to Abu Bakr after the Prophet's death. Also applied to his successors Umar, Uthman and Ali who are referred to as the 'Rightly-Guided Caliphs'. The title remained in use until 1924 after the dissolution of the Ottoman Empire when the secular leader Kemal Atatürk abolished the title. In recent times, some Muslim groups have raised the issue of a revival of the true caliphate.

caliphate The office of leadership that emerged on the death of the Prophet. The definition and role of the caliphate underwent many changes in Islamic history. Primary functions included protecting the people, ensuring the proper application of sharia and the supervision, administration and governance of the territory under his rule.

darura 'Necessity', a situation in which a forbidden action (*haram*) is permitted for the sake of public good.

fatwa (plural fatawa) A legal opinion given by a *mufti* with the requisite training and status to issue such an opinion. In the Shi'i tradition, such scholars are known as *mujtahids*. A fatwa is not binding. *Mufti*s acted in a consultative capacity in Muslim courts as well as interpreting Islamic law as appointed officials of the state. The practice of issuing a fatwa has continued in modern times as a mechanism for dealing with personal, social, legal, political and religious issues.

fiqh	Term for Islamic law as interpreted and understood by legal experts from among the *'ulama* (scholars). While sharia is a comprehensive body of law ordained by God, *fiqh* is its practical understanding, mediated through human agency and coupled with a commitment to implementing sharia.
gharar	An element which creates gain for one party at the cost of another in a contract or commercial arrangement mainly through uncertainty. Its prohibition would require all investment gains and losses to be apportioned in order to avoid excessive uncertainty leading to unjust enrichment.
hadd (plural *hudud*)	The term is used in the Qur'an to refer to those restrictive prescriptions that are considered divine in origin. Also refers to legal punishment imposed for fornication (*zina*), the false accusation of fornication (*qadhaf*), drinking wine (*khamr*), theft (*sariqa*), brigandage (*qat' al-tariq*), apostasy (*ridda*) and highway robbery (*zandaqa*).
hadith	The sayings and actions of the Prophet Muhammad, collected and systematically categorised after his death by scholars dedicated to this task. Hadith forms an important component of Muslim law through the concept of Sunna and complements the Qur'an in interpreting, understanding and applying aspects of Muslim belief and practice. There is a Sunni canonised collection and a separate Shi'i collection.
halal	The Qur'anic term for that which is lawful or allowed. Generally, it refers to the permitted categories of food and drink. Overall, the goal of the concept is to provide rules and guidelines for choices regarding that which is permissible, clean and pure – a moral code showing respect for life in all its forms.
'ibadat	Worship and other acts of personal and communal piety.
'idda	In Islam, *'idda* is the period (normally three months) during which a woman must wait after the death of her spouse or after a divorce, when she may not marry another man. Its purpose is to ensure that any child carried by the woman is not that of the deceased spouse or of the previous husband.
ijma'	Consensus of the learned community of religious scholars and jurists at any given time. One of the foundations of Sunni legal theory.

ijtihad	The act of reflection in legal matters, seen as necessary to elaborate precise rules based on the Qur'an and the Sunna. Different law schools arrive at this in different ways, with their scholars enjoying varying levels of status.
imam	A leader, particularly a prayer leader, whose function might be assumed by any adult male Muslim. In Shi'i Islam, 'Imam' refers to the authoritative head, often from the *ahl al-bayt*, the house of the Prophet from which spring his progeny.
imamat	The office in which the authority to guide the Islamic polity is set. Over time, this belief came to include the idea of a continuing lineage of Imams chosen from direct male descendants of the Prophet designated to hold such office.
Khulafa Rashidun	The Rightly-Guided Caliphs refer to the first four Caliphs, namely Abu Bakr, Umar, Uthman and Ali.
madhhab (plural *madhahib*)	Schools of Islamic law. In Sunni Islam the term is primarily used to refer to one of the four major 'schools' of Islamic law. It also implies the doctrine, creed or philosophy of life to which individual Muslims belong.
mahr	A gift paid by the groom to the bride as part of an Islamic marriage contract. It forms part of the property even in the event of a divorce.
maqasid al-sharia	The higher purpose of the law, generally the larger principles which the law is meant to protect, such as life, intellect, property, offspring and religion.
maslaha	Public interest – general welfare in Muslim juridical thought. The concept allowed legal scholars and the state a degree of flexibility to meet the changing circumstances whereby the welfare of the community as a whole might be compromised.
maysir	Gambling – something that does not create new wealth but amounts to one loser and one winner.
mazalim	Unjust or oppressive actions – the name given to special courts dealing with such actions held only by the Caliph, which dispense justice distinct from that of a *qadi*. They also perform the role of a court of appeal against sentences handed out by the *qadi*s.
mihna	Trial, testing – a term used in reference to the inquisition set up in the 9th century by the Abbasid Caliph, al-Maimun, in an attempt to impose the doctrine of the Mu'tazilites

and their belief in the 'created' Qur'an, as opposed to the Ash'arites, who subscribed to the ideology of the 'uncreated Qur'an'.

muhtasib   Tax- or market-inspector, also known as *agronomus*.

mufti   A person empowered to give a fatwa or judicial opinion on issues of Islamic daily life. Their role in the development of Islamic law has been significant. A *mufti* must be a person of good standing, have legal knowledge and the capacity to use reasoning to solve problems.

mutʿa   A temporary marriage believed to have been allowed under certain circumstances but subsequently legitimised only under Shiʿi law.

nikah   Marriage, but also denotes the contract of marriage in Islamic law – usually accompanied by the recitation of the Qur'an and additional prayers as well as celebrations and exchange of gifts.

qadi   A Muslim judge whose remit is to provide rulings and resolve disputes. Traditionally, he rendered judgements in accordance with the recognised work and practices of each respective school of law. The office is still extant in countries where sharia courts hold sway.

qiyas   Analogical reasoning not unlike *ratio decidendi* in English Common Law. One of the sources of jurisprudence in Sunni legal practice.

raʾy   Personal opinion – used by certain jurists (*faqih*s) opposed to the traditionalists when interpreting religious law (*fiqh*). This form of reasoning has become less prevalent and has been formalised as *ijtihad*.

riba   Unlawful gain resulting from exploitive charges on accrued debt. Generally defined as usury or interest. The concept does not include lawful profit or gain.

sharia   Arabic for 'path' or 'way', encompassing the total sum of duties, obligations and guidelines for Muslims. It includes various relationships – with God, with other human beings as well as ethics. A comprehensive system that guides Muslims in their relationships with each other as well as with non-Muslims.

siyasat al-sharia   Government in accordance with Revealed law – administrative law that developed in Muslim societies dealing with issues of governance and administration of the state apart from sharia.

sukuk	Similar to a conventional bond – the principal being that it is asset-backed. The asset can be leased to the client to yield a return on it.
Sunna	Established customs, precedents, the conduct of life and cumulative tradition. Such tradition encompasses knowledge and practices passed down from previous generations, representing an authoritative, respected and continuous corpus of beliefs and customs. Also refers to the life and example of the Prophet as related through hadith.
takaful	A form of Islamic insurance based on the principle of mutual assistance (*ta'awuni*) – it offers joint risk-sharing in the event of a loss by one of its members.
talaq	Commonly 'repudiation or divorce'. In classical Islamic law this refers to the husband's right to dissolve the marriage by simply announcing to his wife that he repudiates her. It requires neither justification nor court approval, although certain conditions apply as to what constitutes a valid repudiation.
ta'zir	Discretionary sentence imposed by the *muhtasib* for crimes mentioned in the Qur'an but which do not have an overt sanction. Often it was used by the political authority when the rigours of sharia became too exacting and thus impractical.
'ulama	Term used for those educated in the religion and the law.
umma	Term used to refer to the whole community of Muslims.
'urf	Also known as *'ada* or *'adat*, or customary law, which has existed historically side by side with sharia. It includes local practices under the general umbrella of Islamic law and largely pertains to matters of marriage, divorce, inheritance, homicide, crimes of honour, status of women and land tenure.
usul al-fiqh	Arabic for 'roots of law'. The sources or 'roots' of Islamic jurisprudence, which, after al-Shafi'i, are identified as the Qur'an, Sunna, *ijma'* and *qiyas*; Islamic legal theory, legal methodology and theoretical jurisprudence.

Notes

Preface and Acknowledgements

1   S. Hossein Nasr, *The Study Quran: A New Translation and Commentary* (New York, 2015).

Introduction: Islamic Law in the Contemporary World

1   J. Jomier, *How to Understand Islam* (New York, 1989), p. 37.
2   Readers may wish to know what the specific law schools of Islam are. For this we suggest they refer to the Introduction of this book.
3   In Anglo-Saxon law, texts include the Constitution, early legal treatises, law reports, commentaries and so on. For Muslims, 'texts' include the Qur'an, commentaries on the Qur'an, hadith, the writings of exegetes, opinions of jurists, the *fiqh* or positive laws as developed by various legal scholars in early Islam, together with writings contributing to the understanding of the law.
4   The Shi'a are a group of people who regarded Ali as the immediate rightful successor to the Prophet both in his temporal and spiritual aspects. This historical development has subsequently taken on a metaphysical dimension which continues to this day. The Ibadis are one of the surviving communities of the Khariji tradition which considers itself to be neither Sunni nor Shi'i, and whose influence is found today in Oman, East Africa (particularly Zanzibar) and parts of North Africa. For further background, see W. M. Watt, *Islamic Philosophy and Theology* (Edinburgh, 1985), pp. 7–13.
5   See R. Griffith-Jones (2013), 'The "Unavoidable" Adoption of Sharia Law – The Generation of a Media Storm', in R. Griffith-Jones, ed., *Islam and English Law: Rights, Responsibilities and the Place of Shari'a* (Cambridge, 2013), pp. 9–19.

6 See S. Mourad, 'Riddles of the Book', *New Left Review* 86 (2014), p. 30. Available at https://newleftreview.org/II/86/suleiman-mourad-riddles-of-the-book. Accessed 30 March 2017.

7 A. Ahmed, 'Communal Autonomy and the Application of Islamic Law', *Newsletter of the Institute for the Study of Islam in the Modern World*, October 1982, p. 32.

8 A. A. An-Na'im, 'Sharia and Basic Human Rights Concerns', in *Toward an Islamic Reformation: Civil Liberties, Human Rights and International Law* (Syracuse, NY, 1996), pp. 161–181.

9 N. J. Coulson, *A History of Islamic Law* (Edinburgh, 1964), pp. 1–7. Emphasis added by authors.

10 Ibid., p. 1.

11 Ibid., p. 129.

12 The concept of *ijtihad* entails exerting one's mind in order to understand the signs of God in all their multifaceted manifestations. We explain this more fully in Chapter 1.

13 W. B. Hallaq, 'Was the Gate of Ijtihad Closed?', *International Journal of Middle East Studies* 3:16 (1984), pp. 3–41.

14 By positive laws we mean statutes which have been enacted by a legislature, or laws decided by a court or other institutions and which can take whatever form the promulgators wish them to take.

15 N. Feldman, 'Why Shariah?', *New York Times*, 16 March 2008, at http://www.nytimes.com/2008/03/16/magazine/16Shariah-t.html. Accessed 5 January 2017.

16. However, see Baderin, A. Mashood, 'Human Rights and Islamic Law: The Myth of Discord', *European Human Rights Law Review*, 2 (2005), pp. 165–185.

Chapter 1: Sharia – Origin through Revelation, Historical Development and Change

1 For further background see biographies of the Prophet including A. Guillaume, *The Life of Muhammad: Translation of Ibn Isḥāq's Sirat Rasul Allah* (Oxford, 1955); A. Schimmel, *Muhammad is His Messenger: A Veneration of the Prophet in Islamic Piety* (Chapel Hill, NC, 1985); W. M. Watt, *Muhammad: Prophet and Statesman* (Oxford, 1961); K. Armstrong, *Muhammad. Prophet of Our Time* (London, 2006); M. Rodinson, *Mohammed*, tr. Anne Carter (London, 1971).

2 The Qur'an states in 5:48:

'For each we have appointed a divine law (*shir'a*) and a clear way. Had God willed, He could have made you one community. But that He may test you by that which He has given you. So vie with one another in good works. Unto God you will all return, and He will then inform you of that wherein you differ.'

And Qur'an 45:18: 'We have sent you, O Muhammad, on a clear religious path (*sharī'a*) concerning the matter so follow it.'

3   The concept of Caliph/caliphate is discussed in Chapter 7.

4   B. Weiss, *The Spirit of Islamic Law* (Athens, GA, 1998), pp. 7–8.

5   Coulson, *A History of Islamic Law*, p. 12. Furthermore, even when verses in the Qur'an prohibit certain behaviours, sanctions for their violation are largely by way of moral exhortations rather than penal impositions.

6   Qur'an 4:59.

7   The 'straight path' is mentioned in the very first sura of the Qur'an as '*al-sirat al-mustaqim*'.

8   L. Hazleton, *After the Prophet: The Epic Story of the Shia-Sunni Split in Islam* (New York and Toronto, 2009); W. Madelung, *The Succession to Muhammad: A Study of the Early Caliphate* (Cambridge, 1996).

9   While for Sunni Islam consensus was generated through the '*ulama* or clerics, in Shi'i Islam it is the Imam who, as a descendant of the *ahl al-bayt*, or the House of the Prophet, has exclusive authority to interpret the law.

10 Qur'an 4:59.

11 This principle is based upon Q 3:104 of the Qur'an, which includes an exhortation to embrace good and prohibit evil and which guides the ethical behaviour of Muslims.

12 W. B. Hallaq, *The Origins and Evolution of Islamic Law* (Cambridge, 2005), p. 8.

13 Ibid., pp. 15–16.

14 Ibid., pp. 18–19.

15 Qur'an 81:8–14.

16 Hallaq, *Origins and Evolution*, p. 1. See also J. Schacht, *An Introduction to Islamic Law* (Oxford, 1946), p. 1.

17 Schacht, *Introduction to Islamic Law*, p. 1.

18 Ahmed, 'Communal Autonomy', p. 32.

19 Coulson, *History of Islamic Law*, p. 11.

20 Ibid., p. 12.

21 Cf. Richard Bell and W. M. Watt, *Introduction to the Qur'an* (Edinburgh, 1970).

22 Mecca was a traditional pre-Islamic centre of an annual pilgrimage and continued to be so after the advent of Islam, but henceforth as a monotheistic and Islamic centre under the direction of the Prophet.

23 It should be noted that this divine command has different connotations for Shi'is as opposed to Sunnis with regard to who was to provide this guidance after the death of the Prophet. We shall examine this issue in Chapter 7.

24 Qur'an 2:164. See also Qur'an 3:41.

25 *Jāmi' al-Tirmidhī*, ed. Hāfiz Abū Tāhir Zubayr 'Ali Za'i (Riyadh, 2007), *hadith* 1327, vol. 2, p. 124.

26 This is reported by Jabir b.'Abd Allah. See Muhammad b. 'Umar al-Wāqidī, *Kitāb al-Maghāzī*, ed. M. Jones (London, 1966), pp. 329–331.

27 The term 'Caliph' is first used in the Qur'an in reference to Adam in his custodial capacity on earth (Q 2:30) and also to David (Q 38:26). As deputy or successor to the Prophet, the term was first applied to Abu Bakr and subsequently to Umar, Uthman and Ali, who later are jointly referred to as the 'Rightly-Guided Caliphs'. For a fuller background of the term Caliph/caliphate, see Ahmad Pakatchi, 'Caliphate', *EIs*, vol. 5, pp. 407–462.

28 Qur'an 4:59.

29 *Hadd* (plural *huddud*): a set of offences mentioned in the Qur'an, in certain cases with fixed penalties that carried the maximum (*hadd*) punishment. This is more clearly defined in Chapter 11.

30 Literally 'apostasy' – a term associated with the wars against several tribes, who, following the death of the Prophet, refused to pay allegiance to Abu Bakr. This led to a set of skirmishes, the most famous of which was the battle against the tribe of Banu Tamim.

31 An example of such, which is quoted as a precedent by the author al-Mawardi, is the decision of Caliph Ali to introduce the rule of contributory negligence in accidental homicide. See Coulson, *History of Islamic Law*, p. 130.

32 The designation given to the first four Caliphs of Islam, Abu Bakr, Umar, Uthman and Ali, because they were close to the Prophet and took him as a model for their lives and because of the way they governed the newly fledged Muslim community.

33 See Hazleton, *After the Prophet*; W. Madelung, *The Succession to Muhammad*.

34 The Arabic term *sahaba* is generally applied to those who were close to the Prophet in his lifetime. Their closeness to the Prophet and their role in supporting him rendered them historically significant.

They are believed to have played a key role in the transmission of the Prophetic tradition. Their descendants were also selected for privileged treatment with regard to land and property.

35 Feldman, 'Why Shariah?'.

36 Coulson, *History of Islamic Law*, p. 20.

37 For a commentary on Ali's letter to Malik, see R. Shah-Kazemi, *Justice and Remembrance: Introducing the Spirituality of Imam Ali* (London, 2006), p. 109.

38 There are also stories about how Caliphs conducted their public business extolling the virtues of good behaviour and avoiding conflict of interest. These form part of the narrative by which Muslims gauge proper conduct. These stories are found in *Sira* (or Prophetic biography) literature. This is a genre which highlights the life of the Prophet and provides examples of good conduct for the faithful to follow.

39 The United Nations has advised Arab countries to take Ali b. Abi Talib as an example in establishing a regime based on justice and democracy and encouraging knowledge. The United Nations Development Programme in its 2002 Arab Human Development Report, distributed around the world, listed six sayings of Ali on ideal governance. See http://Qur'ansmessage.com/forum/index. php?topic=999.0. Accessed 11 January 2017.

40 Hallaq, *Origins and Evolution of Islamic Law*, p. 2.

41 The word itself means 'cube' and is referred to in the Qur'an as the 'house of God'. The Kaaba is the most important sanctuary in Islam. The structure is now located in the centre of the Great Mosque of Mecca and is the site of the annual pilgrimage, the Hajj. Muslims believe that the first Kaaba was constructed by the prophet Adam and subsequently rededicated to the worship of God by Abraham and his son Ishmael.

42 *Imam* in Shi'i Islam refers to a person from the progeny or household of the Prophet (*ahl al-bayt*) who is designated to guide the faithful in the interpretation of the faith. He is different from the imams of Sunni Islam who are functionaries who generally lead the daily prayers and are the heads of their respective mosques. See also W. Madelung, 'Imāma', *EI2*, vol. 3, pp. 1163–1169.

Chapter 2: Legal Practice under the Umayyads (661–750)

1 The Umayyads, who derived their name from the Quraysh clan of Banu Umayya, ruled in Damascus from 661 to 750. The dynasty came to power when Mu'awiya (d. 680), governor of Syria and

the nephew of Uthman, the third Caliph, challenged Ali b. Abi Talib's claim to the caliphate. The Umayyad dynasty ruled through 14 Caliphs until it was overthrown by the Abbasids, who moved the caliphate from Damascus to Baghdad. Only one Umayyad, 'Abd al-Rahman, escaped the massacre of the clan perpetrated by the Abbasids and managed to escape to Spain where, in 756, he established a Spanish Umayyad dynasty in that country which effectively lasted until 1492.

2 A *qadi* is a Muslim judge who provides rulings and resolves disputes according to the principles of the respective schools of sharia. For further information see E. Tyan, 'Ķāḍī', *EI2*, vol. 4, pp. 373–374.

3 See C. Geertz, *Islam Observed: Religious Development in Morocco and Indonesia* (Chicago, IL, 1971). See also L. Rosen, *The Anthropology of Justice – Law as Culture in Islamic Society* (Princeton, NJ, 1989).

4 Mustafa Akyol, *Islam without Extremes: A Muslim Case for Liberty* (New York, 2011), p. 59.

5 The Mu'tazilites formed a school of Muslim thought that flourished in the 9th-century court of the Abbasid Caliph al-Mamun (r. 813–833). They applied rationalist methods of discourse based on Greek philosophy to questions of Muslim doctrine and Qur'anic interpretation on issues such as the Unity of God, the Justice of God, free will and the createdness of the Qur'an. The Ash'arites, a competing school of scholars, conceived of God as a wholly transcendent entity whose actions could never be circumscribed by human logic.

6 The Abbasids were a Muslim dynasty whose period of rule in varying degrees of dominance lasted from 750 to 1258. They came to power claiming descent through an uncle of the Prophet named al-Abbas.

7 Qadariyya a Sufi order based on the teachings of Abd al-Qadir al-Jilani in the 12th century. Following his death, his sons formalised the Order and spread its teachings to many parts of the Muslim world.

8 Abu Mansur al-Maturidi (853–944) was born in Central Asia and was the founder of a school of Sunni theology. He was a jurist and commentator on the Qur'an. Building on the interpretations of the Hanafi doctrine popular in Balkh and Central Asia at the time, though a polemicist, he did not reject rationalism entirely, but helped in devising a distinctive approach in the context of the debates that were then current. See Azim Nanji and Razia Nanji, *The Penguin Dictionary of Islam* (London, 2008), p. 113.

9 The legal schools of the Shi'a are discussed in greater detail in Chapter 7.

10 See the 1997 case of Saima Waheed reported by Beena Sarwar at http://
    www.ipsnews.net/1997/03/pakistan-saima-wins-case-but-judgement-
    threatens-womens-rights/. Accessed 12 January 2017. Note also the
    statement of Justice S. M. Zubair in the Lahore High Court Case
    upholding the validity of the marriage of Najma Bibi with Mohammad
    Tariq Mahmood, when he states 'Islam allows an adult Muslim woman
    to marry according to her own choice. A *wali* or guardian is bound
    by the will and consent of the woman, not the other way around.'
    The Court noted that society is undergoing major socio-economic
    changes and held that 'it was the duty of jurists and superior court
    judges to give progressive interpretation to Islamic law provisions in
    keeping with the spirit of the law and the needs of the time'.
11 A. Lalani, *Early Shi'i Thought: The Teachings of Imam Muḥammad
    al-Bāqir* (London, 2000).
12 A. Lalani, ibid, pp. 37–57.
13 The word 'occultation' has a technical meaning for the condition of
    anyone who is not visible in the present but is regarded as existing
    but hidden from sight (*ghayba*), and therefore continues to have a
    metaphysical presence.

Chapter 3: Consolidation of the Schools of Law under the Abbasids (750–1258)

1 See Karen Armstrong, *Islam: A Short History* (London, 2000).
2 *Madhahib* (sing. *madhhab*), schools of Islamic law which came about
   through the process of systematising and codifying law undertaken
   by successive generations of Muslim scholars over three centuries
   in the central regions of early Islam. For the benefit of the reader we
   provide a brief outline of these schools in pp. xii–xiv of this book.
3 Muhammad al-Shaybani, (ca. 750–805), a scholar and jurist, was
   known to be a student of Abu Hanifa al-Nu'man, the founder of
   the Hanafi school of Islam. He grew up in Kufa, travelled to Medina
   and studied under Malik ibn Anas. His scholarship attracted the
   attention of the Abbasid Caliph, Harun al-Rashid, who enlisted his
   services for the state.
4 It should be noted that whilst this development was taking place with
   regard to what eventually became Sunni Islam, Shi'i principles of law
   were being conceptualised by the Shi'i Imams such as Muhammad
   al-Baqir and Ja'far al-Sadiq, who were operating outside the context
   of the political authority. Their ideas had a seminal influence on the
   early development of the theories of law.

5 This was the earliest written collection of hadith or sayings of the Prophet, which form the basis of *fiqh* or positive law. It is not only a collection of hadith, as many of the legal precepts it contains are not exclusively based on hadith. The book covers rituals, rites, customs, traditions and laws extant at the time of the Prophet.

6 Coulson, *History of Islamic Law*, p. 43.

7 Ibid., p. 52.

8 Hallaq, *Origins and Evolution*, p. 2.

9 Ibid., p. 205. This point is also emphasised by Mohamed Arkoun in his seminal article in Arabic entitled *al-Fikr al-uṣūlī wa istiḥālat al-taʾṣīl: naḥwa tarīkh ākhar li al-fikr al-islāmī (Foundationalism and the Problem with the Foundationalists)* (Beirut, 1999). This point was underlined in a personal interview with Dr Mohamed Keshavjee on 3 September 1998.

10 In a series of letters to his governors, al-Mamun adumbrated the Caliph's role as the guardian of God's religion and laws. It must be noted that he appeared to draw upon the Shiʿi notion that the Imam-Caliph alone possessed esoteric knowledge and he used this idea to emphasise his role as an educator to lead the people out of ignorance in religious matters. This was an effort on his part to arrogate to himself authority over religious knowledge from the scholars (*'ulama*), notably from traditionalists such as Ahmed ibn Hanbal whose authority to interpret was rooted in his expertise in the Prophet's Tradition. This did not succeed in the long term, as the Shiʿa distanced themselves from al-Mamun and, in the Sunni context, the position of the Caliph with regard to sharia was reduced first to political authority and later became more symbolic.

11 Coulson, *History of Islamic Law*, p. 53.

12 Ibid., p. 61.

13 This whole area about the hadith and its provenance has been the subject of discourse, beginning with the research of Ignaz Goldziher in the early 20th century. See also *I. Goldziher, Vorlesungen über den Islam* (Heidelberg, 1925) and *Etudes islamologiques d'Ignaz Goldziher* (Leiden, 1962), pp. 52–56.

14 Ibid., p. 57.

15 J. Schacht, *The Origins of Muhammadan Jurisprudence* (Oxford, 1950), p. 97.

16 Some Western scholarship on Islam conducted in the 20th century has regarded the majority of hadith as being unreliable and retrojected after the death of the Prophet. Others argue that hadith reflects more the religious discourses of the 2nd and 3rd centuries of Islam rather

than historical reality. Muslim scholars, in general, assert that while the element of invention was always present, the meticulous attention paid by Muslim collectors of hadith to authenticating the content and validating the role of the transmitters has enabled the established part of the tradition to be separated from that which may be regarded as unreliable. In a sense, historical fact is beside the point, as the role of hadith was to give 'body' to the initially meagre legal dispensations set out in the Qur'an. Hadith filled a void and its legitimacy was based upon its acceptance by Islamic scholars and believers.

17 Al-Kulayni was an important Shi'i hadith collector whose most important work, *al-Kafi*, was a seminal Twelver Shi'i hadith collection. Ibn Babawayh, also known as al-Suduk, was a theologian, jurist and an authoritative figure in Imami Shi'i theology and jurisprudence who lived in Baghdad. Muhammad al-Tusi was a Twelver Shi'i scholar who authored two of the four main Shi'i books of hadith. His works on theology and jurisprudence were responsible for the emergence of a strong legal tradition within the Imami Shi'i community.

18 Al-Zahiri was a Sunni Islamic scholar of the 9th century who reacted strongly against metaphorical readings of legal texts, insisting on the principle that law should be based on only the literal and evident meaning (*zahir*) of the holy texts.

19 Extremists refers to legal schools that adhered strictly to the principle of rejection of human reasoning in any form as a source of law by insisting that every legal rule found its authority in the holy texts, which needed to be read literally.

20 Coulson, *History of Islamic Law*, p. 73.

Chapter 4: Developments after Shafi'i

1 Muhammad al-Shatibi (d. 1385) was a scholar and jurist noted for his legal views on contextualising Muslim law and reinterpreting established practices within the social and economic contexts of the time. His greatest contribution was on the notion of *maqasid al-shari'a*, known as the 'higher purposes' of law which, today, is regarded as a concept through which sharia could be made more relevant to the needs of the time.

2 John Esposito, *Women in Muslim Family Law* (Syracuse, NY, 1982), p. 122.

3 See F. Rahman, 'Law and Ethics in Islam', in R. G. Hovannisian, ed., *Ethics in Islam* (Malibu, CA, 1985), pp. 3–15. More generally, see his

Islam and Modernity – Transformation of an Intellectual Tradition (Chicago, IL, 1982).

4   A. Duderija, 'Contemporary Muslim Reformist Thought and Maqāṣid cum Maṣlaḥa Approaches to Islamic Law: An Introduction', in A. Duderija, ed., *Maqāṣid al-Sharīʿa and Contemporary Reformist Muslim Thought: An Examination* (New York, 2014), pp. 1–9.

5   Coulson, *History of Islamic Law*, p. 75.

6   M. Rodinson, *Islam and Capitalism*, tr. Brian Pearce (London, 1973), pp. 137–138.

7   Suleiman Ali Mourad, *Early Islam between Myth and History: al-Ḥasan al-Baṣrī (d. 110 H/728 CE) and the Formation of his Legacy in Classical Islamic Scholarship* (Leiden, 2006), p. 163.

8   Akyol, *Islam without Extremes*, p. 102.

9   For a critique of this theory see A. Sachedina, *Prolegomena to the Qurʾan* (New York, 1998), pp. 186–248.

10 B. Lewis, *The Middle East: 2000 Years of History from the Rise of Christianity to the Present Day* (London, 1995), p. 210.

11 Akyol, *Islam without Extremes*, p. 102.

12 Marshall G. S. Hodgson, *The Venture of Islam: The Classical Age of Islam* (Chicago, IL, 1974), p. 343.

13 Genesis 3:16: 'I will greatly multiply thy sorrow and thy conception; in sorrow thou shalt bring forth children.'

14 Qurʾan 20:115–121.

15 Albert Hourani, *A History of the Arab Peoples* (London, 1991), pp. 5–6.

16 K. Abu al-Fadl, *The Great Theft* (New York, 2007).

17 W. M. Watt, *Freewill and Predestination in Early Islam* (London, 1948), pp. 17–30.

18 O. M. Farooq, 'Riba Interest and Six Hadiths; Do We Have a Definition or a Conundrum?' *Review of Islamic Economics* 13, no. 1, 2009, p. 105.

19 Quoted in Akyol, *Islam without Extremes*, p. 303.

20 A. Afsaruddin, *First Muslims: History and Memory* (Oxford, 2007), p. 116.

21 See An-Naʿim, *Toward an Islamic Reformation*, on how the theory of reverse abrogation could be utilised in the service of a more humane and compassionate *fiqh* relevant to modern times.

22 Quoted in N. J. Coulson, 'Doctrine and Practice of Islamic Law', *Bulletin of the School of Oriental and African Studies*, 18 (1956), p. 211.

23 For an elaboration of these points, see Coulson, *History of Islamic Law*, p. 82.

24 Ya'qub b. Ibrahim al-Ansari (d. 798).
25 Abu al-Hasan b. Muhammad b. Habib al-Mawardi (972–1058), known also as Alboacen.
26 Taqi al-Din Ahmad b. Taymiyya (d. 1328).
27 Burhan al-Din Ibrahim b. 'Ali al-Ya'mari ibn Farhun (ca. 1358–1397).
28 N. J. Coulson, *Conflicts and Tensions in Islamic Jurisprudence* (Chicago, IL, 1969), p. 60.

Chapter 5: Further Geographical Expansion and Cultural Accommodation

1 Coulson, *History of Islamic Law*, p. 123.
2 Marshall G. S. Hodgson, *The Venture of Islam: The Gunpowder Empires and Modern Times* (Chicago, IL, 1974).
3 See the report 'Prenuptial Agreement that Can End a Marriage', Mai Noman, 29 July 2014, at http://www.bbc.co.uk/news/magazine-28526103. Accessed 19 January 2017.
4 Coulson, *History of Islamic Law*, p. 137.
5 D. Powers, *Law Society, and Culture in the Maghreb, 1300–1500* (Cambridge, 2002), pp. 206–228.
6 A. Fakhri, *Fatwas and Court Judgments: A Genre Analysis of Arabic Legal Opinion* (Columbus, OH, 2004), p. 9.
7 Coulson, *History of Islamic Law*, p. 142.
8 A collection of fatwas of the Hanafi school of law compiled during the 17th century in India and influential in the subcontinent to this day.
9 G. Abdo, *New Sectarianism: The Arab Uprisings and the Rebirth of the Shia-Sunni Divide* (Oxford, 2017), p. 68.
10 See G. R. Bunt, *Islam in the Digital Age: E-Jihad, Online Fatwas and Cyber Islamic Environments* (London, 2003).
11 Coulson, *History of Islamic Law*, p. 143.
12 Ibid., p. 144.
13 Coulson, *History of Islamic Law*, p. 148.

Chapter 6: Call for Reform – from the *Tanzimat* to the Arab Spring

1 Where we speak of the West historically we are largely referring to Western Europe, though today the term is more broadly used to cover America and other countries such as Australia, Canada and New Zealand.
2 G. Pultar, ed., *Islam ve Modernite* (Istanbul, 2007), p. 195.

3   B. Lewis, *The Emergence of Modern Turkey* (Oxford, 1961), p. 130.

4   These had been ongoing since the mid-fifteenth century.

5   The Turkish Capitulations were grants made by successive Sultans to Christian nations, conferring rights and privileges in favour of their subjects resident or trading in Ottoman dominions; this policy mirrored that adopted by the Byzantine Empire. For further explanation see Maurits H. van den Boogert, *The Capitulations and the Ottoman Legal System: Qadis, Consuls and* Beraths *in the 18th Century* (Leiden, 2005).

6   Private law is that part of the legal system which deals with the relationships between individuals (including incorporated bodies) such as contracts and torts as described in Common Law, and the law of obligations under civil legal systems. In the case of the Capitulations this included family laws for Europeans.

7   For more detailed background to this topic see P. J. Vatikiotis, *The Modern History of Egypt* (London, 1985), and Hourani, *History of the Arab Peoples*.

8   Al-Sanhuri (1895–1971) was an Egyptian legal scholar who drafted the revised Egyptian Civil Code of 1948. He helped draft the Civil Codes of pre-Baathist Syria, Jordan and Libya, and the Commercial Code of Kuwait. Al-Sanhuri was known for attempting to recreate a 'pure Islamic law' by modernising sharia using Western civil law and inspired by its American and French enactments. A controversial figure, his place in the legal history of the modern Middle East is firmly established. See G. Bechor, *The Sanhuri Code, and the Emergence of Modern Arab Civil Law (1932 to 1949)* (Leiden, 2007).

9   Coulson, *History of Islamic Law*, p. 153.

10   Ibid., p. 155.

11   Ibid.

12   See footnote 7 above.

13   *Rector of the Azhar University v The President of the Republic, The President of the Council of Ministers, The President of the Legislative Committee of the People's Assembly, and Atef Fouad Goudah.* Supreme Constitutional Court of Egypt: Case No. 20 of Judicial Year 1985, 1 Arab L. Q 100, 104 (Saba Habachy trans. 1986).

14   Civil Shariat Review Petition No. 1 of 2000 at http://www.supremecourt.gov.pk/web/user_files/File/JR_Detailed_Judgment_in_Riba_Case.pdf. Accessed 22 March 2017.

15   In Moroccan law *mudawana* denotes the personal status code or family code. It covers the regulation of marriage, polygamy, divorce, inheritance and child custody.

16 Fatayat is the arm of the Nahdlatul Ulama established in 1950 which deals with women's issues, including gender equality and female participation in public life.

17 See I. Coleman, 'Women, Islam and the New Iraq', *Foreign Affairs* (Jan/Feb 2006), pp. 24–38.

18 The phrase is from a hadith of the Prophet: Abu Bakr al-Sarakhsī, *Uṣūl al-Sarakhsī* (Beirut, 1993), vol. 2, p. 313.

19 'Alā' al-Dīn 'Alī b. 'Abd al-Malik Ḥusām al-Dīn al-Mutaqqī al-Hindī, *Kanz al-'ummāl fī sunan al-aqwāl wa al-afʿāl* (Beirut, 1998), vol. 10, p. 36.

20 Coulson, *History of Islamic Law*, p. 201.

21 J. N. D. Anderson, *Islamic Law in the Modern World* (New York, 1959).

22 In *Itwari v Asghari*, an Indian law case, the judge stated 'that Muslim Law as enforced in India has considered polygamy as an institution to be tolerated but not encouraged, and has not conferred upon the husband any fundamental right to compel the first wife to share his consortium with another woman in all circumstances. In that case the circumstances in which his second marriage took place are relevant and material in deciding whether his conduct in taking a second wife was in itself an act of cruelty to the first. A Muslim husband has the legal right to take a second wife even while the first marriage subsists, but if he does so, and then seeks the assistance of the civil court to compel the first wife to live with him against her wishes on pain of severe penalties including attachment of property, she is entitled to raise the question whether the court, as a court of equity, ought to compel her to submit to co-habitation with such a husband. In that case the circumstances in which his second marriage took place are relevant and material in deciding whether his conduct in taking a second wife was in itself an act of cruelty to the first.' See: https://indiankanoon.org/doc/1456722/. Accessed 19 January 2017. See also *Mohd. Ahmed Khan v Shah Bano Begum* (1985 SCR (3) 844) at https://en.wikipedia.org/wiki/Mohd._Ahmed_Khan_v._Shah_Bano_Begum. See also *Khurshid Bibi v Muhammad Amin* in Women's Rights Case Law at https://wrcaselaw.wordpress.com/2012/09/04/khul-divorce-khurshid-bibi/. Accessed 19 January 2017.

23 M. Keshavjee, *Islam, Sharia and Alternative Dispute Resolution – Mechanisms for Legal Redress in the Muslim Community* (London, 2013). See also S. Sardar Ali, *Modern Challenges to Islamic Law* (Cambridge, 2016), and The Boyd Commission Report (2004)

Dispute Resolution in Family Law: Protecting Choice, Promoting Inclusion – Executive Summary at https://www.attorneygeneral. jus.gov.on.ca/english/about/pubs/boyd/executivesummary.html. Accessed 19 January 2017.

Chapter 7: Shi'i Legal Understanding and Theory of Law

1　F. Daftary and G. Miskinzoda, eds, *The Study of Shi'i Islam: History, Theology and Law* (London, 2014), p. 271. This book aims to address the problem of lack of primary sources by attempting to examine the *fiqh* of minority Muslim communities on the basis of what is expounded by their own practitioners of the law.

2　A Caliph is a deputy or successor to the Prophet. The title was first applied to Abu Bakr who led the Muslim community after the death of the Prophet. The term was also applied to the other immediate three successors – Omar, Uthman and Ali – known as the Rightly-Guided Caliphs. For a fuller description see Pakatchi, 'Caliphate'. The last caliphate came to end on 3 March 1924 after the dissolution of the Ottoman empire.

3　With the occultation of the Imam in the majoritarian Shi'i Ithna 'ashari school and later in other Shi'i *tariqa*s or interpretations, the law in itself also became more rigid in the absence of a living hereditary Imam to guide the legal process and its evolution.

4　Benefit or interest to be enjoyed by the public in different contexts such as the economy, justice and mutual treatments. These should be in line with the higher objectives of sharia.

5　Public benefits which serve the essentials required to protect a person's spiritual and material well-being. These (life, intellect, property, offspring and religion) are called '*al-daruriyyat*'.

6　See A. Abdalla, 'Principles of Islamic Interpersonal Conflict Intervention: A Search within Islam and Western Literature', *Journal of Law and Religion* 15 (2001), pp. 151–184; M. Keshavjee, 'Alternative Dispute Resolution (ADR) and its Potential for Helping Muslims Reclaim the Higher Ethical Values (*Maqasid*) Underpinning the Sharia', in H. Tiliouine and R. J. Estes, eds, *The State of Social Progress in Islamic Societies* (Basel, 2016), pp. 607–622; and Keshavjee, *Islam, Sharia and Alternative Dispute Resolution*. Furthermore, work in this field is exemplified by the Muslim Law Sharia Council UK established by the eminent scholar Zaki Badawi. See also S. N. Shah-Kazemi, *Untying the Knot: Muslim Women, Divorce and the Shariah* (London, 2001), at http://www.nuffieldfoundation.org/untying-knot-muslim-women-divorce-and-shariah. Accessed 30 January 2017.

7 See M. Keshavjee and R. Abdulla, 'Modern Developments Concerning a Purpose-Based Understanding of Sharia', in *The Shari'a: History, Ethics and Law*, ed. A. Sajoo (forthcoming).

8 See footnote 12 in Chapter 2.

9 Coulson, *History of Islamic Law*, p. 107.

10 But see *Hadith al-Thaqalayn*, a Sunni source in al-Tirmidhi, *Sunan al-Tirmidhī*, ed. Muḥammad Ibn 'Īsā (Beirut, 2000), vol. 5, pp. 433–434.

11 Madelung, *The Succession to Muhammad*. For a more accessible account of this narrative see Hazleton, *After the Prophet*.

12 Coulson, *History of Islamic Law*, p. 105.

13 These were Twelver Shi'ism's most authoritative commentators on law and doctrine and they compiled what came to be referred to as the 'Four Books'. Abu Ja'far Muhammad b. Ya'qub al-Kulayni (d. 941) and Ali b. Babawayh al-Qummi, also known as Ibn Babawayh (d. 991), wrote *al-Kāfī* and *Risālat al-I'tiqādāt*, respectively, which provide useful points of comparison with the contemporary *Da'ā'im al-Islām* of al-Qadi al-Nu'man. These works show the differences between Twelver and Ismaili Shi'i doctrines of Imamat. See also S. Hamdani, *Between Revolution and State: the Path to Fatimid Statehood* (London, 2006), p. 57.

14 We have taken the Ithna 'ashari school of Shi'i Islam since it is the largest school in this branch of the religion. The Ithna 'asharis follow a line of 12 Imams beginning with Ali b. Abi Talib and ending with Muhammad al-Mahdi, who went into occultation (*ghayba*) and whose reappearance as the Mahdi is awaited. The Mahdi represents the redemptive messianic figure at the end of time.

15 If readers want to know more about this concept see S. Haeri, *The Law of Desire* (Syracuse, NY, 1989). The book, based inter alia on academic field studies conducted in Iran, contrasts in detail the difference between permanent marriage (*nikah*) and temporary marriage (*mut'a*) and highlights the legal consequences of each type of relationship.

16 For further background see E. Francesca, 'Constructing an Identity: The Development of Ibadi Law', in A. al-Salimi and H. Gaube, eds, *Studies on Ibadism and Oman* (Hildesheim, 2014), vol. 3, pp. 109–131. For readers who wish to know more about Ibadi law, this can be found at: https://hajarmulder.wordpress.com/2008/11/15/ibadi-ahadith/. Accessed 4 December 2017.

17 Al-Baqir had a prestigious genealogy in that both his maternal and paternal grandfathers, al-Hasan and al-Husayn, were grandsons of the Prophet. He was the father of Ja'far al-Sadiq who succeeded him as Imam of the Shi'i Muslims. On both see A. Lalani, *Early Shi'i Thought: The Teachings of Imam Muḥammad al-Bāqir* (London, 2000), pp. 37–57.

18 Ibid., p. 156, nn 2, 3, 4 and 5.

19 Ibid., p. 103. It is said that at that time there were some influential Sunni jurists known as the 'Seven Lawyers of Medina'. They were famous because they featured prominently in most of the tracts of Sunni law during a formative period.

20 Ibid., pp. 102–103.

21 Duderija, *Maqāṣid al-Sharī'a*.

22 See F. Daftary, *Historical Dictionary of the Ismailis* (Lanham, MD, 2012), pp. 90–92.

23 A Shi'i Ismaili dynasty that ruled in Egypt and North Africa from 909 to 1172. The name derives from the connection of its rulers to Fatima, the daughter of the Prophet and wife of Ali b. Abi Talib. At its height Fatimid sovereignty extended to many parts of the Middle East, the Mediterranean, parts of India as well as to Iran and Central Asia. Their rule was characterised for its cultural, scientific and economic achievements.

24 The Fatimid notion of authority was novel in the sense that the Shi'i Imam held a dual position as both head of faith and head of state. This has an important bearing on the development of sharia, though it must be remembered that the Fatimids did not supplant Sunni Maliki law in Egypt but had Shi'i functionaries operating the legal system alongside Sunni judges.

25 Bohras, also known as Ismailis, live largely in the Indian subcontinent. They converted to Islam from about the 11th century onwards and belong to the line of Ismailism that gave their allegiance to al-Musta'li after 1094; they are also known as Musta'li Tayyibi Ismailis. In 1539, their head, known by the title of *da'i al-mutlaq*, moved from Yemen to India, and their headquarters is now in Mumbai.

26 The Alamut period is named after the mountain fortress which became the seat of the Nizari Ismaili state. In 1090, the Ismaili *da'i* Hasan-i Sabbah seized Alamut, situated in Persia about 35 kilometres north-east of Qazwin in the region of Daylam, and established the Nizari Ismaili state, later also founding a major library there. In 1256, Alamut was conquered by the Mongols.

27 In Ithna 'ashari cosmology, the Imam, though in occultation, is referred to as *Imam-i Zaman*, which signifies 'Lord of the Age', connoting that, although he is physically absent, he is spiritually present. The interpretation of the law is under his metaphysical oversight.

28 See http://iis.ac.uk/news/message-international-islamic-conference. Accessed 23 March 2017. *Zahir* signifies the outer meaning of the holy texts as opposed to *batin* which connotes the inner meaning.

Chapter 8: The Multiple Manifestations of Sharia

1 The Runnymede Trust, *Islamophobia: A Challenge for Us All* (London, 1997).

2 See R. Griffith-Jones, 'The 'Unavoidable' adoption of *shari'a* law' pp. 9–18.

3 Ayatollah Khomeini (1902–1989) was the religious leader of Iran who overthrew the Shah, bringing to an end a long period of monarchy.

4 For further elaboration on this important issue see M. Ruthven, *A Satanic Affair: Salman Rushdie and the Rage of Islam* (London, 1990). See also R. Webster, *The History of Blasphemy* (London, 1990); and Z. Sardar and M. W. Davies, *Distorted Imagination: Lessons from the Rushdie Affair* (London, 1990).

5 See 'Afghan on Trial for Christianity', 20 March 2006. Available at http://news.bbc.co.uk/go/pr/fr/-/2/hi/south_asia/4823874.stm. Accessed 28 June 2017.

6 Constitution of Afghanistan Art. 130, *Official Gazette* No. 818 (28 January 2004) at http://www.Afghan-web.com/politics/current_constitution.html. Accessed 28 June 2017.

7 Knust Rassekh Afshar, 'The Case of an Afghan Apostate – The Right to a Fair Trial between Islamic Law and Human Rights in the Afghan Constitution', in *Max Planck Yearbook of United Nations*, vol. 10, 2006, pp. 591–605. Available at http://www.mpil.de/files/pdf3/mpunyb_13_knust1.pdf. Accessed 28 June 2017.

8 See 'Afghanistan: Pressure Mounts Over Afghan Conversion Case', 23 March 2006, Radio Liberty. Available at https://www.rferl.org/a/1067028.html. Accessed 27 June 2017.

9 See Syed Saleem Shahzad, 'Losing Faith in Afghanistan', *Asia Times on Line*, 24 March 2006. Available at http://www.Atimes.com/atimes/South_Asia/HC25Df02.html. Accessed 28 June 2017.

10 See Abdul Waheed Wafa and David Rhode, 'Kabul Judge Rejects Calls to End Trial of Christian Convert', *New York Times*, 24 March 2006. Available at http://www.nytimes.com/2006/03/24/world/asia/kabul-judge-rejects-calls-to-end-trial-of-christian-convert.html?mcubz=1. Accessed 28 August 2017.

11 See 'Afghan Convert May Be Released', BBC News, 25 March 2006, at http://news.bbc.co.uk/1/hi/world/south_asia/4841812.stm. Accessed 28 June 2017.

12 Ron Synovitz, 'Afghanistan: Pressure Mounts Over Afghan Conversion Case', 23 March 2006, Radio Free Europe/Radio Liberty. Available at https://en.wikipedia.org/wiki/Abdul_Rahman_(convert). Accessed 28 June 2017.

13 See https://en.wikipedia.org/wiki/Abdul_Rahman_(convert). Accessed 28 June 2017.

14 Resistance to change in the 20th century was not new to Afghanistan. In 1929 Habibullah Kalakani deposed King Amanullah with the help of various Afghan tribes who opposed the modernisation of Afghanistan. Amanullah had returned from Europe in 1928 convinced of the need to modernise Afghanistan rapidly, a notion that upset the ultra-conservative Shinwari tribe of eastern Afghanistan, who began calling for Amanullah's banishment from Afghanistan. On taking power, Kalakani closed schools for women and all Western education centres. He was vanquished soon thereafter, and by late October 1929 Nadir Khan's army defeated him and took up the reins of power. See Vartan Gregorian, *The Emergence of Modern Afghanistan: Politics of Reform and Modernization, 1880–1946* (Stanford, CA, 1969), and Rhea Talley Stewart, *Fire in Afghanistan 1914–1929: The First Opening to the West Undone by Tribal Ferocity Years Before the Taliban* (Garden City, NY, 1973).

15 Note that the Hebrew scripture does not use the word 'blaspheme' but the euphemism 'bless' – as in the Book of Job or Kings – as the Masoretes obviously felt that even to write the word 'blaspheme' with reference to God was not acceptable. Hence the idea of blasphemy has a long history of being such a capital crime that it could hardly be uttered. See http://biblehub.com/text/1_kings/21-10.htm. Accessed 29 June 2017.

16 C. Ernst, 'Blasphemy: Islamic Concept', *Encyclopedia of Religion*, ed. L. Jones (Detroit, MI, 2005), pp. 974–977.

17 See footnote 3 above.

18 See https://tribune.com.pk/story/99277/taseers-remarks-about-blasphemy-law/. Accessed 29 June 2017.

19 The Ahmadiyya movement was founded by Mirza Ghulam Ahmad (ca. 1835–1908), who is accorded messianic and prophetic status. Because of this claim, the movement is regarded as heretical and is proscribed in Pakistan and various other Muslim countries.

20 For further details of this, see the leading article in the *Guardian*, 3 March 2016, entitled: 'Religious Intolerance: a Sin against Freedom'. Available at https://www.theguardian.com/commentisfree/2016/mar/03/the-guardian-view-on-religious-intolerance-a-sin-against-freedom. Accessed 23 January 2017.

21 See Emont John, 'Jakarta's Christian Governor Sentenced to Prison in Blasphemy Case', *Washington Post* – World Views (Analysis), 9 May 2017. Available at https://www.washingtonpost.com/news/worldviews/wp/2017/05/09/jakartas-christian-governor-sentenced-to-prison-in-blasphemy-case/?utm_term=.4cb0ebdd75ec. Accessed 29 June 2017.

22 See the *Guardian*, 11 October 2016, at https://www.theguardian.com/world/2016/oct/11/asia-bibi-pakistan-blasphemy-law-supreme-court-death-sentence-salmaan-taseer. Accessed 29 June 2017.

23 *Dawn*, 'Blasphemy: What You Need to Know about Asia Bibi's Trial', reported and updated on 13 October 2016, at https://www.dawn.com/news/1289700. Accessed 29 June 2017.

24 See Naeem Shakir in *Lapidomedia*, 7 October 2016, at http://www.lapidomedia.com/authors/111. Accessed 27 March 2017.

25 Ibid.

26 This law in the United Kingdom was last invoked in 1977 when the magazine *Gay News* and its editor Denis Lemon were found guilty of blasphemous libel in a private prosecution brought by Mary Whitehouse, who was the secretary of the National Viewers' and Listeners' Association, where she objected to a poem and illustration about a homosexual centurion's love for Christ at the crucifixion. It should be noted that Mrs Whitehouse succeeded in proving blasphemy. See http://news.bbc.co.uk/onthisday/hi/dates/stories/july/11/newsid_2499000/2499721.stm. Accessed 19 September 2017.

27 It should also be noted that the judge who passed sentence on Salman Taseer's murderer has had to leave Pakistan for fear of his own life, and also that the offence has been successively rewritten and widened while the punishment has been made more stringent.

28 See Dan Isaacs 'Nigerian Woman Fights Stoning' on BBC News, 8 July 2002. Available at http://news.bbc.co.uk/1/hi/world/africa/2116540. stm. Accessed 29 June 2017.

29 See Mukhtar Mai, *In the Name of Honour* (London, 2007).

30 Similar advocacy of women's rights with particular reference to education has arisen in the case of Malala. See M. Yousafzai, *I Am Malala* (New York, 2014).

31 See M. A. Chaudary, *Justice in Practice: Legal Ethnography of a Pakistani Punjabi Village* (Karachi, 1999).

32 *Lina Joy v Majlis Agama Islam Wilayah Persekutuan & 2 Ors 2005* [CA] at http://www.malaysianbar.org.my/selected_judgements/lina_joy_v_majlis_agama_islam_wilayah_persekutuan_2_ors_2005_ca.html. Accessed 29 June 2017.

33 Nathaniel Tan and John Lee, *Religion Under Siege? Lina Joy, The Islamic State and Freedom of Speech* (Kuala Lumpur, 2008), p. 12.

34 It may be interesting to note that Judaism does not recognise apostasy. The Talmud (*Shulchan Aruch, Even Haezer* 44:9) does not state this in so many words but considers a marriage between a Jewish man and a Jewish woman, who have both converted to another religion, as completely valid, and their children are considered Jewish.

35 For a view on the full implications of this case, see the lecture of Dato Cyrus Das to the Malaysian Bar Council in S. Ang, M. Choon and L. Fong, 'Report on the State of Religious Liberty in Malaysia for the Year 2007', in *Religious Liberty After 50 Years of Independence* (Petaling, 2008), pp. 41–50. See also T. Thomas, 'Is Malaysia an Islamic State', in T. Thomas, *Anything but the Law – Essays on Politics and Economics* (Selangor, 2016), pp. 105–141.

36 See Coleman, 'Women, Islam and the New Iraq', pp. 24–38.

37 A. A. An-Na'im, *Islamic Family Law in a Changing World: A Global Resource Book* (London, 2002), p. 170.

38 *Rector of al-Azhar University v The President of the Republic, The President of the Council of Ministers, The President of the Legislative Committee of the People's Assembly, and Atef Fouad Goudah.* Supreme Constitutional Court of Egypt: Case No. 20 of Judicial Year 1985 – 1 Arab L.Q 100,104 (Saba Habachy trans. 1986).

39 Civil Shariat Review Petition No. 1 of 2000 at http://www.supreme-court.gov.pk/web/user_files/File/JR_Detailed_Judgment_in_Riba_Case.pdf. Accessed 22 March 2017.

40 See W. M. Ballantyne, *Essays and Addresses on Arab Laws* (London, 1999).

41 Human Rights Watch, 'Integration of the Human Rights of Women and the Gender Perspective: Violence against Women and "Honor" Crimes', 5 April 2001, quoted on www.wikigender.org/wiki/honour-crimes/.

42 Murat Gezer Şanliurfa in *Today's Zaman*, 28 July 2008.

43 Quoted in Elaine Storkey, *Scars Across Humanity: Understanding and Overcoming Violence Against Women* (London: SPCK, 2015).

44 The question of sexuality in the modern world demands a new approach towards understanding the various legal issues affecting the LGBTQ community. Although homosexual acts are regarded as unlawful and punishable under Islamic law, especially by those who invoke scriptural prohibitions as interpreted by them, in the contemporary world such prosecutions assume human rights dimensions which cannot be ignored. LGBTQ people who act without discretion in Muslim societies could face social and legal hostility. A great deal more research needs to be undertaken in the light of modern scientific knowledge concerning possible genetic predispositions coupled with ethics, human rights law and the broader sharia principles. Whilst some work has been done by a few Muslim academics who point out that there is no consensus of opinion on the status of the LGBTQ community in the Muslim world, more work needs to be carried out.

45 Quoted from http://assembly.coe.int/nw/xml/XRef/Xref-XML2 HTML-en.asp?fileid=17106&lang=en. Accessed 29 August 2017.

46 Eric K. Silverman, 'Anthropology and Circumcision', *Annual Review of Anthropology*, 33 (2004), pp. 419–445.

47 See, however, Nawal El Saadawi, 'I Am Going to Carry on this Fight Forever', *Independent*, 15 October 2011. The Senegalese director Ousmane Sembène in his award-winning 2004 film *Moolaadé*, shows how it is the female elders in a village who actually carry out the practice of FGM.

48 N. M. Nour, K. B. Michels and A. E. Bryant, 'Defibulation to Treat Female Genital Cutting', *Obstetrics & Gynecology*, 108 (2006), pp. 55–60.

49 See https://www.theguardian.com/society/video/2017/mar/17/jaha-dukureh-promise-fgm-video. Accessed 20 March 2017.

50 See Sandra Laville, 'Doctor Found not Guilty of FGM on Patient at London Hospital', *Guardian*, 4 February 2015.

51 See Keshavjee, *Islam, Sharia and Alternative Dispute Resolution*, pp. 133–134.

52 A judge in the Outer House of the Scottish Court of Session.
53 M. Keshavjee, *Islam, Sharia and Alternative Dispute Resolution*, p. 135. Also see *Sohrab v Khan* (2002) SLT, p. 1255.
54 https://www.theguardian.com/uk-news/2018/may/29/couple-found-guilty-attempted-forced-marriage-daughter
55 https://www.theguardian.com/global-development/2018/may/28/thousands-enslaved-in-forced-marriages-across-uk-investigation-finds
56 http://www.ipsnews.net/1997/03/pakistan-saima-wins-case-but-judgement-threatens-womens-rights/. See also Martin Lau, *The role of Islam in the Legal System of Pakistan* (Leiden, 2006), p. 206.
57 Quoted in Declan Walsh, 'The Rescuers', *Guardian*, 5 December 2005.
58 Sira Abdul Rahman, 'Religion and Animal Welare — An Islamic Perspective', *Animals*, 7, 11, 2017.
59 For a background on how Z. A. Badawi was able to place Islamic precepts into a modern context, see Keshavjee, *Islam Sharia and Alternative Dispute Resolution*, pp. 82–85.
60 Duderija, 'Contemporary Muslim Reformist Thought and Maqāṣid cum Maṣlaḥa Approaches to Islamic Law: An Introduction', in Duderija, ed., *Maqāṣid al-Sharīʿa*, pp. 1–9.

Chapter 9: Neo-*Ijtihad*

1 See I. Asaria, 'Influencing Transformational Change Through Governance: Engaging Public Policy Makers and Legislators in Islamic Finance'. Lecture given in March 2016 at the 7th [Malaysian] Security Commission – Oxford Centre for Islamic Studies Roundtable.
2 Duderija, 'Contemporary Muslim Reformist Thought', pp. 1–9.
3 We should note that Islamic finance has no particular 'home' in that it is not supported by a national or international legal system as such but is free-floating inasmuch as sharia itself is not tied to a particular state but applied by many states in various manifestations. For an up-to-date understanding of some of these issues on a continuing basis, see Mushtak Parker, 'Basel III Standard Moots IFI's Ability to Meet LCR', *Islamic Banker*, 204, January 2013, pp. 6–7; 'A Global Sharia Authority of Last Resort: Time to Nail Apex Shariah Body for Islamic Finance', *Islamic Banker*, 208, May 2013, p. 2; 'Shariah Transparency Key to Demystifying Tawarruq', *Islamic Banker*, 210, July 2013, pp. 12–13; and 'Malaysia Edges towards Law Harmonization for Islamic Finance', *Islamic Banker*, 213, October 2013, p. 16. See

also Mushtak Paker, 'Continued Islamic Banking Surveillance Vital', *New Straits Times*, 27 June 2017.

4 See footnote 1 above.

5 Q 2:275; 2;276; 2:278; Q 3:130; Q 4:161; Q 3:39.

6 See N. Saleh, *Unlawful Gain and Legitimate Profit in Islamic Law: Riba, Gharar and Islamic Banking* (Cambridge, 1986). See also Ballantyne, *Essays and Addresses.*

7 C. Mallat, 'Tantawi on Banking Operations in Egypt', in K. Masud, B. Messick and D. Powers, eds, *Islamic Legal Interpretation: Muftis and their Fatwas* (Cambridge, MA, 1996), pp. 286–287.

8 R. Riḍā, 'Ribḥ ṣundūq al-tawfīr', *al-Manār*, 19, 1917, p. 528.

9 R. Riḍā, 'Ṣundūq al-tawfīr fī idārat al-barīd', *al-Manār*, 19, 1917, pp. 28–29.

10 Mallat, *Tantawi on Banking Operations in Egypt*, pp. 286–287. See also Malcolm H. Kerr, *Islamic Reform: The Political and Legal Theories of Muhammad Abduh and Rashid Rida* (Berkeley, CA, 1966).

11 Nabil Saleh, 'Financial Transactions and the Islamic Theory of Obligations and Contracts', in C. Mallat, ed., *Islamic Law and Finance* (London, 1988), p. 26.

12 See W. M. Ballantyne, 'Islamic Law and Financial Transactions in Contemporary Perspective', in his *Essays and Addresses*, p. 178.

13 Ballantyne, *Essays and Addresses*, p. 276.

14 This notion sets out the freedom of choice between parties.

15 Quotations from Saleh in this and the following paragraph are from: N. Saleh, 'Financial Transactions and Contracts', pp. 26–27.

16 W. M. Ballantyne, 'The Sharia: Bridges or Conflict?', in his *Essays and Addresses on Arab Laws* (London, 1999), p. 278.

17 Mallat, 'Tantawi on Banking Operations', p. 288.

18 Ibid.

19 Ibid., p. 294.

20 Ibid., p. 295.

21 Ibid., p. 296.

22 Ibid.

23 See M. Rasekh, 'Sharia and Law in the Age of Constitutionalism', *The Journal of Global Justice and Public Policy*, 2 (2016), pp. 274–275.

24 See http://blogs.worldbank.org/arabvoices/vaccine-sukuks-islamic-securities-deliver-economic-and-social-returns. Accessed 24 January 2017.

25 See Duderija, *Maqāṣid al-Sharīʿa*, and more specifically his chapter 'Islamic Law Reform and *Maqāṣid al-Sharīʿa* in the Thought of Mohammad Hashim Kamali', pp. 13–38.

26 Some of these professionals have begun to write books on the topic, but there is still much work to be done at a greater depth. See M. D. Bakar, *Shariah Minds in Islamic Finance* (Kuala Lumpur, 2016).

27 See Timur Kuran, *Islam and Mammon: The Economic Predicaments of Islamism* (Princeton, NJ, 2004); ibid. *The Long Divergence: How Islamic Law Held Back the Middle East* (Princeton, NJ, 2010).

28 See I. Asaria, *Influencing Transformational Change Through Governance: Engaging Public Policy Makers and Legislators in Islamic Finance.* Lecture given in March 2016 at the 7th [Malyasian] Security Commission – Oxford Centre for Islamic Studies Roundtable.

29 A rhetorical question posed by Iqbal Asaria during his presentation 'From Halal to Halal to Tayyib' at an Institute of Islamic Banking and Insurance seminar held at Ernst & Young on 12 May 2015.

30 One example of a transnational dispute resolution system is the Conciliation and Arbitration Board system of the Ismaili Muslim community, an international system operating under the Ismaili Muslim Constitution, which is the governing structure for Ismailis worldwide. See M. Keshavjee, *Family Mediation in the Shia Imami Ismaili Muslim Community: Institutional Structures, Training and Practice* (London, 2009). See http://iis.ac.uk/family-mediation-shia-imami-ismaili-muslim-community-institutional-structures-training-and-practice. Accessed 24 July 2017.

31 See the Report on *Access to Justice Final Report*, by The Right Honourable The Lord Woolf, Master of the Rolls, July 1996, *Final Report to the Lord Chancellor on the Civil Justice system in England and Wales* at https://en.wikipedia.org/wiki/Civil_Procedure_Rules. Accessed 24 January 2017.

32 The Law Dictionary at http://thelawdictionary.org/article/what-percentage-of-lawsuits-settle-before-trial-what-are-some-statistics-on-personal-injury-settlements. Accessed 5 July 2017.

33 See M. Keshavjee, 'Alternative Dispute Resolution: Its Resonance in Muslim Thought and Future Directions', a talk given at the Ismaili Centre, London, 2 April 2002. Available at http://akdn2stg.prod.acquia-sites.com/sites/default/files/keshavjee_adr-144515351.pdf. Accessed 24 January 2017.

34 See A. Othman, 'And Amicable Settlement Is Best: Sulh and Dispute Resolution in Islamic Law', *Arab Law Quarterly* 21 (2007), pp. 64–90.

35 It should be noted that in Islamic law a husband has to grant a *talaq* to his wife regardless of whether she has been divorced by a civil or secular court.

36 This is also discussed by al-Ghazali and Ibn Taymiyya. See Duderija, 'Contemporary Muslim Reformist Thought', pp. 1–9.

37 Keshavjee, *Islam, Sharia and Alternative Dispute Resolution*.

38 See S. N. Shah-Kazemi, *Untying the Knot*.

39 See Abdalla, 'Principles of Islamic Interpersonal Conflict Intervention', pp. 151–184. See also 'Independent Review into Sharia Law Launched' at https://www.gov.uk/government/news/independent-review-into-sharia-law-launched. Accessed 24 January 2017.

40 See D. MacEoine, *Sharia Law or 'One Law for All'?* (London, 2009).

41 See M. Boyd, *Dispute Resolution in Family Law: Protecting Choice, Promoting Inclusion* at https://www.attorneygeneral.jus.gov.on.ca/english/about/pubs/boyd/executivesummary.html. Accessed 24 January 2017.

42 See T. Fatah, *Pakistan: The Tragic Illusion of an Islamic State* (Mississauga, ON, 2008).

43 See. Griffith-Jones, ed., *Islam and English Law*. See also A. Korteweg and J. Selby J., eds, *Debating Sharia: Islam, Gender Politics, and Family Law Arbitration* (Toronto, 2012). See also, Keshavjee, *Islam, Sharia and Alternative Dispute Resolution*.

44 M. Phillips, 'May Needs to Wake Up to the Reality of Sharia', *The Times*, 2 August 2016. In autumn 2016 debates commenced in the UK Parliament with regard to the role of such councils and their relationship with the national laws of the country. See also S. Bano, *An Exploratory Study of Shariah Councils*. J. R. Bowen, 'How Could English Courts Recognise the Shariah?', pp. 411–435 gives a fuller background on the work of sharia councils in the United Kingdom.

45 For the full text, see http://www.lawandreligionuk.com/2018/02/01/sharia-in-england-and-wales-report-of-the-independent-review/. Accessed 19 February 2018.

46 See A. Othman, 'And Amicable Settlement is Best', pp. 64–90.

47 Abdur Rahman I. Doi, *Shariah: The Islamic Law* (London, 1984), pp. 14–15.

48 R. Shah-Kazemi, *Justice and Remembrance*, p. 229.

49 Ibid., p. 109.

50 Ibid.

51 Ronald C. Jennings, 'Kadi, Court and Legal Procedures in 17th C. Ottoman Kayseri: Kadi and the Legal System', *Studia Islamica*, 48 (1978), pp. 133–172. Keyseri was one of the largest cities in Anatolia in the 16th century, and it was the administrative centre of the region.

52 See D. S. El Alami and D. Hinchliffe, *Islamic Marriage and Divorce Laws in the Arab World* (London, 1998).

53 See W. B. Hallaq, *Sharīʿa: Theory Practice and Transformations* (Cambridge, 2009), pp. 162–163.

54 See Abdalla, 'Principles of Islamic Interpersonal Conflict Intervention', pp. 151–184.

55 See Rahman, *Islam and Modernity*. See also, his 'Law and Ethics in Islam', pp. 3–15.

56 See Duderija, ed., *Maqāṣid al-Sharīʿa*, and more specifically his chapter 'Islamic Law Reform and Maqāṣid al-Sharīʿa in the Thought of Mohammad Hashim Kamali', pp. 13–38.

57 See M. Keshavjee, 'Dispute Resolution', in A. Sajoo, ed., *A Companion to Muslim Ethics* (London, 2010), pp. 151–166. See also Keshavjee, 'Alternative Dispute Resolution', p. 607.

58 See Keshavjee, *Islam, Sharia and Alternative Dispute Resolution*, and also S. N. Shah-Kazemi, *Untying the Knot*.

59 See M. Keshavjee, 'Cross-Border Child Abduction Mediation in Cases Concerning Non-Hague Parental Child Convention Countries', in C. Paul and S. Kiesewetter, eds, *Cross-Border Family Mediation: International Parental Child Abduction, Custody and Access Cases* (Frankfurt, 2014), pp. 95–114.

60 From Judge Jillani's speech to the Conference on 7 May 2016, a copy of which was sent to Dr Mohamed Keshavjee who was present at the Conference.

Chapter 10: Sharia and Human Rights

1 J. Bentham, 'Anarchical Fallacies; Being an Examination of the Declaration of Rights Issued during the French Revolution', in *The Works of Jeremy Bentham*, ed. J. Bowering (Edinburgh, 1843), vol. 2, p. 501.

2 A. Sen, *Development as Freedom* (Oxford, 1999), pp. 227–232.

3 Ibid., pp. 228–232.

4 D. Selbourne, *The Principle of Duty* (London, 2009).

5 See Introduction, n. 16.

6 M. Ahmad, ed., *State and Politics in Islam* (Washington, DC, 1986).

7 A. An-Naʿim, 'Sharia and Basic Human Rights Concerns', in C. Kurzman, ed., *Liberal Islam: A Sourcebook* (New York, 1998), p. 222.

8 Ibid., p. 224.

9 B. Tibi, *The Challenge of Fundamentalism: Political Islam and the New World Disorder* (Berkeley, CA, 1998), p. 195. See also p. 41.

10 B. Tibi, *Islam Between Culture and Politics* (London, 2001), p. 132. See also his *The Challenge of Fundamentalism*, p. 183.

11 C. Bennett, *Muslims and Modernity* (London, 2005), pp. 64–65.

12 A. Maududi, *Human Rights in Islam* (Lahore, 1977).

13 A reform movement initiated by al-Afghani and Muhammmad Abduh in the 19th century. They are described more fully in the last chapter of this book on pp. 189–190.

14 H. Bielefeldt, 'Muslim Voices in the Human Rights Debate', in *Human Rights Quarterly*, 7 (1995), pp. 585–617.

15 Ibid., p. 604.

16 C. Bennett, *Muslims and Modernity*, p. 67.

17 Baderin, A. Mashood, 'Human rights and Islamic Law: The Myth of Discord', *European Human Rights Law Review*, 2 (2005), pp. 165–185.

18 http://www.alhewar.com/ISLAMDECL.html. Accessed 14 July 2017.

19 R. Shaham, *The Expert Witness in Islamic Courts: Medicine and Crafts in the Service of the Law* (Chicago, IL, 2010), pp. 48–49.

20 Ibid.

21 See A. An-Na'im, *Toward an Islamic Reformation*. See also S. Sardar Ali, 'Exploring New Directions in the Islamic Legal Traditions: Re-Interpreting Sharia from Within?', *Journal of Islamic State Practices in International Law* 9 (2013), pp. 13–14.

22 A. An-Na'im, 'Shari'a and Basic Human Rights Concerns', p. 222.

23 The Rushdie affair is mentioned in Chapter 8.

24 B. Tibi, *Islam between Culture and Politics*, p. 158.

25 B. Tibi, *The Challenge of Fundamentalism*, pp. 28 and 81.

26 A. Soroush, *Reason, Freedom and Democracy in Islam* (Oxford, 2000), p. 129.

27 M. Charfi, *Islam and Liberty: The Historical Misunderstanding* (New York, 1998), p. 65.

28 Ibid.

29 Interview with M. Arkoun by M. Keshavjee on 9 September 1998.

30 F. Gerges, ed., *The New Middle East: Protest and Revolution in the Arab World* (Cambridge, 2004), p. 1. Also see Masooda Bano and Hanane Benadi, who describe the manner in which the Egyptian government has co-opted the prestigious institution of al-Azhar to support the Sisi government's political agenda, in Masooda Bano and Hanane Benadi, 'Regulating religious authority for political gains: al-Sisi's manipulation of al-Azhar in Egypt', *Third World Quarterly*, September 2017, n.p.

31 Ann Elizabeth Mayer, 'The Islam and Human Rights Nexus: Shifting Dimensions', *Muslim World Journal of Human Rights*, 4 (2007), p. 8.

32 A. E. Mayer, 'The Islam and Human Rights Nexus: Shifting Dimensions', *Muslim Journal of Human Rights*, 4 (2007), pp. 1–27.

Chapter 11: Criminal Justice in Islam

1 A. Giddens, *The Nation State and Violence: Volume Two of A Contemporary Critique of Historical Materialism* (Berkeley, CA, 1985). See also Masooda Bano and Hanane Benadi, who describe the manner in which the Egyptian government has co-opted the prestigious institution of al-Azhar to support the Sisi government's political agenda, in Masooda Bano and Hanane Benadi, 'Regulating religious authority for political gains: al-Sisi's manipulation of al-Azhar in Egypt', *Third World Quarterly*, September 2017, n.p.

2 W. B. Hallaq, *Sharī'a: Theory, Practice and Transformations*, p. 308.

3 Ibid., pp. 310–311.

4 See F. E. Vogel, 'The Trial of Terrorists under Classical Islamic Law', *Harvard International Law Journal*, 43 (2002), pp. 53–60.

5 Halil İnalcik, 'Meḥemmed II', *EI2*, vol. 6, p. 901.

6 Information on the following two sections has been based upon our reading of R. Peters, *Crime and Punishment in Islamic Law*.

7 On the present debate, see Mashood A. Baderin, 'Islam and the Realization of Human Rights in the Muslim World: A Reflection on Two Essential Approaches and Two Divergent Perspectives', *Muslim World Journal of Human Rights*, 4 (2007).

8 R. Peters, *Crime and Punishment in Islamic Law*, pp. 182–183.

9 Ibid.

Chapter 12: Islam and Ethics

1 A. Siddique, 'Ethics in Islam: Key Concepts and Contemporary Challenges', *Journal of Moral Education*, 26 (1997), pp. 423–431.

2 See Azartash Azarnoosh, 'adab', *EIs*, 3, pp. 1–20.

3 Muḥammad b. Ismā'īl al-Bukhārī, *al-Jāmi' al-Ṣaḥīḥ al-musnad* (Cairo, 1400/1979), Book 1, Hadith 625.

4 A. Nanji, 'Medical Ethics and the Islamic Tradition', *Journal of Medicine and Philosophy*, 13 (1988), pp. 257–275.

5 F. Rahman, *Health and Medicine in the Islamic Tradition: Change and Identity* (New York, 1987), p. 107.

6 See Q 22:5: 'and among you is he who is taken in [early] death, and among you is he who is returned to the most decrepit [old] age so that he knows, after [once having] knowledge, nothing'.

7 See Report on Charlie Gard case in the *Telegraph* at http://www.telegraph.co.uk/news/2017/04/11/high-court-rules-doctors-can-withdraw-life-support-treatment/. Accessed 24 July 2017.

8 For the working of the AKDN, and more particularly its ethical framework, see A. Sajoo, *Muslim Ethics – Emerging Vistas* (London, 2004), pp. 99–107.

9 C. Mathewes, *Understanding Religious Ethics* (Oxford, 2010), p. 5.

10 'Aus so krummem Holze, als woraus der Mensch gemacht ist, kann nichts ganz Gerades gezimmert werden'; Immanuel Kant, *Gesammelte Schriften*, vol. 8 (Berlin, 1912), p. 23.

Chapter 13: Critique

1 A. Duderija, ed., *Maqāṣid al-Sharī'a*. See particularly the chapter 'Islamic Law Reform and Maqāṣid al-Sharī'a in the Thought of Mohammad Hashim Kamali', pp. 13–37.

2 See R. Abdulla, 'A Muslim Reading', in M. Forward, ed., *Ultimate Visions: Reflections on the Religions We Choose* (Oxford, 1995), pp. 13–21.

3 See W. B. Hallaq, *The Impossible State: Islam, Politics, and Modernity's Moral Predicament* (New York, 2013). See also T. Thomas, 'Is Malaysia an Islamic State?' Paper delivered at the 13th Malaysian Law Conference in 2005. Available at http://www.malaysianbar.org.my/constitutional_law/is_malaysia_an_islamic_state_.html. Accessed 20 February 2017.

4 A. An-Na'im, 'Sharia and Basic Human Rights Concerns', pp. 236–237.

5 As for a citizen's right to change their faith in accordance with the Constitution of Malaysia, see Dato Cyrus Das to the Malaysian Bar Council in S. Ang, M. Choon and L. Fong, 'Report on the State of Religious Liberty in Malaysia', pp. 41–50.

6 See M. D. Bakar, *Shariah Minds in Islamic Finance*. See also A. Duderija, ed., *Maqāṣid al-Sharī'a*.

7 See C. Geertz, *Islam Observed*.

8 See M. Arkoun, *The Unthought in Contemporary Islamic Thought* (London, 2002).

9 M. Lilla, *The Shipwrecked Mind on Political Reaction* (New York, 2017).

10 Promulgated by Muhammad in 622 and aimed 'to establish pluralist governance as an imperative for the founding of a civic umma'. See A. Sajoo, *Muslim Ethics*, p. 73.

11 See A. Duderija, ed., *Maqāṣid al-Sharīʿa*.

12 Ibid., p. 3.

13 Ibid., p. 5.

14 Ibid., p. 6.

15 G. E. Attia, *Towards Realization of the Higher Intent of Islamic Law (Maqasid al-Sharia): A Functional Approach* (Kuala Lumpur, 2010), pp. 116–151.

16 See M. Keshavjee and R. Abdalla, 'Modern Developments'.

17 See G. Bunt, *Islam in the Digital Age*.

18 Rachid al-Ghannouchi, 'Secularism in the Arab Maghreb', in J. Esposito and A. Tamimi, eds, *Islam and Secularism in the Middle East* (London, 2002), p. 99.

19 Ibid., p. 104.

20 See Tim Adams, 'Welcome to the New World Order of Adam Curtis, Searching for Meaning in a Century of Chaos', *The Observer*, 9 October 2016.

21 See J. Wolff, 'In a World of Fake News and Bilious Reaction, Give Thanks for the Revival of the PPE Degree', *Guardian*, 4 April 2017.

22 A. Barlas, *'Believing Women' in Islam: Unreading Patriarchal Interpretations of the Qur'an* (Austin, TX, 2002).

23 F. Mernissi, *Beyond the Veil: Male–Female Dynamics in Modern Muslim Society* (Bloomington, IN, 1987); eadem, *The Veil and the Male Elite: A Feminist Interpretation or Women's Rights in Islam* (New York, 1990).

24 See Chapter 10.

25 See Z. Mir-Hosseini, 'Muslim Women's Quest for Equality between Islamic Law and Feminism', *Critical Inquiry*, 32 (2006), pp. 626–654; and also Z. Mir-Hosseini, 'Moral Contestations and Patriarchal Ethics: Women Challenging the Justice of Muslim Family Laws', in Robert Heffner, ed., *Shariʿa and Islamic Ethics in Transition* (Indianapolis, IN, 2016), pp. 62–82.

26 Ibid., p. 636.

27 Ibid., p. 637.

28 Z. Mir-Hosseini, 'Moral Contestations and Patriarchal Ethics: Women Challenging the Justice of Muslim Family Laws', in Robert W. Hefner, ed., *Shariʿa Law and Modern Muslim Ethics* (Bloomington, IN, 2016), p. 79.

29 Z. Mir-Hosseini, unpublished paper entitled 'Contesting Patriarchal Ethics in Muslim Legal Traditions', presented at a seminar on 1 July 2017 at the Institute for the Study of Muslim Civilisations in London.

30 Ibid., p. 14.
31 Ibid.
32 Ibid.
33 See Q 3:104.
34 Q 3:169.
35 Q 4:29 which prevents killing each other but not suicide per se.
36 Abū'l-Fidā' Ismāʿīl b. ʿUmar Ibn al-Kathīr, *al-Bidāya wa al-Nihāya* (Beirut, 1408/1988), vol. 3, p. 126, hadith no. 3276.
37 al-Bukhārī, *Ṣaḥīḥ*, vol. 3, p. 32.
38 The proponents of suicide killings argue that the term 'suicide' is a derogatory one invented by the West; for them such acts are an obligation to kill infidels. Those killed who are innocent are regarded as not having died but gone directly to paradise. A notion similar to this was expressed by the Bishop of Narbonne during the crusade against the Cathars in France when he was asked whether it was right to set fire to a church where women and children had sought refuge – his answer was: 'God will know his own'.
39 Cited in Muḥammad b. al-Ḥasan al-Shaybānī, *Sharḥ al-Siyār al-kabīr*, ed. Muḥammad Ḥasan Muḥammad Ḥasan al-Shāfiʿī (Beirut, 1977), vol. 4, pp. 151–152.
40 Q 8:58.
41 Q 2:190.
42 Q 9:7 and Q 2:194.
43 M. Munir, 'Suicide Attacks and Islamic Law', *International Review of the Red Cross*, 90 (2008), p. 89.
44 Islamic law recognises the practice whereby one Muslim may declare another as a non-believer (*kāfir*). However, this form of accusation is regarded very seriously, and whoever carries out this act must be certain of what they are doing since an ill-founded *takfir* accusation is forbidden in sharia.
45 Thus in June 2007 Pakistan's acting Minister of Religious Affairs, Muhammad Ijaz-ul-Haq, called for the death of Salman Rushdie, who had been awarded a knighthood, by a suicide attack against him.
46 Q 17:33.
47 See S. Ahmed, *What is Islam? The Importance of Being Islamic* (Princeton, NJ, 2016).

Bibliography

Standard Abbreviations

EI2 = *The Encyclopaedia of Islam*. Leiden, 1986.
EIs = *Encyclopaedia Islamica*. Leiden, 2015.

Abdalla, A. 'Principles of Islamic Interpersonal Conflict Intervention: A Search within Islam and Western Literature', *Journal of Law and Religion*, 15 (2000), pp. 151–184.

Abdo, G. *New Sectarianism: The Arab Uprisings and the Rebirth of the Shia-Sunni Divide*. Oxford, 2017.

Abdulla, R. 'A Muslim Reading', in M. Forward, ed., *Ultimate Visions: Reflections on the Religions We Choose*. Oxford, 1995, pp. 13–21.

Afsaruddin. A. *First Muslims: History and Memory*. Oxford, 2007.

Ahmad, M. ed. *State and Politics in Islam*. Washington, DC, 1986.

Ahmed, A. 'Communal Autonomy and the Application of Islamic Law', *Newsletter of the Institute for the Study of Islam in the Modern World*, October 1982, p. 32.

Ahmed, S. *What is Islam? The Importance of Being Islamic*. Princeton, NJ, 2016.

Akyol, Mustafa. *Islam without Extremes: a Muslim Case for Liberty*. New York and London, 2013.

Ali, S. Sardar. 'Exploring New Directions in the Islamic Legal Traditions: Re-Interpreting Sharia from Within?', *Journal of Islamic State Practices in International Law* 9 (2013), pp. 13–14.

—— *Modern Challenges to Islamic Law*. Cambridge, 2016.

Anderson, N. J. D. *Islamic Law in the Modern World*. New York, 1959.

Ang, S. M. Choon and L. Fong. 'Report on the State of Religious Liberty in Malaysia for the Year 2007', in *Religious Liberty after 50 Years of Independence*. Petaling, 2008, pp. 41–50.

An-Na'im, A. 'Sharia and Basic Human Rights Concerns', in C. Kurzman, ed., *Liberal Islam: A Sourcebook*. New York, 1998, pp. 222–238.

—— *Toward an Islamic Reformation: Civil Liberties, Human Rights and International Law.* Syracuse, NY, 1999.

Arkoun, M. *Arab Thought*, tr. J. Singh. New Delhi, 1988.

—— *al-Fikr al-uṣūlī wa istiḥālat al-ta'ṣīl: naḥwa tarīkh ākhar li al-fikr al-islāmī* (*Foundationalism and the Problem with the Foundationalists*). Beirut, 1999.

—— *The Unthought in Contemporary Islamic Thought.* London, 2002.

Armstrong, K. *Islam: A Short History.* London, 2000.

—— *Muhammad. Prophet of Our Time.* London, 2006.

Attia, G. E. *Towards Realization of the Higher Intent of Islamic Law. Maqasid al-Sharia: A Functional Approach.* Kuala Lumpur, 2010.

Azarnoosh, A. 'Adab', *EIs*, vol. 3, pp. 1–20.

Baderin, Mashood A., 'Islam and the Realization of Human Rights in the Muslim World: A Reflection on Two Essential Approaches and Two Divergent Perspectives', *Muslim World Journal of Human Rights* (2007), 1 Art. 5.

Bakar, M. D. *Shariah Minds in Islamic Finance: An Inside Story of a Shariah Scholar.* Kuala Lumpur, 2016.

Ballantyne, W. M. *Essays and Addresses on Arab Laws.* London, 2000.

—— 'Islamic Law and Financial Transactions in Contemporary Perspective', in W. M. Ballantyne, *Essays and Addresses on Arab Laws.* London, 2000, pp. 177–185.

—— 'The Sharia: Bridges or Conflict?', in *Essays and Addresses on Arab Laws.* London, 1999, pp. 276–281.

Bano, S. *An Exploratory Study of Shariah Councils in England with Respect to Family Law.* Reading, 2012.

Barlas, A. 'Believing Women' in Islam: Unreading Patriarchal Interpretations of the Qur'an.* Austin, TX, 2002.

Bechor, G. *The Sanhuri Code, and the Emergence of Modern Arab Civil Law (1932 to 1949).* Leiden, 2007.

Bell, R. and W. M. Watt. *Introduction to the Qur'an.* Edinburgh, 1970.

Bennett, C. *Muslims and Modernity.* London, 2005.

Bentham, J. *The Works of Jeremy Bentham*, ed. J. Bowering. Edinburgh, 1843, 11 vols.

Bielefeldt, H. 'Muslim Voices in the Human Rights Debate', *Human Rights Quarterly*, 7 (1995), pp. 585–617.

Bowen, J. R. 'How Could English Courts Recognise the Shariah?', *University of St. Thomas Law Journal*, 7, (Spring, 2010), pp. 411–435.

The Boyd Commission Report. *Dispute Resolution in Family Law: Protecting Choice, Promoting Inclusion* – Executive Summary (2004) at https://www.attorneygeneral.jus.gov.on.ca/english/about/pubs/boyd/executivesummary.html.

Boyd, M. *Dispute Resolution in Family Law: Protecting Choice, Promoting Inclusion* at https://www.attorneygeneral.jus.gov.on.ca/english/about/pubs/boyd/executivesummary.html.

al-Bukhārī, Muḥammad b. Ismāʿīl. *al-Jāmiʿ al-Ṣaḥiḥ al-musnad*. Cairo, 1400/1979.

Bunt, G. *Islam in the Digital Age: E-Jihad, Online Fatwas and Cyber Islamic Environments*. London, 2003.

Charfi, M. *Islam and Liberty: The Historical Misunderstanding*. New York, 1998.

Chaudary, M. A. *Justice in Practice: Legal Ethnography of a Pakistani Punjabi Village*. Karachi, 1999.

Coleman, I. 'Women, Islam and the New Iraq', *Foreign Affairs* (Jan/Feb 2006), pp. 24–38.

Coulson, N. J., *Conflicts and Tensions in Islamic Jurisprudence* (Chicago, IL, 1969).

—— 'Doctrine and Practice of Islamic Law', *Bulletin of the School of Oriental and African Studies*, 18 (1956), pp. 211–226.

—— *A History of Islamic Law*. Edinburgh, 1964.

Daftary, F. *Historical Dictionary of the Ismailis*. Lanham, MD, 2012.

Daftary, F. and G. Miskinzoda, ed. *The Study of Shiʿi Islam: History, Theology and Law*. London, 2014.

Doi, Abdur Rahman I., *Shariah: The Islamic Law*. London, 1984.

Duderija, A., ed. *Maqāṣid al-Sharīʿa and Contemporary Reformist Muslim Thought: An Examination*. New York, 2014.

El Alami, D. S. and D. Hinchliffe. *Islamic Marriage and Divorce Laws in the Arab World*. London, 1998.

Ernst, C. 'Blasphemy: Islamic Concept', *Encyclopedia of Religion*, ed. L. Jones. Detroit, MI, 2005, pp. 974–977.

Esposito, J. *The Oxford Dictionary of Islam*. Oxford, 2003.

—— *Women in Muslim Family Law*. Syracuse, NY, 1982.

al-Fadl, Abu. *The Great Theft*. New York, 2007.

Fakhri, A. *Fatwas and Court Judgments: A Genre Analysis of Arabic Legal Opinion*. Columbus, OH, 2004.

Farooq, O. M. 'Riba Interest and Six Hadiths; do we have a definition or a conundrum?' *Review of Islamic Economics* 13 (2009), pp. 105–141.

Fatah, T. *Pakistan: The Tragic Illusion of an Islamic State*. Mississauga, ON, 2008.

Feldman, N. 'Why Shariah?', *New York Times*, 16 March 2008.

Francesca, E. 'Constructing an Identity: The Development of Ibadi Law', in A. al-Salimi and H. Gaube, ed., *Studies on Ibadism and Oman*. Hildesheim, 2014, vol. 3, pp. 109–131.

Geertz, C. *Islam Observed: Religious Development in Morocco and Indonesia*. Chicago, IL, 1971.

Gerges, F. ed. *The New Middle East: Protest and Revolution in the Arab World*. Cambridge, 2004.

al-Ghannouchi. 'Secularism in the Arab Maghreb', in J. Esposito and A. Tamimi, ed., *Islam and Secularism in the Middle East*. London, 2002, pp. 97–123.

Giddens, A. *A Contemporary Critique of Historical Materialism*, vol. 2: *The Nation State and Violence*. Berkeley, CA, 1985.

Gregorian, Vartan. *The Emergence of Modern Afghanistan: Politics of Reform and Modernization, 1880–1946*. Stanford, CA, 1969.

Griffith-Jones, R. ed., *Islam and English Law: Rights, Responsibilities and the Place of Shari'a*. Cambridge, 2013.

Guillaume, A. *The Life of Muhammad: Translation of Ibn Isḥāq's Sirat Rasul Allah*. Oxford, 1955.

Haeri, S. *The Law of Desire*. Syracuse, NY, 1989.

Hallaq, W. B. *The Impossible State: Islam, Politics, and Modernity's Moral Predicament*. New York, 2013.

—— *The Origins and Evolution of Islamic Law*. Cambridge, 2005.

—— *Sharī'a: Theory Practice and Transformations*. Cambridge, 2009.

—— 'Was the Gate of Ijtihad Closed?', *International Journal of Middle East Studies*, 3, (1984), pp. 3–41.

Hamdani, S, *Between Revolution and State: The Path to Fatimid Statehood*. London, 2006.

Hazleton, L. *After the Prophet: The Epic Story of the Shia-Sunni Split in Islam*. New York and Toronto, 2009.

Ibn al-Kathīr, Abu al-Fidā' Ismā'īl b. 'Umar. *al-Bidāya wa al-Nihāya*. Beirut, 1408/1988.

al-Hindī, 'Alā' al-Dīn 'Alī b. 'Abd al-Malik Ḥusām al-Dīn al-Mutaqqī. *Kanz al-'ummāl fī sunan al-aqwāl wa al-af'āl*. Beirut, 1998.

Hodgson, Marshall G. S. *The Venture of Islam*, 3 vols. Chicago, IL, 1974.

Hourani, A. *A History of the Arab Peoples*. London, 1991.

Jennings, Ronald C. 'Kadi, Court and Legal Procedures in 17th C. Ottoman Kayseri: Kadi and the Legal System', *Studia Islamica*, 48 (1978), pp. 133–172.

Jomier, J. *How to Understand Islam*. New York, 1989.

Kerr, Malcolm H. *Islamic Reform: The Political and Legal Theories of Muhammad Abduh and Rashid Rida*. Berkeley, CA, 1966.

Keshavjee, M. 'Alternative Dispute Resolution. ADR and its Potential for Helping Muslims Reclaim the Higher Ethical Values. *Maqasid* Underpinning the Sharia', in H. Tiliouine and R. J. Estes, eds, *The State of Social Progress in Islamic Societies*. Basel, 2016, pp. 607–622.

—— 'Cross-Border Child Abduction Mediation in Cases Concerning Non-Hague Parental Child Convention Countries', in C. Paul and S. Kiesewetter, eds, *Cross-Border Family Mediation: International Parental Child Abduction, Custody and Access Cases*. Frankfurt, 2014, pp. 95–114.

—— 'Dispute Resolution', in A. Sajoo, ed., *A Companion to Muslim Ethics*. London, 2010, pp. 151–166.

—— *Family Mediation in the Shia Imami Ismaili Muslim Community: Institutional Structures, Training and Practice*. London, 2009.

—— *Islam, Sharia and Alternative Dispute Resolution: Mechanisms for Legal Redress in the Muslim Community*. London, 2013.

——, and R. Abdulla. 'Modern Developments concerning a purpose-based Understanding of Sharia', in A. Sajoo, ed., *The Shariʿa: History, Ethics and Law*. London, 2018.

Korteweg A., and J. Selby J., ed. *Debating Sharia: Islam, Gender Politics, and Family Law Arbitration*. Toronto, 2012.

Kuran, T. *The Long Divergence: How Islamic Law Held Back the Middle East*. Princeton, NJ, 2010.

Kurzman, C., ed. *Liberal Islam: A Sourcebook*. New York, 1998.

Lalani, A., *Early Shiʿi Thought: The Teachings of Imam Muḥammad al-Bāqir*. London, 2000.

Lambton, A. 'A Nineteenth Century View of Jihād', *Studia Islamica*, 32 (1970), pp. 180–192.

Lewis, B. *The Emergence of Modern Turkey*. Oxford, 1961.

—— *The Middle East: 2000 Years of History from the Rise of Christianity to the Present Day*. London, 1995.

Lilla, M. *The Shipwrecked Mind on Political Reaction*. New York, 2017.

MacEoine, D. *Sharia Law or 'One Law for All'?* London, 2009.

Madelung, W. 'Imāma', *EI2*, vol. 3, pp. 1163–1169.

—— *The Succession to Muhammad: A Study of the Early Caliphate*. Cambridge, 1997.

Mai, Mukhtar. *In the Name of Honour*. London, 2007.

Mallat, C. 'Tantawi on Banking Operations in Egypt', in K. Masud, B. Messick, and D. Powers, eds, *Islamic Legal Interpretation: Muftis and their Fatwas*. Cambridge, MA, 1996, pp. 286–287.

Masud, K., B. Messick, and D. Powers, ed. *Islamic Legal Interpretation: Muftis and their Fatwas*. Cambridge, MA, 1996.

Mathewes, C. *Understanding Religious Ethics*. Oxford, 2010.

Maududi, A. *Human Rights in Islam*. Lahore, 1977.

Mayer, A. E. 'The Islam and Human Rights Nexus: Shifting Dimensions', *Muslim Journal of Human Rights*, 4 (2007), pp. 1–27.

Mernissi, F., *Beyond the Veil: Male-female Dynamics in Modern Muslim Society*. Bloomington, IN, 1987.

—— *The Veil and the Male Elite: A Feminist Interpretation or Women's Rights in Islam*. New York, 1990.

Mir-Hosseini, Z. 'Moral Contestations and Patriarchal Ethics: Women Challenging the Justice of Muslim Family Laws', in Robert Heffner, ed., *Shari'a and Islamic Ethics in Transition* (Indianapolis, IN, 2016), pp. 62–82.

—— 'Muslim Women's Quest for Equality between Islamic Law and Feminism', *Critical Inquiry*, 32 (2006), pp. 626–654.

Mourad, Suleiman Ali. *Early Islam between Myth and History: al-Ḥasan al-Baṣrī. d. 110 H/728 CE and the Formation of his Legacy in Classical Islamic Scholarship*. Leiden, 2006.

—— 'Riddles of the Book', *New Left Review*, 86 (2014), pp. 15–52.

Munir, M., 'Suicide Attacks and Islamic Law', *International Review of the Red Cross*, 90, 869 (2008), p. 89.

Nanji, Azim. 'Medical Ethics and the Islamic Tradition', *Journal of Medicine and Philosophy*, 13 (1988), pp. 257–275.

—— and Razia Nanji, *The Penguin Dictionary of Islam*. London, 2008.

Nasr, S. Hossein. *The Study Quran: A New Translation and Commentary*. New York, 2015.

Othman, A. 'And Amicable Settlement Is Best: Sulh and Dispute Resolution in Islamic Law', *Arab Law Quarterly* 21 (2007), pp. 64–90.

Pakatchi, A. 'Caliphate', *EIs*, vol. 5, pp. 407–462.

Peters, R. *Crime and Punishment in Islamic Law: Theory and Practice from the Sixteenth to the Twenty-First Centuries*. Cambridge, 2005.

Powers, D. *Law Society, and Culture in the Maghreb, 1300–1500*. Cambridge, 2002.

Pultar, G. ed., *Islam ve Modernite*. Istanbul, 2007.

Rahman, F. *Health and Medicine in the Islamic Tradition: Change and Identity*. New York, 1987.

—— *Islam and Modernity: Transformation of an Intellectual Tradition*. Islamabad, 1984.

—— 'Law and Ethics in Islam', in R. G. Hovannisian, ed., *Ethics in Islam*. Malibu, CA, 1985, pp. 3–15.

Rasekh, M. 'Sharia and Law in the Age of Constitutionalism', *The Journal of Global Justice and Public Policy*, 2 (2016), pp. 274–275.

Riḍā, R. 'Ribḥ ṣundūq al-tawfīr', *al-Manār*, 19 (1917), p. 528.

—— 'Ṣundūq al tawfīr fī idārat al-barīd', *al-Manār*, 19 (1917), pp. 28–29.

Rodinson, M. *Islam and Capitalism*, tr. Brian Pearce. London, 1973.

—— *Mohammed*, tr. Anne Carter. London, 1971.

Rosen, L. *The Anthropology of Justice – Law as Culture in Islamic Society*. Princeton, NJ, 1989.

The Runnymede Trust. *Islamophobia: A Challenge for Us All*. London, 1997.

Ruthven, M. *A Satanic Affair: Salman Rushdie and the Rage of Islam*. London, 1990.

Sachedina, A. *Prolegomena to the Qur'an*. New York, 1998.

Sajoo, A., ed. *A Companion to Muslim Ethics*. London, 2010.

——, *Muslim Ethics – Emerging Vistas*. London, 2004.

Saleh, N. 'Financial Transactions and Contracts', in C. Mallat, ed., *Islamic Law and Finance*. London, 1988, pp. 13–30.

—— *Unlawful Gain and Legitimate Profit in Islamic Law: Riba, Gharar and Islamic Banking*. Cambridge, 1986.

al-Sarakhsi, Abū Bakr. *Uṣūl al-Sarakhsī*. Beirut, 1993.

Sardar, Z., and M. W. Davies. *Distorted Imagination: Lessons from the Rushdie Affair*. London, 1990.

Schacht, J. *An Introduction to Islamic Law*. Oxford, 1946.

—— *The Origins of Muhammadan Jurisprudence*. Oxford, 1950.

Schimmel, A. *Muhammad is His Messenger: A Veneration of the Prophet in Islamic Piety*. Chapel Hill, NC, 1985.

Selbourne, D. *The Principle of Duty*. London, 2009.

Sen, A. *Development as Freedom*. Oxford, 1999.

Shaham, R. *The Expert Witness in Islamic Courts: Medicine and Crafts in the Service of the Law*. Chicago, IL, 2010.

Shah-Kazemi, R. *Justice and Remembrance: Introducing the Spirituality of Imam Ali*. London, 2006.

Shah-Kazemi, S. N. *Untying the Knot: Muslim Women, Divorce and the Shariah*. London, 2001.

al-Shaybānī, Muḥammad b. al-Ḥasan *Sharḥ al-Siyār al-kabīr*, ed. Muḥammad Ḥasan Muḥammad Ḥasan al-Shāfi'ī. Beirut, 1977.

Siddique, A. 'Ethics in Islam: Key Concepts and Contemporary Challenges', *Journal of Moral Education*, 26 (1997), pp. 423–431.

Silverman, Eric K. 'Anthropology and Circumcision', *Annual Review of Anthropology*, 33 (2004), pp. 419–445.

Soroush, A. *Reason, Freedom and Democracy in Islam*. Oxford, 2000.

Stewart, Rhea Talley. *Fire in Afghanistan 1914–1929: The First Opening to the West Undone by Tribal Ferocity Years before the Taliban*. Garden City, NY, 1973.

Storkey, E. *Scars across Humanity: Understanding and Overcoming Violence against Women*. London, 2015.

Tan, Nathaniel, and John Lee. *Religion under Siege? Lina Joy, The Islamic State and Freedom of Speech*. Kuala Lumpur, 2008.

Thomas, T. *Anything but the Law – Essays on Politics and Economics.* Selangor, 2016.

Tibi, B. *The Challenge of Fundamentalism: Political Islam and the New World Disorder.* Berkeley, CA, 1998.

—— *Islam between Culture and Politics.* London, 2001.

al-Tirmidhī, Abū 'Īsā Muḥammad. *Jāmi' al-Tirmidhī,* ed. Ḥāfiz Abu Tāhir Zubayr 'Alī Zā'ī. Riyadh, 2007.

—— *Sunan al-Tirmidhī,* ed. Muḥammad Ibn 'Īsā. Beirut, 2000.

Tyan, E., 'Ḳāḍī', *EI2,* vol. 4, pp. 373–374.

Vatikiotis, P. J. *The Modern History of Egypt.* London, 1985.

Vogel, F. E. 'The Trial of Terrorists under Classical Islamic Law', *Harvard International Law Journal,* 43 (2002), pp. 53–60.

al-Wāqidī, Muḥammad b. 'Umar. *Kitāb al-Maghāzī,* ed. M. Jones. London, 1966.

Watt, W. M. *Freewill and Predestination in Early Islam.* London, 1948.

—— *Islamic Philosophy and Theology.* Edinburgh, 1985.

—— *Muhammad: Prophet and Statesman.* Oxford, 1961.

Webster, R. *The History of Blasphemy.* London, 1990.

Weiss, B. *The Spirit of Islamic Law.* Athens, GA, 1998.

Yousafzai, M. *I Am Malala.* New York, 2014.

Index